The HUMAN LIFE of JESUS

By John Erskine

WILLIAM MORROW AND COMPANY, NEW YORK

This book is manufactured under wartime
conditions in conformity with all government regulations controlling the use of
paper and other materials.

Printed in the United States of America

CONTENTS

Preface   vii
I. The Birth and the Childhood   1
II. Joseph and Mary   15
III. The Years of Which Nothing Is Known   26
IV. John the Baptist   32
V. The Beginning of the Ministry   44
VI. The Messiah and the Kingdom of God   64
VII. The Twelve Companions   73
VIII. The Beatitudes and the Maledictions   95
IX. The Parables   105
X. The Miracles   131
XI. The Lord's Prayer   144
XII. Mission to the Gentiles   156
XIII. The Mission to Jerusalem   166
XIV. The Growth of the Revelation in Jesus   176
XV. Who Were His Enemies?   187
XVI. The Passover in Jerusalem   200
XVII. The Last Supper   210
XVIII. The Betrayal, the Trial, the Crucifixion   219
XIX. The Resurrection   236
Bibliography   241

Preface

THE CENTRAL doctrine of Christianity is the Incarnation. Jesus is the God who became Man. He took our nature upon him, and knew by experience our happiness, our sorrows, our temptations, our little strength. Assuming our limitations, he showed us how to live. He revealed to us our own possibilities.

Yet the Christian usually studies the supernatural rather than the human character of Jesus. In the face of his clear doctrine we persuade ourselves that religion has to do with the next world rather than with this. We think of the kingdom of God as a state to be entered only after death, though he taught us to pray, "Thy kingdom come . . . on earth."

It is unfortunate that Christians leave to unbelievers or half-believers the privilege of emphasizing the humanity of Jesus. For most of us, apparently, the doctrine of the Incarnation is very difficult. We are familiar with human persons, but we decline to believe in a divine person; or we can believe in a divine person, but not in a divine person who is also human. Those who deny the divinity of Jesus yet admire his human character, are half-believers, and so are those who think themselves orthodox yet base their faith in Jesus on those incidents told of him which could be true of no other human being.

I call this book *The Human Life of Jesus,* not because I don't believe in him, but because I do. My subject is not a philosophical idea, but a historical event, a stupendous apparition, the significance of which men recognized at the time, and still recognize, either by a lifting up of their hearts or by an instinctive antagonism. The portrait of this apparition is fairly clear in the Gospels, but ages of piety and adoration, inclining more often than not to the one-sided interpretation, have obscured the simple beginnings. He came among men as one of them, as just another man. He was not introduced to society as a god, nor were his contemporaries asked to subscribe to a creed before they could meet him. But when they had made his acquaintance and had caught through his presence and his words a glimpse of his spirit, they felt he was more than man, and knowing him still better, they believed he was divine.

At least some of them did. Of all who first heard him, perhaps only a few were convinced. Others saw at once that he would be dangerous. It would seem that the number of his friends and the number of his foes increased at an equal pace, until the enemies for a moment got the upper hand and killed him.

I wish I knew just how in his mortal days he used the opportunities and solved the problems which are mine. At first sight the question seems not altogether answerable. The record of what he said and did is for no period of his life as complete as we could wish, and we have no account at all of his boyhood and youth. But we can supply the gap, in part at least, by using our imagination. We don't need to help ourselves out by fanciful guesses. If we read attentively we shall find the material in the Gospels richer than we perhaps supposed.

For my own instruction in writing this book I have compared the King James version of the Gospels with the version in the Douay Bible. These two great translations—the one chiefly read by English-speaking Protestants, the other read by English-speaking Catholics—have been revised for greater accuracy during the three centuries and more since they were first published. With other translations they are discussed in the Bibliography.

For the sake of speed in getting at the story, I have postponed to the Bibliography a discussion of those who first told the life and the sayings and the works of Jesus. The origin of the Gospel tradition and of the four authorized accounts is of profound interest, but it is not here my theme. First and last I have tried to tell the human life of Jesus. I appeal to no ancient manuscripts, but rather to your heart and mine, and to the experience of our own human needs which enables us to recognize the healing wisdom in what Jesus taught.

JOHN ERSKINE

i

The Birth and the Childhood

NO DOUBT Mary told Jesus what a great man he was to be. Would any mother keep such a secret from her child, even if it had been a secret? Gabriel had spoken as though all the world were to know.

She was living obscurely in Nazareth, engaged to marry Joseph, and one morning when she was alone at her work the Angel astonished her by appearing in the house and saying, "Hail, thou that art highly favoured, the Lord is with thee: blessed art thou among women. . . . Fear not, Mary: for thou hast found favour with God. And, behold, thou shalt conceive in thy womb, and bring forth a son, and shalt call his name Jesus. He shall be great, and shall be called the Son of the Highest: and the Lord God shall give unto him the throne of his father David: And he shall reign over the house of Jacob forever; and of his kingdom there shall be no end."

A prophecy of honor and power in this world! However fantastic and improbable, it would come true if God so willed. Certainly her son, if she had a son, would be extraordinary. What woman's child is not? She would train him from the first. She would whisper over his cradle that he had a destiny.

It makes little difference whether we can see the Angel standing there, bringing the message in person straight from the presence of God, or whether we hear the words as a whisper in

Mary's heart. In whatever form, it would still be the Angel, the bringer of good tidings. The human life of Jesus begins with a revelation to his mother. She had a dream for her child.

2

M A R Y was young, but Joseph was an old man, or at least he was advanced in years, a widower, with sons and daughters. He needed a wife of suitable age. Perhaps, as legend tells, he foresaw the peril of marriage to a mere girl, but he loved her and convinced himself it was the thing to do. Mary and he were betrothed. It *is* said of him also that he was a just man, and the story proves it. When Mary was found to be with child, he married her at once, though the child was not his. Did he blame himself, indirectly, for her plight? Was his devotion to her, from that moment, all the greater? His troubled heart had its own messages, straight from heaven; he must trust and love. But Jesus, as the neighbors knew, was not quite like other children. There may have been whispering about his birth, though the four authentic Gospels do not mention it. Mary watched over him with all the more care.

It was by an accident, as we say, that the child was born in Bethlehem rather than in Nazareth. Joseph took his wife with him, at the time of the great taxing, to be registered in the city of David, since he was of David's line. St. Luke tells about it.

"It came to pass in those days, that there went out a decree from Cæsar Augustus, that all the world should be taxed. And this taxing was first made when Cyrenius was Governor of Syria. And all went to be taxed, every one into his own city. And Joseph also went up from Galilee, out of the city of Nazareth, into Judæa, unto the city of David, which is called Bethlehem; because he was of the house and lineage of David: to be taxed with Mary, his espoused wife, being great with child.

"And so it was, that, while they were there, the days were accomplished that she should be delivered. And she brought forth her firstborn son, and wrapped him in swaddling clothes, and laid him in a manger; because there was no room for them in the inn."

This passage is challenged by skeptical historians. They say the census referred to occurred ten years later, and in any case Joseph didn't need to go to Bethlehem to register. Critics of this school conclude, therefore, that Jesus was born, not in Bethlehem, but in Nazareth, and a few go so far as to hint that he may never have been born at all. But a scholar who is skeptical in one field is likely to be skeptical in another. If there was a census, Joseph and his contemporaries knew as much about it as we know of what happens around us today—and we sometimes are confused in our memories. The scholars who search into the far past must rely on records, on inscriptions or fragments of inscriptions, which also may be confused. There was an inscription which seemed to confirm St. Luke's date for the census, but the experts now question its genuineness. For myself, I lean to the man who speaks as an eyewitness, or who had his story from an eyewitness, rather than to the man who contradicts him two thousand years later.

What really needs comment here is the manger cradle where Jesus was laid, because there was no room in the inn. Was the innkeeper a mean soul? At sight of the elderly carpenter coming down the road leading a donkey with a sick woman on it, did he decide to put them out in the barn, where they wouldn't annoy the well-paying guests? Or was the main house really crowded to the eyelids, and did he, with some effort and out of true sympathy, clear a corner of the stable and improvise a straw bed? With the increase of comfort in the western world the poverty of the birth scene in Bethlehem startles us, as though it were exceptional, but the difference then between the inn and the stable was small, as in some parts of the East it still is. Folk carols remind us that the Christ child had for warmth only the breath of the cattle and the heat of their bodies. The carols neglect to say, however, that the guests inside the inn had no heat at all.

We shall never have the whole truth about the innkeeper. His profession obscures his character. Hospitality is the one universal sacrament among all mankind, and since an innkeeper lives by dispensing hospitality for money, he is cut off from the humane reputation which he perhaps deserves. If he gives freely, dispensing the kind of hospitality which is a sacrament, we say he charges it up to advertising. This point can be illustrated by any famous story involving an innkeeper, by Chaucer's *Canterbury Tales*, for instance, where the host of the Tabard Inn joins the pilgrimage, and we don't know whether it's for religion or for business. Innkeepers came to be known in our speech as publicans, because they kept public houses, but also because the name suggested the mercenary tax collectors of the Gospels.

Aside from this prejudice there is no reason for supposing that Jesus was born in an atmosphere of unkindness, or that his first welcome was only from his mother and Joseph and from the wondering eyes of the ass and the cattle. Yet when the old painters portrayed this scene, they left the innkeeper out; they put in the Wise Men from St. Matthew's Gospel, and the shepherds from St. Luke's, the learned and the plain folk, brought there by science and by a voice from heaven, but equally adoring. We can't think of the manger without the Wise Men or without the shepherds; together they give the inclusive significance of the Christ child, the God-in-man, who took all of our nature upon him, the reaches of the mind as well as the instinctive yearnings of the heart.

Sincere believers have been at some pains to prove that there was indeed a particularly bright star at the moment when Jesus was born, and that it led the Wise Men to the child. Their effort is in my opinion regrettable. Whatever the original facts were, the Wise Men, like the shepherds, are remembered for ideal significance rather than for literal truth. What St. Matthew says about the star provides small basis for the legend usually told. By his account, the Wise Men had to come to Jerusalem and ask questions of Herod before the star began to act as their guide. Having seen a particularly bright star in the east, they concluded that a king was about to be born somewhere. They may have concluded further that the king was to be born in Judæa, or they may have made inquiries in all lands, wherever a royal heir might be expected. In any case they went through the city of Jerusalem saying, "Where is he that is born King of the Jews? for we have seen a star in the east, and are come to worship him." The people were excited by this inquiry, and the news of it reached Herod. Having considerable respect for astrologers, he asked the chief priests and the scribes where the Jews expected their promised saviour to appear, and the chief priests and the scribes quoted or paraphrased the prophet Micah: "And thou Bethlehem, in the land of Juda, art not the least among the princes of Juda: for out of thee shall come a Governor, that shall rule my people Israel."

So Herod sent the Wise Men to Bethlehem. It was not the star which brought them there, but as they left Jerusalem, "Lo, the star, which they saw in the east, went before them, and came and stood over where the young child was. When they saw the star, they rejoiced with exceeding great joy." Evidently the star had not been in sight during their previous journeys.

St. Matthew does not say how many Wise Men there were, but he tells us that when they saw the young child with Mary, his mother, they fell down and worshiped, and when they had opened their treasures they presented unto him gifts—gold and frankincense and myrrh. Since there were three gifts, legend long ago decided there were three Wise Men. Legend also gave them three beautiful names—Gaspar, Melchior, and Balthasar. In many old paintings one of them is shown as a Negro, to indicate that Jesus came to all men of whatever race and color.

When did the Wise Men appear at Bethlehem? Unless we read carefully we slip into the tradition, encouraged by many religious paintings, that they came at the same time as the shepherds. But St. Matthew does not say so. Jesus was circumcised on the eighth day, and after the forty days of purification Joseph and Mary presented him at the temple in Jerusalem. Obviously they had no reason as yet to fear Herod, and the slaughter of the Bethlehem infants had not yet occurred. St. Luke says Joseph and Mary went directly from the purification ceremony to Nazareth; St. Matthew says they went to Nazareth after the return from Egypt. The difficulty is disposed of by assuming that the Wise Men reached Jerusalem after the purification ceremony, while Joseph and Mary were still living at Bethlehem. The flight from Herod would then be logical and easy, since the inn where Jesus was born happened to be the usual gathering point for travelers taking the road to Egypt. Evidently Herod understood that the child had been born some weeks or months before the Wise Men appeared, for in his insane fear he ordered the killing of "all from two years and under, according to the time he had diligently inquired of the Wise Men." The Church has always separated the two visits to the manger, remembering the shepherds at Christmas and the Wise Men at the Feast of the Epiphany.

Of the shepherds we know little. Sheep intended for sacrifice in the temple were pastured on the fields of Bethlehem; the men to whom the angels revealed themselves may have been in charge of such a flock, in the service of the temple, and therefore by temperament predisposed to profound religious experience. In any case they had the privilege, we must believe, of hearing the Christmas message correctly stated. Our English Bibles usually have it, "Glory to God in the highest, and on earth, peace, good will toward men." But the good will of heaven to man might well be taken for granted; we don't need the multitude of the heavenly host to announce blessings to passive recipients. Jesus taught men on what terms they may earn the right to enter the kingdom of heaven. The spirit of the Christmas tidings, as correctly stated, is active rather than passive—"on earth peace, to men of good will."

3

HEROD occupies an unenviably high place in the records of human depravity. He lacked anything resembling moral sense.

His besetting fear was a loss or diminution of his authority. Thinking of his own sons as potential rivals, who might be a little too eager to succeed him, he murdered them. Knowing well the Jewish hope for a Messiah, he was ready to make short work of any too-promising child. He invited the Wise Men to stop again at Jerusalem on their way home and let him know just where in Bethlehem they found the new-born King of the Jews, so that he could join in the worship. But the Wise Men, being wise, went home another way, and Herod, to be on the safe side, killed every infant in Bethlehem.

He probably didn't consider the episode worth a second thought, since the village was small, and his executioners couldn't have found more than twenty little throats to cut, but the Slaughter of the Innocents remains the archetype of all atrocities. The good tidings of the angels, only a few weeks before, were now turned cruelly ironical. Peace on earth? Jesus was born in Bethlehem—and the other children had to die. Years afterward he said, with whatever tone of sadness, "I came not to send peace, but a sword." (St. Matthew, chapter 10, verse 34.)

The visit of the shepherds may have astonished Joseph and Mary, but the visit of the Wise Men disturbed them. If distinguished foreigners were to bring royal gifts to the child, first making a commotion in Jerusalem, Joseph knew too much about Herod to linger in the neighborhood. St. Matthew says he was warned in a dream to leave quickly. Those who wished to avoid Herod usually went to Egypt, if only across the border. How far Joseph went or how long he stayed, we can only guess. We believe Herod died soon after the killing of the children in Bethlehem; if so, the flight and the exile were brief. There are no authentic details of the journey, but apocryphal legends fill the interval with romance, with fantastic miracles, with grotesque absurdities.

One episode stands out from the conglomeration because of its significance and beauty. A band of robbers fell on the travelers, and the young chief pulled away the shawl Mary held around her, trying to protect the child. When he saw the face of Jesus, he was disarmed, and let the family go unhurt, saying, "Child, if some day it is your turn to have mercy, remember me."

Years afterward one of the thieves on Calvary, the good thief, turning his head to the cross beside him, saw there, even in agony, the unforgettable look of the child on the Saviour's face. "Lord, remember me when thou comest into thy kingdom."

4

O F the childhood of Jesus in Nazareth, St. Luke gives us his tantalizingly brief account: "And when they had performed all things according to the law of the Lord, they returned into Galilee, to their own city of Nazareth. And the child grew, and waxed strong in spirit, filled with wisdom: and the grace of God was upon him.

"Now his parents went to Jerusalem every year at the feast of the passover. And when he was twelve years old, they went up to Jerusalem after the custom of the feast."

From infancy, then, until his twelfth year we have the first large gap in the record, yet it is not impossible to make for ourselves a fairly accurate picture of his boyhood. We know something about the Nazareth of his time and something about the education he received. We can imagine the influence of his home. If we wished, we could draw on apocryphal stories of his school days, of his relation to his teachers or to the other boys, but this fabulous material is of no value, historical or otherwise. It is best to make what we can of the few certain facts.

Galilee as Jesus knew it was a rich and beautiful country, fair to the eye and extremely stimulating to the mind. The soil was so productive that the cost of living was about one-fifth the cost in Judæa. There was little wealth, but life was easy, unless the Nazarene went south to Jerusalem, where his normal expenditures would at once be multiplied by five. At the presentation of Jesus in the temple his parents offered the sacrifice of a pair of

noble character of this man, admired him far beyond ordinary filial devotion. The influence of Joseph, they say, can be traced in the parable of the Prodigal Son, or in other stories which portray a magnanimous father. These commentators sometimes add that the affection which Jesus showed for the young, was something he learned by observing his mother's husband. But to push the argument so far is unnecessary. Jesus had in himself a deeper nature than Joseph's, and larger reservoirs of love. It is enough that Joseph was an extraordinary man, and that Jesus knew it. We wish we were told much more about the other children, Joseph's own sons and daughters. In what ways did he show affection for them? Were they devoted to him? Though neither the authentic nor the apocryphal Gospels furnish answers to these questions, their silence should not be interpreted unfavorably; the purpose of all the Gospels was to spread the story of Jesus, not of his relatives.

In one detail the apocryphal account is uncomplimentary to Joseph. It tells an incident which seems to prove that he was not a very good carpenter. One day when Jesus was still a small child he was helping his father in the carpenter shop, and Joseph ran into what was for him an insuperable difficulty. He had received a commission to make a table or, in variants of the legend, a bed, and he needed a number of boards each cut to precisely the same length. No matter how hard he tried, the boards always came out a little too long or a little too short. Jesus advised his father to lay the boards one on top of the other and to make them absolutely even at one end. When this was done, by pushing them against an upright plank, it was found that at the other end also the boards had become absolutely even.

This story, I am sure, is not, as it seems, a libel on Joseph's craftsmanship, but rather an unconscious testimony that the makers of the fable were themselves bad amateurs, who at some time had tried to cut with a saw two boards of equal length. If you've ever addressed yourself to this elementary problem you understand why it has remained a classic test of carpentering skill from the time when Noah built the Ark. The legend-makers wished to show that their fabulous Jesus used miraculous power to get around difficulties and to avoid the ordinary disciplines of life. Such stories seemed to the early Christians, as to us, immoral, and for that among other reasons the Gospel versions which exploited them were declared apocryphal. Joseph apparently had steady employment and could support his rather large family. He must have been competent at his trade.

A few references in the authentic Gospels indicate his position among the neighbors. When the people heard the preaching of Jesus and saw his works, they exclaimed, "Is not this the carpenter's son?" The question implies that the carpenter was well known. His life was not solitary. He associated with men of other trades and occupations, with men like the fisherman Zebedee, with the important citizens of Nazareth. Jesus too met his neighbors daily, except for those periods when he deliberately retired into solitude. So far as we know, Joseph had no opportunity for retirement or for uninterrupted meditation. He was a busy man, and he worked hard.

We hear of him last when he and Mary look for Jesus in the temple and find him among the doctors. He was not at the wedding at Cana. Before that event, in all probability, Mary had become a widow. Perhaps it was because of Joseph's death that she took her family there. It may even be that Cana was originally her home, and in her widowhood she returned to the scene and to the friends of her youth.

3

T H E legends about the mother of Jesus are far too many to summarize here. I shall try merely to indicate what are for me the illuminating clues to her remarkable character.

Some of these clues come to us from the apocryphal legends which, however inaccurate in detail, may yet be founded upon fact. According to legend, she was the daughter of Joachim and Anne. At the age of three she was dedicated to service in the temple, and the temple authorities recognized in her at once an extraordinary purity and elevation of thought and character. I hope they saw also the independence and courage and ardor of her temperament.

When she was fourteen, still following the legend, she was given in marriage to a husband miraculously chosen. An angel bade the high priest to assemble all the widowers, and let each widower bring a rod. Joseph, summoned with the rest, went up to the temple carrying a rod. The high priest took the rods, and having prayed, returned them, one by one, and last of all he took up Joseph's rod to hand it back, but out of the end of it flew a dove and lighted upon Joseph's head. The high priest then declared that Joseph should marry the child Mary. Joseph at first refused, saying that he had sons and was an old man, and she was but a girl; if he took her to wife he would become a laughingstock. But the high priest persuaded him.

This fable illustrates our natural tendency to attribute a remarkable background to those whom we greatly admire. I repeat the story here to indicate how early the admiration for the mother of Jesus stimulated the myth-making faculty.

We are on firmer ground when we come to Mary's visit to her cousin Elisabeth. The fact that she turned at once to this relative tells us a great deal. Elisabeth, the wife of Zacharias, was evidently a woman of unusual character, of independence, and originality, with the gifts of eloquence and the aptitude for leadership which reappeared in her son John the Baptist. If a similarity of temperament and character can be traced between John and Jesus, it can be traced still more easily between Elisabeth and Mary. I think it important for an understanding of the Virgin as she is portrayed in the Gospels to recognize the energy and independence of her character. If we accept only the accounts in later centuries which stress naturally enough the sorrowing aspects of her love, we may forget that in the early years of Christendom, down as far as the Middle Ages, she fascinated the imagination with her beauty, with her generous boldness, even at times with her sense of humor. In all reverence we may say that she was adored for her own sake, as well as for her relation to Jesus.

The places in the Gospels where her words to her son are given, and his replies to her, have troubled devout readers. We wish we were told more often what she said; unless we have been taught to read carefully, we are a little shocked that Jesus should address her always abruptly, sometimes with apparent harshness. The childhood incident in the temple, among the doctors, provides one example, the wedding at Cana provides another. Some of those who have written about Jesus have taken satisfaction, it seems, in building upon this evidence a legend that he did not greatly love his mother, even that there was a definite hostility between them. The casual reader can be pardoned for such misinterpretation if he depends, as many of us do, on a faulty translation, or if he fails to imagine the tone of voice and the expression of the face which went with the speech, but there is no adequate excuse for scholars.

At the wedding at Cana, for example, when the modest supply of wine proved inadequate for the number of guests, Mary called her son's attention to the embarrassment of their host. In the familiar English text, the King James version, Jesus replies, "Woman, what have I to do with thee? mine hour is not yet come." The text of the earliest Greek version, and the text of the great Latin translation, the Vulgate, are both entirely clear. Jesus said, "Woman, what is that to me and thee?" "Woman" is in these old versions a courteous form of address, and if Jesus spoke in an affectionate tone, or with a smile, as we have no reason for thinking he did not, the effect was much as though he had said "Dear Woman." The rest of the sentence was equivalent to, "This need not worry us," or perhaps, "What difference does it make?" However the words are paraphrased, the intention was to reassure Mary.

"Mine hour is not yet come." These words are correctly translated, and they might be difficult to understand if we did not follow the theory which I have already suggested, that the mother of Jesus, from his early childhood, urged him to fulfill the august destiny which the Angel had foretold. She interpreted the promise perhaps too literally; Jesus was to re-establish the independence and the prosperity of his people, and eventually was to sit on the throne of David, an earthly king. As the child grew she discovered in him powers of another kind—psychological and spiritual gifts beyond the wisdom expected of even the ablest monarchs. The first manifestations of these powers perhaps did not disturb her; on the contrary, they encouraged her to expect from him a remedy even for minor difficulties, even for a miscalculation in the housekeeping. Her words to the servants are full of motherly pride and confidence—"Whatsoever he saith unto you, do it."

It need not surprise us that Jesus had a clearer understanding of his mission. He was not in this world to be a magical source of supply when ordinary catering failed. This problem had no spiritual significance; his hour was not yet come. Yet after all he did what she asked, and she knew he would. Perhaps she had asked such help before, and he had given it, though with reluctance. Perhaps the reluctance was greater each time she asked. "This beginning of miracles did Jesus in Cana of Galilee." Perhaps Mary knew in her heart it was an end rather than a beginning. He would use his power no more for material or physical satisfaction; he would perform only the miracles which belonged to him, the miracles of life.

I speak here of the wedding at Cana to illustrate the love between Mary and Jesus. She did not at once understand what kind of empire he would reign over, but neither did the apostles. When she saw clearly at last, there is no reason to believe she recoiled from this second revelation, though its immeasurable significance would be attended by incalculable tragedy. For her it would be personal tragedy, for him the tragedy of mankind. He would become in a sublime sense a Messiah, a saviour, but she would remain only his mother.

In a later chapter we shall have the opportunity to discuss

miracles in general. It is enough here to stress simply the miracle of mother love, the creative love which dedicates the child and watches over it, which continues to watch and sacrifice even after the child is grown. In all religions the worship of motherhood finds somewhere a place, since motherhood is itself a religion. Some Christian believers accept theological doctrines about the Virgin Mary which other Christian believers reject, but the division is less than it seems; in our hearts we all crave the maternal as well as the paternal elements of love. Since the Gospels were in their origin primarily reports of a public ministry, they contain less information than we could wish about the mother of Jesus, but here as elsewhere tradition supplements and interprets the Scriptures. The disciples, as soon as Jesus was gone from them, turned at once to the inspiration of his mother. She was present at their important gatherings, as we have already noticed in the quotation from The Acts of the Apostles. It is not thought that she took any direct part in the affairs of the early Church, but she was there with her memories and thoughts. How could she be anything but an object of reverence?

For me, as I believe for most people, it is impossible to think of her as caring much, if at all, for theological explanations of her son. She understood her child through love. She is the symbol of whatever is constructive in life through love and faith. It is a curious but illuminating paradox that a pessimistic skeptic like Henry Adams, having studied enviously the achievements of the Middle Ages, should in his autobiography praise the Virgin as a greater source of energy and strength than the modern dynamo.

Perhaps no more need be said on this point. Many Christians try to understand the life and the work of Jesus without recognizing the importance of his mother, but such an attempt takes a good deal of the heart out of Christianity.

Of the end of the Virgin's life, or of her age when she died, we know nothing. Like most of the apostles, she was glorified by a host of stories which completely obscured the biographical

themselves by inevitable consequence. We have no evidence that John grasped the implications of this doctrine, but he followed Jesus part way; like the older prophets he could understand that our moral weakness brings misfortune upon us, and he could call men to repentance. But what the kingdom of heaven on earth was to be, what way of life would remain to preach and to practice after sinners had repented, he either did not perceive or he left for one greater than he to tell.

It would doubtless be a mistake to imagine that Jesus himself was at this time clear in his mind about the philosophy which should guide his course. He too learned from the ancient prophets to denounce sin and to call men to repentance, but he did not share John's apparent inclination toward asceticism or toward any other denial of life, or any retreat from it. More than John he would have favored in his youth an out-and-out war against the enemies of his people; the warmth of his emotions and the manliness of his character would seem to make this conclusion inescapable. But during these years, which we like to think were years of a full life, full of happiness, full of trouble, full of thought, he was moving toward the only purpose which could satisfy in him all that was human and all that was divine. As a child he grew in stature. As a young man his growth was of the mind and the heart. What those experiences were which both wounded and taught his heart, we do not know, and perhaps it is as well. Enough that for him the secret of the kingdom of heaven was to be what John never mentioned, love.

iv

John the Baptist

ALL FOUR of the Gospels give prominence to John the Baptist as the herald and forerunner of Jesus. The tributes which Jesus himself paid to his cousin are unforgettable. "Among those that are born of women, there is not a greater prophet than John the Baptist." And after John's death, "He was a burning and a shining light." This burning quality in John, the flame of his ardor and perhaps of his impatience, may have led him to begin his ministry before Jesus was quite ready to begin his. At first it might be thought that Jesus, coming to be baptized, was a follower rather than the leader. John himself tried to dispel this impression, but to some extent it remains, at least in the question here suggested, that perhaps John arrived at his minor decision before Jesus saw precisely through what door he should enter upon his majestic destiny.

St. Matthew introduces John dramatically. "In those days came John the Baptist, preaching in the wilderness of Judæa, and saying, Repent ye: for the kingdom of heaven is at hand."

St. Luke introduces him with a careful setting of the historical moment. "Now in the fifteenth year of the reign of Tiberius Cæsar, Pontius Pilate being governor of Judæa, and Herod being tetrarch of Galilee, and his brother Philip tetrarch of Ituræa and of the region of Trachonitis, and Lysanias the tetrarch of Abilene, Annas and Caiaphas being the high priests, the word of God came unto John the son of Zacharias in the wilderness. And he came into all the country about Jordan, preaching the baptism of repentance for the 'remission of sins.'"

In the first of these quotations the herald announces the opening of the drama; in the second we have a list of ominous persons in the cast—Pontius Pilate, Herod, Annas, and Caiaphas. Herod was to be the death of John. Annas and Caiaphas, through Pontius Pilate, were to bring about the crucifixion of Jesus.

John came out of the wilderness, the thinly populated region in the southern valley of the Jordan. The legend is that both his parents died when he was quite young, a supposition based on no other fact than that they were no longer young when he was born. Assuming that he was bereaved early, it is probable enough that he retired to the desert surrounding the western shores of the Dead Sea; he would go there for study and meditation, but not for entire solitude, since hermits and teachers made their home in these sands and were sought out there by devotees and pupils. Through the years of his youth John did not necessarily avoid altogether the village life in which Jesus grew up. Like others who made the desert their retreat, he probably came out at intervals on various errands.

He learned to subsist in hermit fashion on meager food, and his appearance was uncouth. He "had his raiment of camel's hair, and a leathern girdle about his loins; and his meat was locusts and wild honey." The camel's hair garment may have been inspired by the description of Elijah in the second book of Kings, chapter 1, "He was an hairy man, and girt with a girdle of leather about his loins." John the Baptist thought of himself as a successor to the old prophets, a second Elijah. By temperament he was a zealot; now, in contrast to his cousin, he had become a thoroughgoing fanatic.

The kingdom of heaven which he announced was to be a moral house-cleaning on a grand scale. Since all men were sinners, he summoned them to public confession and immediate reform. By presenting themselves for the rite of baptism, they were to acknowledge their sinfulness, and the clean water poured on the head would symbolize forgiveness. But against those who did not repent, John, like all authentic prophets, leveled terrible threats of the wrath to come.

Why was Jesus one of the crowd who came to John for baptism? At sight of him, John said, "I have need to be baptised of thee, and comest thou to me?" Perhaps Jesus wished to support his cousin in a work with which he sympathized, though it did not take the same form as his own mission. Or perhaps he was not yet decided on his course. But in his own preaching, shortly to begin, he made no use of baptism as a symbolic ceremony; in fact, he seems to have avoided ceremonies of all kinds as much as possible. John's phrase, the kingdom of heaven, he made his own, but in a new sense. Others before these two had been waiting for the kingdom, or searching for it, but gropingly. John described it plainly enough, but Jesus, having listened to the thunders by the banks of Jordan, must have gone away unsatisfied. The kingdom of heaven must be more than this.

John's career was inevitably brief. His sincerity, his honesty, and his passionate zeal were bound to be the end of him. It was like him to carry his preaching to the one place where it would not be tolerated. The famous story is told with most detail in the Gospel of St. Mark, chapter 6.

"For Herod himself had sent forth and laid hold upon John, and bound him in prison for Herodias' sake, his brother Philip's wife: for he had married her. For John had said unto Herod, It is not lawful for thee to have thy brother's wife. Therefore Herodias had a quarrel against him, and would have killed him; but she could not: for Herod feared John, knowing that he was a just man and an holy, and observed him; and when he heard him, he did many things, and heard him gladly.

"And when a convenient day was come, that Herod on his birthday made a supper to his lords, high captains, and chief estates of Galilee; and when the daughter of the said Herodias came in, and danced, and pleased Herod and them that sat with him, the king said unto the damsel, Ask of me whatsoever thou wilt, and I will give it thee. And he sware unto her, Whatsoever thou shalt ask of me, I will give it thee, unto the half of my kingdom. And she went forth, and said unto her mother, What shall I ask? And she said, The head of John the Baptist. And she came in straightway with haste unto the king, and asked, saying, I will that thou give me by and by in a charger the head of John the Baptist. And the king was exceeding sorry; yet for his oath's sake, and for their sakes which sat with him, he would not reject her.

"And immediately the king sent an executioner, and commanded his head to be brought: and he went and beheaded him in the prison, and brought his head in a charger, and gave it to the damsel: and the damsel gave it to her mother."

We must keep our various Herods straight. The one who ruled when Jesus was born, and who killed the children of Bethlehem, was Herod the Great. The murderer of John was Herod Antipas, a son of the Great Herod. There was also another son, Herod Aristobulus, half brother to Antipas, and still a third son, Philip, half brother to Aristobulus and to Antipas. Herod the Great married ten times, and his miscellany of families vied with each other for a record in envy, hatred and incest. The unspeakable Herodias was the daughter of brother Aristobulus; she became the wife of brother Philip; with her cordial consent she was stolen from Philip by brother Antipas, who was the heir of Herod the Great and therefore the most promising husband among the blood relatives.

To marry Herodias, Antipas discarded the wife he already had, the daughter of Aretas, an Arab king, and Aretas promptly declared war on him. Had it not been for Roman aid, Herod Antipas would have met disastrous defeat, for his army did not enjoy risking life to defend this concentrated practice of desertion, incest and adultery. Some of Herod's soldiers in this shameful campaign appeared at the river Jordan, to repent and be baptized; it was to them that John said, Do violence to no man, and be content with your wages.

Knowing the moral horror which stirred not only the soldiers but even more the civil population, the common decent folk of

Judæa, John could do nothing less than denounce Herod's marriage. He may have spoken directly to the tetrarch, making a special journey to the court for this courageous purpose. He probably did not stop with saying the match was unlawful; it is thought he laid the blame on the woman, as the agent of the devil. Such a point of view would have been in the hermit tradition even if Herodias had been an innocent character, but her anger at John was from that moment so intense that no one doubts he told the truth about her.

The daughter of Herodias was named Salome. Modern writers have made her the evil heroine of the story, intimating that she had a passion for John which he did not return, and that her request for his head was inspired by a perverted and thwarted love. This twist in the plot is without basis in the Gospel story, or in other Jewish legend. Salome's depravity needs no mythical additions. She must have been singularly lacking in self-respect to dance, as the Bible intimates she did, nude at a drunken orgy where even Herodias, hardened though she was, did not care to appear. Salome had to consult her elsewhere for instruction as to the proper reward to ask for the dancing. Apparently there had been no plot between mother and daughter; Salome had danced purely for art's sake, and the murderous command of Herodias was an inspiration of the moment.

But the supposition that Salome had been strangely attracted by the uncouth, dynamic prophet from the desert is interesting because of another legend that Herodias herself had felt his charm. For dramatic purposes a modern writer would transfer this passion to the girl whose dancing led directly to John's death, but it is more probable, if the legend has any foundation at all, that the mature woman, jaded in heart and body, who had followed her ambition from one husband to another, would be drawn against her will to the strong, self-disciplined young man with the clear and terrible eyes, who knew her for what she was. The fact that he disapproved of her marriage is hardly enough to explain her determination to kill him. Others much nearer to the court circle also disapproved, but she reserved her revenge for the man she couldn't dismiss from her thoughts.

What Herod thought of the prophet, we'd like very much to know. Beyond question he admired him, so far as his weak nature permitted. St. Mark says that he "feared John, knowing that he was a just man and an holy, and observed him; and when he heard him he did many things, and heard him gladly." The translation, "he did many things," is an error; it should be "he was perplexed." We can understand why he feared John, perhaps even wished to do away with him, since the very soldiers came to be baptized, but why should he listen to him gladly? And on what occasion did he listen?

In The Acts of the Apostles, at the beginning of chapter 13, we read, "Now there were in the church that was at Antioch certain prophets and teachers; as Barnabas, and Simeon that was called Niger, and Lucius of Cyrene, and Manaen, which had been brought up with Herod the tetrarch, and Saul."

This Manaen, who had been brought up with Herod, is supposed to have been his foster brother. He became a disciple of John, and later a disciple of Jesus, and through him St. Luke is supposed to have had his information about Herod. From him also Herod is supposed to have learned to respect John the Baptist. If the lover of Herodias was at all willing to discuss with Manaen the new and austere doctrine, we must think he had, among his other qualities, a streak of decency, some capacity for remorse, some fear of retribution.

When Jesus began his mission, Herod, according to St. Luke, chapter 9, "heard of all that was done by him: and he was perplexed, because it was said of some, that John was risen from the dead. . . . And Herod said, John have I beheaded: but who is this, of whom I hear such things? And he desired to see him."

He did see Jesus at last in circumstances to the highest degree dramatic and ironic, during the trial before the Crucifixion. St. Luke tells us that as soon as Pilate knew that Jesus was a Galilean, and therefore belonged to Herod's jurisdiction, he sent him to Herod, who happened to be in Jerusalem at the time. "And when

Herod saw Jesus, he was exceeding glad: for he was desirous to see him of a long season, because he had heard many things of him; and he hoped to have seen some miracle done by him. Then he questioned with him in many words; but he answered him nothing." Jesus, standing there, may have been remembering his cousin, and Herodias, and Salome.

2

JOHN's denunciation of Herodias and his consequent imprisonment brought about a crisis in the fellowship between him and Jesus. Their ideals were the same, but their methods were different. John had the temperament to strike out at evil wherever he saw it, to reform the world by reforming the individuals in it, taking one case at a time. Jesus, like his cousin, had the gift of moral indignation, and on occasion could overwhelm wrongdoers with righteous anger, but he preferred to teach the principles of good and evil, and to prepare others to teach. Time is too short and the world too large for John's way of sifting mankind, heart by heart. The cousins may have argued the problem out, each according to his conviction, before John administered to Herod a public rebuke. He did what he believed he must do, but his career was over, and Jesus went on without him.

St. Mark leaves no doubt about the resemblance and also the contrast between the two ministries. John had proclaimed that the kingdom of God was at hand, he had called sinners to repentance, he had taken his station at Jordan's banks to baptize them, and he had personally and finally rebuked Herod. Followers and disciples inevitably attached themselves to him, but his temper was to work alone, single-handed, without provision for the spread of his teaching. His program seems impulsive, insufficiently thought out, and though Jesus supported it by coming to John for baptism, it seems more than likely he had argued against it, if the two cousins consulted about their plans, as I believe they did. Jesus began his mission less dramatically, but with foresight:

"Now after that John was put in prison, Jesus came into Galilee, preaching the gospel of the kingdom of God, And saying, The time is fulfilled, and the kingdom of God is at hand: repent ye, and believe the gospel. Now as he walked by the sea of Galilee, he saw Simon and Andrew his brother casting a net into the sea: for they were fishers. And Jesus said unto them, Come ye after me, and I will make you to become fishers of men. And straightway they forsook their nets, and followed him." (St. Mark, chapter 1.)

It would have been natural enough for John to feel some resentment of a program resembling his, yet in a short time more successful. His few disciples were jealous of this attempt, as they would think, at imitation. They carried to John the news that already, so soon after receiving baptism, Jesus was preaching and baptizing, and multitudes were crowding to hear him. If I am right in believing that the cousins were not in entire accord as to their methods, then John's reply to the would-be troublemakers is doubly fine: "Ye yourselves bear me witness, that I said, I am not the Christ, but that I am sent before him. He that hath the bride is the bridegroom: but the friend of the bridegroom, which standeth and heareth him, rejoiceth greatly because of the bridegroom's voice: this my joy therefore is fulfilled. He must increase, but I must decrease." (St. John, chapter 3.)

John's loyalty was to be further tested by those jealous admirers of his. He had imposed on them the extreme discipline to which in his hermit philosophy he was committed; there was to be no enjoyment of food and drink, not even the soberest pleasure of the table, with gracious talk and the sacrament of hospitality. John approved of whatever was necessary to sustain life, and of nothing more. His diet was locusts and wild honey; neither etiquette nor ceremony delayed him in his feeding. In direct contrast, Jesus practiced and taught the rituals which human beings have always used to give the soul room, so distinguishing the experiences of man from those of beasts. Jesus was present at weddings, on occasions of mourning, and frequently with a wide variety of friends at dinners and feasts. Out of a quiet supper he made a supreme sacrament. The value of self-discipline none knew better than he, and on occasion he fasted, but he told us to fast in private, not as a public way of life. This is one matter in which he and John were temperamentally opposed.

It was the disciples of John, as on the earlier occasion, who brought up this question, and their purpose was not the promotion of harmony. They took their complaint now to Jesus himself. "Why do the disciples of John and of the Pharisees fast, but thy disciples fast not?" Jesus must have known his cousin's fine answer to the previous fault-finding, for he made use of John's metaphor: "Can the children of the bridechamber fast, while the bridegroom is with them? As long as they have the bridegroom with them, they cannot fast. But the days will come, when the bridegroom shall be taken away from them, and then shall they fast in those days." (St. Mark, chapter 2.)

What John thought of this episode, we can only guess. From the glimpses we have of his disciples, they were in no frame of mind to report accurately what Jesus said. They had not told the precise fact when they said that Jesus personally was administering the rite of baptism; the Gospel of St. John explains that Jesus himself did not baptize, but his disciples. In the question of fasting, the Baptist could say nothing to support the answer of Jesus, even if that answer had reached him unmodified. He was not a man to surrender his convictions.

Did he and Jesus ever talk to each other again? We know of only one communication, challenging and tragic. Once more John's disciples, two of them, came to Jesus with a question, but now John himself had sent them. From his prison he had heard of healings and cures, and the gift of performing miracles, as the Gospel tells us, had never been his. Imprisonment, week after week, was breaking him down. He could live in solitude, but not in a cage. He began to doubt—first to doubt himself, perhaps, then to question whether Jesus was after all the Messiah for whom he had prepared. Could anyone be the authentic Saviour whose behavior and whose accomplishments varied so far from the pattern his forerunner would have chosen? He would himself have asked Jesus for his opinion; being in chains he sent two disciples, carefully chosen. "Art thou he that should come, or do we look for another?"

We should read in these words no unworthy criticism or attack, certainly no despair of the ideal which John and Jesus had shared. There are few stronger characters in history than the Baptist; though he had small prospect of life, though he was defeated, he knew the Messiah would come. He turned to Jesus, counting on the same faith and the same willingness to face facts. Did Jesus still believe himself the destined Saviour of their people, or should they both fortify their faith with long patience?

The question revealed, of course, his lack of faith in this wonderful person, joined to him in ties of family and in the will to bring on earth the kingdom of God, but reaching far beyond him in mind and soul. It is fantastic that a man like John the Baptist should have been the herald or forerunner of Jesus Christ, and in order to smooth away the sharper edges of the paradox we usually attribute to John certain Christlike qualities he did not possess. I have tried rather to point up the lack of resemblance between them, following the few but clear indications in the Gospel, and I have tried to present this lack of resemblance as something of which Jesus was keenly aware.

This last question of John's, for example, is honest and searching, also pathetic and tragic, and it may be many other things, but it isn't tactful. John could be loyal but not considerate. He was a good man, but so far as I know, he has never been thought a pleasant one. By way of contrast, the answer which Jesus sent to him is full of understanding and kindness and divine tact. "Go and shew John again those things which ye do hear and see: the blind receive their sight, and the lame walk, the lepers are cleansed, and the deaf hear, the dead are raised up, and the poor have the gospel preached to them."

Since Jesus knew well enough that these works of his had been the very cause of John's distrust, perhaps also of his envy, some word of reproach might have been added, in the usual logic of human emotions, but Jesus converted the reprimand into a beatitude: "Blessed is he, whosoever shall not be offended in me." (St. Matthew, chapter 11.)

We hear no more of John till Salome danced and Herodias told her what reward to ask. When his disciples learned of his execution, St. Mark says, they came and took up his corpse, and laid it in a tomb. But as Jesus proceeded in his ministry, and the number of believers grew, John was not forgotten. His memory was in the landscape wherever he had preached. Once when Jesus was in the place beyond Jordan where John at first baptized, "many resorted to him, and said, John did no miracle: but all things that John spake of this man are true."

3

THE high priests Annas and Caiaphas, who for what they considered the good of their people were shortly to bring about the death of Jesus, watched in prudent silence Herod's marriage with Herodias and his murder of the Baptist. High priests were to all intents appointed by the Roman governor of the province, who would remove them promptly if they gave trouble. Annas had reason to know; he had failed to give satisfaction, and his son-in-law Caiaphas now held office in his place. The older man had as much courage and independence as can be expressed in stubbornness, and therefore he maintained in private that he was still high priest, and Pontius Pilate, the cynical governor, indulged him in his humor. The names of Annas and Caiaphas are for this reason joined, in their own informal arrangement, as partners in the spiritual direction of their people. Annas had no real authority, but neither had Caiaphas, so long as he took orders from Rome. They both were careful not to provoke the enmity of Herod, who as tetrarch under Pilate ruled one fourth of the province.

A high priest might be expected to encourage resistance to the Roman domination, and Annas and Caiaphas doubtless were patriots, so far as was convenient, but open revolt meant martyrdom, and for martyrdom neither had any talent. In the Gospels they do not cut a pretty figure, but in secular history they fare worse; their own people thought of them as trimmers, as appeasers, as hypocrites, and they were supposed to be adepts in the manipulation of Roman justice to their own ends by bribery. Since John the Baptist never was a threat to the ancient tradition, they might have supported him—or rather, they could not in conscience do otherwise. When they played safe and held aloof, no doubt the disciples of John laid an extra malediction or two on their well-cursed heads.

Annas and Caiaphas have their place with Judas as betrayers of their kind. By naming them at the beginning of the story, at the moment when the Baptist appeared with his message that the kingdom of heaven was at hand, St. Luke opens an ironic prospect; these very men who put up with Herodias and Salome, through fear of Pilate, would one day ask Pilate to crucify Jesus, whom they could not tolerate.

One more stroke of irony. The name Caiaphas is another form of the name Cephas, "Rock"—Peter's name.

v

The Beginning of the Ministry

AS SOON as Jesus was baptized, he withdrew into the desert near by, and there fasted for forty days. St. Matthew, St. Mark, and St. Luke tell this episode with only slight variation. St. John does not mention it. When Jesus was weakened by hunger, the devil besieged him with three separate temptations, all designed to wreck his ministry before it began.

We who call ourselves modern need not be bothered by the psychological imagery employed in an earlier age. Our own psychological terms will in time sound quaint enough. We do not now say that the devil tempts us, yet we are still tempted, and it may be after all that it's the devil who does the tempting. Again we need not be bothered by the fact that the Evangelists who tell the story give the very words of the temptation, and the words with which Jesus replied. To be sure, the Evangelists were not present, but the experience was of a kind which Jesus would remember as momentous, and it is natural to suppose he told it to his disciples. For him as for them it had a deep human meaning.

Why did he go into the wilderness immediately after the baptism? Because, even when he came to John at the river Jordan, he was still in doubt how to follow his destiny. His mission was to save his people, but what form should the salvation take? John's conception of the wished-for Messiah was too narrow. Certainly the sinners in the neighborhood should be called to repentance, and wicked men like Herod should be branded, but what should be done further? How should salvation be carried to the whole people, to all the world? Just because the scope of the task was so large, to think of it at all might prove a form of temptation; the challenge might seem to call for practical organization and earthly power. Herod could not be touched in his wickedness because of Rome. Annas and Caiaphas might offer Rome as excuse for their moral degradation. If Israel were to be restored spiritually, would it not first be necessary in a literal and political sense to set Israel free? Were those dear people, like his mother, who looked for Jehovah to send them an earthly champion, another David, to bring down the giant with one miraculous shot—were they right after all?

He himself had the power to perform miracles of the commonest sort, miracles of healing. His friends knew he had it. Could he extend this gift indefinitely? In the countryside in which he was brought up, the healing power resided so obviously in certain personalities that a doubter would have been laughed at. But only those could heal whose nerves were whole, who radiated an immense vitality, who attracted by an irresistible magnetism, who themselves were health incarnate. With this power he knew he was exceptionally endowed. Could there be a more beneficent mission, or a pleasanter, than to deserve and receive gratitude and praise by mending the broken and the sick, especially since the cure could be wrought simply by being himself?

And if the work of healing is blessed, is it not blessed also to remain in health, to rejoice in strength, to accept with thanksgiving the continuing miracle of life? This retreat to the desert, this painful thirst and hunger, this bleak and lonely discomfort— were they truly an exercise to free the spirit, or were they not rather a cowardly denial of the will of God? Are we to keep the mind out of mischief by weakening the body, or are we to find the way of salvation in the very center of a full life?

If Jesus had been indeed what the traditional portrait too frequently makes him, a grieving spirit, wise only in sadness; if the shocking calumny were true, that he never smiled; if the Comforter never was cheerful—then the temptation in the wilderness would have no human meaning. The outward beauty or the inner joy of life could hardly mislead a man who was totally unaware of either. But if Jesus began his mission in the zest of youth, alert in every faculty to every appeal, and possessing a charm of body and mind that drew all men to him—then indeed it would be a temptation to pause in the midst of good fortune and heaven-sent happiness, and to neglect the call to a hard errand and to sacrifice. We have not read the Gospel attentively if we fail to realize that Jesus indeed grew in favor with God and man, with man as well as with God; that he was beautiful to the eye, or handsome, if that is the better word; that his voice had masculine undertones and overtones which stirred his hearers to the depths; that he loved the company of men and women who likewise were good, and good-looking, and good-mannered, and in every wise and noble sense good companions. I believe it was not piety alone, but a true report of the fact, that first described Mary, the mother of Jesus, as beautiful. The life of sacrifice and sorrow, the infinite love and the immeasurable tragedy, can be understood only if we realize the human price which Jesus paid—and which for a moment he was tempted not to pay.

"When he had fasted forty days and forty nights, he was afterward an hungred. And when the tempter came to him, he said, If thou be the Son of God, command that these stones be made bread. But he answered and said, It is written, Man shall not live by bread alone, but by every word that proceedeth out of the mouth of God.

"Then the devil taketh him up into the holy city, and setteth him on a pinnacle of the temple, and saith unto him, If thou be the Son of God, cast thyself down: for it is written, He shall give his angels charge concerning thee: and in their hands they shall bear thee up, lest at any time thou dash thy foot against a stone. Jesus said unto him, It is written again, Thou shalt not tempt the Lord thy God.

"Again, the devil taketh him up into an exceeding high mountain, and sheweth him all the kingdoms of the world, and the glory of them; and saith unto him, All these things will I give thee, if thou wilt fall down and worship me. Then saith Jesus unto him, Get thee hence, Satan: for it is written, Thou shalt worship the Lord thy God, and him only shalt thou serve.

"Then the devil leaveth him, and, behold, angels came and ministered unto him."

2

"THE bread of angels"—Dante's name for it—is the wisdom of God. Jesus, wrestling with himself, learned his mission. The heart of his later teaching is in his first answer, "Man shall not live by bread alone." He was saying, of course, that there is another kind of bread, the bread of life, and by implication he was saying also that on the various levels, from the most physical to the most spiritual, there are different orders of hunger, different needs, different problems—and that a problem which presents itself on a low level can be solved on a higher. Hunger is a craving for food; it can be satisfied by hearty eating, or within reasonable limits it can be cured by moderation and self-restraint. Or to take an example from the field where the Messiah's mission was supposed to lie—the problem of Israel at the moment was the Roman Empire. From the power of Rome, how could a small country of farmers and shepherds and fishermen ever get free? In the wishful thoughts of the people a miracle would happen some day, a champion would come, no stronger apparently than the boy David, who by some sleight of hand would destroy or cancel out the Empire's armies, its wealth, its superb organization. The hope was to accept the Roman challenge on its own terms, and to conquer Rome on its own level—thanks to a miracle. But there was a kind of power Rome did not know. The Roman liked to keep his feet on the ground, with a solid road under his feet, and he made himself happier by digging his roads deeper and more solid. He had common sense; he prided himself on being without wings. His wasn't the soaring temperament. Jesus saw clearly where the Roman Empire was strong, but also where it was defenseless, in the higher flights of the soul. It would at last be conquered by ideas and ideals.

The teachings of Jesus were based on insights which, belonging to his personality, can therefore be organized into a consistent philosophy, yet some of us believe they are most convincing in their original form as insights. The three temptations are held together by an implied logic, but the sequence is not important; the truths remain, no matter which one is stated first. The insight into the different levels on which man lives, is followed—it might just as well be preceded—by the insight that to enter a moral world we must first accept the laws governing the physical world. Moral law is far higher than physical law; man is not a beast and need not model his behavior upon the behavior of beasts; but moral law cannot be stable if it indulges the wish or the hope from time to time to suspend or contradict the physical law.

The devil takes Jesus to a pinnacle of the temple, and challenges him to jump down. If he is divinely appointed to his mission, he will no doubt be saved by a miracle. The reply of Jesus, "Thou shalt not tempt the Lord thy God," gives his judgment on any hope or wish for a short-cut in either the moral or the physical world. He perceived as part and parcel of natural law that man, having a soul as well as a body, might live on different levels, but in the strictly physical realm the physical law holds. Even if we could make exceptions to it for our benefit, we ought not to do so; an inconstant, variable universe would be a madhouse. Repeatedly in his later teaching Jesus called attention to the material and physical conditions in the midst of which the spirit of man must work out its destiny.

The devil then takes Jesus to the top of a high mountain, shows him all the kingdoms of the world, and states on what conditions they may be his. Jesus at that terrible moment sees how difficult it would be to accept his own insight, that we may live on the higher as well as the lower levels, and that existence on every

law. Why not cling to the lowest
ial satisfactions and brute force?
to flourish on wealth and force,
nd of power which is easiest to
must be slave to the big ones,
sarily deplored? Would it be
ciled to Rome, accept Roman
swallowed up and lost in the Empire?
then be less hostility in the world, less violence, a
sharing of cultures, a better distribution of comforts;
messiahs would no longer be needed anywhere, and Jesus, with
his youth, his good looks, and his extraordinary gifts, could find
a place near the top, perhaps at the very top, wherever the best
men gather to take charge of their fellows and to make sure they
are as happy as they deserve to be.

This idea, the realization that his own mind for a second entertained this idea, is for Jesus a deep shock. "Get thee hence,
Satan."

3

T H E more we study these three temptations of Jesus, the more
confidently we draw from them certain conclusions. In the first
place he knew he possessed unusual powers, some of them of a
kind which might persuade him he could perform the very
miracles of which he did not approve. In the second place he
accepted his human life whole-heartedly, as the scene created in
time for the drama of man's eternal soul. No matter how high
the spirit might reach above it, this world on its own level is full
of beauty and may be filled with graciousness, and Jesus would
never deny that truth. Once for all he put behind him the asceticism of John the Baptist. In the third place he saw that the higher
we rise on the different levels of existence, the broader and fuller
becomes our life. He could not imagine the material world as an
ample base from which rises a pyramid of being, the narrow apex
of which is spirit. On the contrary, the material base is narrow,

and above it rises, level above level, an expandin[...]
verse. He would say later, in plain terms, that his [...]
lead men to a more abundant life. And he would ad[...]
the most abundant, the most rewarding life must be [...]
suffering. The higher we climb, the harder it is to climb[...]

If there is a fourth conclusion to be drawn from the te[...]
tions and the answers of Jesus to them, it is that he was defi[...]
the good life in a contrast between time and eternity, rather tha[...]
in the more familiar opposition of matter and spirit. Not that
time and eternity are unfamiliar terms, but by time we usually
mean the period in which our earthly life extends itself, and by
eternity we usually mean the perpetual condition in which we
hope to exist after death. In the childish egotism which seems
natural to mankind we have the feeling—though we know better—that time comes to an end and eternity begins when we die.
Yet eternity is not a stretch of duration infinite at one end and
finite at the other; there is no beginning to eternity, and there
is no end to time. Between time and eternity we may choose
now; we may live in either. We may occupy ourselves, that is,
with temporary things, or we may concentrate on matters which
in their quality are immortal. To busy ourselves chiefly or only
with the labors or the pleasures which we would gladly continue
forever, would be to simplify our lives, and in those thoughts,
hungers and searchings which have the immortal quality, lie the
answers to our temporary problems. It was the devil's hope, in
the symbolic account of the temptation, that Jesus would try to
demonstrate his divine origin by strictly temporal choices, no
one of them a permanent solution of any problem. When Jesus
put the temptation from him, his decision was made to live at
once as he wished to live always, to live in eternity now.

After the baptism, the temptation; after the temptation and the
victory, the beginning of the ministry, for which the thirty years
had been a preparation. We are eager to know, naturally, what
was the first thing Jesus did when he came out of the wilderness. St. Mark gives the shortest account: "He was there in the
wilderness forty days, tempted of Satan; and was with the wild

beasts; and the angels ministered unto him. Now after that John was put in prison, Jesus came into Galilee, preaching the Gospel of the kingdom of God, and saying, The time is fulfilled, and the kingdom of God is at hand: repent ye, and believe the Gospel."

St. Matthew makes the same report, a little more fully: "Now when Jesus had heard that John was cast into prison, he departed into Galilee; and leaving Nazareth, he came and dwelt in Capernaum, which is upon the sea coast, in the borders of Zabulon and Nephthalim. . . . From that time Jesus began to preach, and to say, Repent: for the kingdom of heaven is at hand."

St. Luke agrees that the mission of Jesus began with his preaching: "And Jesus returned in the power of the Spirit into Galilee: and there went out a fame of him through all the region round about. And he taught in their synagogues, being glorified of all."

St. John omits all account of the temptation, and proceeds directly from the baptism to the calling of the disciples, of which episode, as we shall see, he gives his fine but personal version. The other Evangelists agree that Jesus began his work by spreading the message he had learned from his conquest of himself. His mother had perhaps left Nazareth, as we said before, when Joseph died, and she was now living at Cana, but after the baptism and the temptation Jesus moved from place to place, seeing his family only at intervals.

4

N O R T H of Nazareth lay Cana, and further north on the Sea of Galilee, lay Magdala, Bethsaida, and Capernaum. Magdala was the home of Mary Magdalene. Bethsaida was the birthplace of Peter, Andrew and Philip; in Capernaum for a short time the mother of Jesus resided. In these little towns, therefore, all within a day's journey of each other, the ministry began, the first disciples were chosen, the first miracles performed, and the doctrine was first taught. Hand in hand with the teaching went the healing, the fame of which spread rapidly. Indeed, if the testimony were not against us, we might suppose that the works of healing, at least in some casual instances, came before the preaching. In every glimpse we have of his early appearances, he seems to be already known. But the order of events given by St. Mark is convincing. After John the Baptist was imprisoned, Jesus went through Galilee, preaching; as he walked along the Sea of Galilee, near Bethsaida, he saw Peter and Andrew casting their nets, and a little farther on, James and John, the sons of Zebedee. They left their work to follow him, and with them he proceeded to Capernaum. There on the Sabbath day he entered the synagogue and taught. In the synagogue was a man with an unclean spirit, a demented person, who recognized Jesus and called to him wildly. Jesus merely by a word, we are told, restored the sick mind to sanity. It was the kind of healing in which from the first his powers of rescue were most frequently revealed.

St. Luke, chapter 4, places the scene of this incident in Nazareth, "where he had been brought up," giving to the preaching in the synagogue a special significance; Jesus was revisiting the home of his youth, and the old neighbors would be coming out to hear him, even the town lunatic, whose ability to recognize him is thus explained. In the synagogue a man of known piety and intelligence might be permitted to read the lessons, one from the Law, the other from the Prophets. A layman in good standing might also be permitted to preach. Jesus had perhaps read the lessons on some earlier Sabbath, while he was still a resident of Nazareth, but now the congregation wished to hear the new doctrine which rumor attributed to him.

"He went into the synagogue on the sabbath day, and stood up for to read. And there was delivered unto him the book of the prophet Esaias. And when he had opened the book, he found the place where it was written, [Isaiah, chapter 61] The Spirit of the Lord is upon me, because he hath anointed me to preach the gospel to the poor; he hath sent me to heal the brokenhearted, to preach deliverance to the captives, and recovering of sight to the blind, to set at liberty them that are bruised, To preach the acceptable year of the Lord.

"And he closed the book, and he gave it again to the minister, and sat down. And the eyes of all them that were in the synagogue were fastened on him.

"And he began to say unto them, This day is this scripture fulfilled in your ears."

At this point, just as the sermon starts, the record fails us. Either St. Luke did not know what Jesus went on to say, or something is missing from the early manuscripts. St. Luke, I have no doubt, gave completely the discourse which charmed the congregation, as he says, by its words of grace. But immediately after the preaching something happened—we wish we knew what it was—which prompted Jesus to rebuke the Nazarenes, and his words, no longer gracious, stung the crowd into an attempt to lynch him. Had there been any previous quarrel between him and the people of Nazareth? So far as we know he had come on this visit with memories steeped in kindly sentiments, and he had been received with respect and with apparent good will. But in a moment we hear him repeat a bitter proverb, connected forever with this little town:

"Verily I say unto you, No prophet is accepted in his own country. But I tell you of a truth, many widows were in Israel in the days of Elias [Elijah], when the heaven was shut up three years and six months, when great famine was throughout all the land; but unto none of them was Elias sent, save unto Sarepta [Zarephath], a city of Sidon, unto a woman that was a widow. And many lepers were in Israel in the time of Eliseus [Elisha] the prophet; and none of them was cleansed, saving Naaman the Syrian.

"And all they in the synagogue, when they heard these things, were filled with wrath, and rose up, and thrust him out of the city, and led him unto the brow' of the hill whereon their city was built, that they might cast him down headlong. But he passing through the midst of them went his way, and came down to Capernaum."

Why Jesus rebuked his former neighbors for lack of faith in him, we don't know, but we understand without difficulty why these words of his maddened them. In Galilee, the country through which foreign traders passed on their way to Jerusalem or to Egypt, the devout Jew felt his religion exposed to a constant attrition; defending loyally what he believed in, he permitted himself some violent prejudices; he cultivated his contempt for all Gentiles. Now Jesus tells him that in the eyes of God he ranks far below the Gentiles, that it was a Sidonian woman who gave Elijah food during the great famine, and that it was a Syrian leper who came to Elisha and was healed.

St. Luke then says that Jesus, having escaped from Nazareth to Capernaum, taught there on the Sabbath days. And in the synagogue was a man who had a spirit of an unclean devil. Is this the same episode which St. Mark gave as the first preaching of Jesus? Did Jesus do his first preaching in Nazareth, as St. Luke seems to say? Assuming the fuller version to be the correct one, I should like to think the lunatic belonged in Nazareth, and that only through a confusion of places is Jesus credited with two appearances in different synagogues in similar circumstances. But if the record were complete, perhaps there would be essential distinctions between the two sermons, one of which we have lost entirely, and the other we have only in part.

5

WE have already discussed the language of Jesus at the wedding at Cana, and later we shall have something to say about the miracle of water turned to wine, but the beautiful story deserves study as a whole. Brief though it is, it contains drama and character, neither of which could well be spared in any attempt to understand the ministry of Jesus.

"There was a marriage in Cana of Galilee; and the mother of Jesus was there: and both Jesus was called, and his disciples, to the marriage.

"And when they wanted wine, the mother of Jesus saith unto him, They have no wine. Jesus saith unto her, Woman, what have I to do with thee? [Woman, what is that to me and thee?] mine hour is not yet come. His mother saith unto the servants, Whatsoever he saith unto you, do it.

"And there were set there six waterpots of stone, after the manner of the purifying of the Jews, containing two or three firkins apiece. Jesus saith unto them, Fill the waterpots with water. And they filled them up to the brim. And he saith unto them, Draw out now, and bear unto the governor of the feast. And they bear it.

"When the ruler of the feast had tasted the water that was made wine, and knew not whence it was: (but the servants which drew the water knew;) the governor of the feast called the bridegroom, and saith unto him, Every man at the beginning doth set forth good wine; and when men have well drunk, then that which is worse: but thou hast kept the good wine until now." (St. John, chapter 2.)

If for a moment we take our attention from the miracle and consider the picture here given of human sympathy and friendliness, we see the relation of Mary to the household in which the wedding occurred, her relation to her son, his attitude toward the feast in general, the courtesy of the "governor" or "ruler" to the bridegroom. The disciples were present, but they remain in the background.

There is dispute as to what is meant by the governor or ruler of the feast. He couldn't have been an *arbiter bibendi*, a toastmaster in the Roman sense, seeing to it that every guest did his share of the drinking; perhaps his position was somewhat that of a head waiter, or he may have been simply a friend of the family with an executive turn, self-appointed to run the party. In any case he does not seem to have known that the wine supply was low. It was Mary who really watched over the evening's progress. The household was not rich, and even a few guests more than had been planned for would exhaust the provisions, to the mortification of bride and groom. It was to save them from embarrassment that Mary and Jesus planned together. The bridegroom may be pardoned for not having his thoughts on the refreshments; he accepts the compliments of the governor of the feast, perhaps without knowing what he is talking about.

The significance of the story for us is that Jesus was present at the wedding and shared the happiness of his friends. He began and ended his ministry, he carried it out at every stage, in examples of social-mindedness. There was to be no place in the kingdom of God for narrow or isolated hearts; to think of him as a lonely Saviour, a Prometheus, is a great error. When his mother came to him with the problem of the wine, we are sure she had to interrupt a cheerful conversation with some other guests.

What was in Mary's thought when she told the servants to obey any order of Jesus? And why should they first of all obey her? Evidently she had already gained authority among the neighbors in Cana—the authority of her character, of her kindness and her charm. And by this time she must have seen many evidences of her son's rare abilities. Her words to the servants do not imply that she expected a miracle, but certainly she expected action of some sort. She knew that no appeal was made to him in vain.

6

THOUGH the complete text of the sermon in the synagogue is lacking, we have an example of his early teaching, at the beginning of his ministry, in what he said to Nicodemus. His words here should be compared with his answers in the temptation; the ideas in both cases are the same.

"There was a man of the Pharisees, named Nicodemus, a ruler of the Jews: the same came to Jesus by night, and said unto him, Rabbi, we know that thou art a teacher come from God: for no man can do these miracles that thou doest, except God be with him.

"Jesus answered and said unto him, Verily, verily, I say unto thee, Except a man be born again, he cannot see the kingdom of God.

"Nicodemus saith unto him, How can a man be born when he is old? can he enter the second time into his mother's womb, and be born?

"Jesus answered, Verily, verily, I say unto thee, Except a man be born of water and of the Spirit, he cannot enter into the kingdom of God. That which is born of the flesh is flesh; and that which is born of the Spirit is spirit." (St. John, chapter 3.)

Evidently Nicodemus was impressed by this young prophet; he addresses Jesus by a title that implies reverence though not necessarily adherence to his views. But it is equally evident that Nicodemus was cautious, to say the least, since he came to Jesus after dark. He was a respectable person with a reputation to maintain. He wanted to know how to get into the kingdom of God, and Jesus told him he must be born again. From that point the talk elaborates the idea implied in the answers to the temptations; the kingdom of God is to be entered only on the high level of the spirit. Nicodemus seems to find this doctrine a little obscure, or perhaps he was bothered by the way he was addressed. Jesus spoke to him with a degree of bluntness if not harshness. When he says "Except a man be born of water and of the Spirit, he cannot enter into the kingdom of God," he is referring to baptism, either to the baptism of John or to the rite as administered by his own disciples. We are not forced to conclude that he is here instituting a preliminary qualification for membership in a church; the speech can be taken merely as comment on the timidity of Nicodemus. He came by night, secretly; those who sought baptism at the hands of John or the disciples of Jesus presented themselves publicly. Jesus is telling Nicodemus to be a man—to stand up and be counted.

Some readers of the Gospel discover in Nicodemus an amiable character, a sensitive nature who recognized truth, however gropingly. That may be, but his visit to Jesus was an unheroic performance and it provoked Mary's son to some uncomplimentary remarks. By implication at least he called Nicodemus a coward, and in one sentence, realistic and somewhat hard, he suggested a doctrine which he repeated in the parable of the Last Judgment. "That which is born of the flesh is flesh; and that which is born of the Spirit is spirit." In the parable the sheep are separated from the goats, but the metaphor leaves us wondering whether the sheep were sheep of their own choice, or whether the goats ever had a chance to escape being goats. Is Jesus telling Nicodemus that some of us are born of the flesh, and therefore are lost from the very start? Such a statement would contradict the spirit of his mission, yet in moments of quite human exasperation he could say severe words and perhaps, for the time, mean them. His vitality and the generosity of his heart rose to quick anger at a revelation of meanness or of unwillingness to live. For myself I treasure the incidents in which explosions of this kind occur, not because they betray a human weakness, but because they reveal a strength which only great human beings possess.

7

THE humanness of his character, along with his spiritual vision, is indicated again by the talk with the woman of Samaria at Jacob's well. Samaria was a district lying westward of the Jordan, midway to the Mediterranean, and practically an equal distance south of Nazareth and north of Jerusalem. As St. John says, when Jesus traveled from Judæa to Galilee he had to pass through Samaria. The people of this district were of a mixed race, and though they worshiped Jehovah, they were unorthodox. Their "high place" was not the temple in Jerusalem, but their local hill, Mt. Gerizim. An orthodox Jew would despise a Samaritan.

Jesus, passing through Samaria, rested by the famous well which tradition associated with the patriarch Jacob. His disciples had left him for the moment. While he sat there, a Samaritan woman came to the well to draw water. Jesus asked her for a drink, and their remarkable conversation followed. This incident, we are told, occurred at noon, not the hour when women usually came to draw water, and we notice that this woman came alone. I believe she was attracted by the handsome, virile young man, and made an occasion for talk with him; I believe also that Jesus, with all the impulses of his human nature, made occasion for talk with her. Men and women will signal to each other till the end of time. Jesus and his companions, traveling through a dusty land where thirst could be quenched from occasional wells, would take with them on the journey, like other travelers, some means of drawing water; he didn't need the woman's aid. The episode should be read as a spirited conversation between two human beings of striking character and opposite sex who, in this one encounter of their lives, could not pass each other by.

"There cometh a woman of Samaria to draw water: Jesus saith unto her, Give me to drink. (For his disciples were gone away unto the city to buy meat.)

"Then saith the woman of Samaria unto him, How is it that thou, being a Jew, asketh drink of me, which am a woman of Samaria? for the Jews have no dealings with the Samaritans.

"Jesus answered and said unto her, If thou knewest the gift of God, and who it is that saith to thee, Give me to drink; thou wouldest have asked of him, and he would have given thee living water.

"The woman saith unto him, Sir, thou hast nothing to draw with, and the well is deep: from whence then hast thou that living water?

"Art thou greater than our father Jacob, which gave us the well, and drank thereof himself, and his children, and his cattle?

"Jesus answered and said unto her, Whosoever drinketh of this water shall thirst again:

"But whosoever drinketh of the water that I shall give him shall never thirst; but the water that I shall give him shall be in him a well of water springing up into everlasting life.

"The woman saith unto him, Sir, give me this water, that I thirst not, neither come hither to draw.

"Jesus saith unto her, Go, call thy husband, and come hither.

"The woman answered and said, I have no husband.

"Jesus said unto her, Thou hast well said, I have no husband:

"For thou hast had five husbands; and he whom thou now hast is not thy husband: in that saidst thou truly.

"The woman saith unto him, Sir, I perceive that thou art a prophet.

"Our fathers worshipped in this mountain; and ye say, that in Jerusalem is the place where men ought to worship.

"Jesus saith unto her, Woman, believe me, the hour cometh, when ye shall neither in this mountain, nor yet at Jerusalem, worship the Father.

"Ye worship ye know not what: we know what we worship: for salvation is of the Jews.

"But the hour cometh, and now is, when the true worshippers shall worship the Father in spirit and in truth: for the Father seeketh such to worship him.

"God is a Spirit: and they that worship him must worship him in spirit and in truth.

"The woman saith unto him, I know that Messias cometh, which is called Christ: when he is come, he will tell us all things.

"Jesus saith unto her, I that speak unto thee am he.

"And upon this came his disciples, and marvelled that he talked with the woman: yet no man said, What seekest thou? or, Why talkest thou with her?

"The woman then left her waterpot, and went her way into the city, and saith to the men, Come, see a man, which told me all things that ever I did." (St. John, chapter 4.)

This little scene is a poem. It concentrates a great deal of history and a great deal of human nature. If I read it correctly, it expresses also much humor and not a little irony. Whether we realize it or not, much of its charm comes from the impact of these two very different personalities.

I am tempted to remind the reader what was said about those years in the life of Jesus of which we know nothing. It seems to me clearly indicated in all the meetings of Jesus with women who were not his relatives, that somewhere in his life in some episode of which we are told nothing, a woman had hurt him deeply. He is invariably kind to those women who have any degree of warm-heartedness, the slightest share of decent cordiality; he is bitter against those who are mean or mercenary. It may be that some girl in his youth admired him for his physical attractiveness, even for his character, but was afraid of his spiritual greatness. Or it may be that he once cared deeply for a woman who in some petty way was false to him. What we can be sure of from the record is that he on no occasion was harsh to a woman who had lived fully, however recklessly, and on no occasion was he severe with any man who similarly had tried to live to the utmost. Immorality he condemned, of course, but he made a distinction between those whose faults are the product of generosity and those who have kept themselves in good repute by not living at all or by living as little as possible. If I presume to say that this woman was one of the people for whose untidy life he could find an excuse, my reason is that in the midst of the talk about exalted spiritual principles, he interrupted himself to make a shrewd guess about her private life. He recognized the type. We shall notice again how often he recognized it.

The conversation began with his request for a drink of water. The woman countered with a question which sounds slightly coquettish. How is it, she asked, that you, a Jew, beg a drink of me, a Samaritan? I thought you Jews had nothing to do with Samaritans. Jesus answered in the key of his great doctrine, that if she knew who he was, she would ask him for a drink, and he would give her living water. She was puzzled by the expression; evidently she thought he referred to the clear water at the bottom of a well like Jacob's, which was extremely deep. She doubted if he had any means for drawing from such a depth. Besides, she asked, are you so much better than Jacob, that you cannot use his well just as it is? Jesus answered that those who drink of the water to which he referred, will never thirst again. Her reply can be read in two ways. "Sir, give me some of this everlasting drink, so that I shan't have to do any more water-carrying." Had she so simple a mind that she took him literally, and hoped to simplify the housework? Or was she incredulous and therefore disposed to treat his words lightly?

I believe that a mocking tone in her question caused him to change the subject and strike back at her. He suggested that she call her husband; she said she had none. We might expect such an answer if, as I think, she was in a slightly flirtatious mood. But Jesus exclaims that she has told the truth, since she has had five husbands and she is not married to the man she happens to be living with at the moment. If the guess was not altogether accurate, it was close enough to startle her. She was shocked for the first time into a serious mood. She hailed Jesus as a prophet, and not having met a prophet before, she seized the occasion to ask whether the Samaritans or the Jews were right in their choice of a place to worship. Her ancestors worshiped in Mt. Gerizim, but the Jews worshiped in the temple at Jerusalem. The great answer of Jesus shows how fast his vision of his mission was growing. The hour is coming, he told her, when true worshipers shall worship the Father, neither in the mountain nor at Jerusalem, but in spirit and in truth. In this statement he commits himself to a religion which in essence is independent of place, of ritual and of ceremony. He seems to recall the exclamation of Jacob waking from his dream in the open desert, with nothing around him but the wide earth, and no roof above but the wide heaven—"This verily is the house of God."

The profound doctrine is lost on the woman. Still in a serious mood but confused and fumbling, she remarks, as if to herself, that she knows the Messiah is coming some day, and when he arrives he will explain all things plainly. As she speaks, Jesus sees his disciples returning from the city of Samaria where they have been buying provisions. The interview is about to end; there is time to say just one thing more. He tells her that he with whom she has talked, is the Messiah. Then the disciples arrive, a little astonished to see him in conversation with a Samaritan woman, but knowing him too well by this time to make any comment.

They did not ask the woman what she wanted; they did not presume to ask him why he talked with her.

The woman had been so deeply stirred by the incident that she forgot the water for which she came—indeed, we are told that in her haste she left the waterpot by the well. What the interview chiefly meant to her is shown by her words to the neighbors: "Come, see a man who told me everything I ever did."

vi

The Messiah and the Kingdom of God

THE NAME JESUS, another form of Joshua, means Saviour. Messiah or Messias means Anointed. The name Christ is a Greek translation of Messiah. Jewish thought for centuries before the birth of Jesus was filled with the hope and dream of a Messiah, who originally was to rescue the people from whatever calamity they suffered at the time, but who gradually became a racial ideal. The Messiah, when at last he arrived, was to usher in the golden age of God's chosen people. He was to represent in himself all the remarkable talents of the race, and by his graciousness as well as by his power he was to recall in his single person the great lawgivers and prophets, the noblest heroes and the most holy priests.

It has been said of the Jews, as it might equally be said of other Oriental peoples, that they have a deep-rooted respect for childhood and old age. In the extremes of life they look for miraculous revelations. Old experience does attain to something like prophetic strain, and very young children surprise by their inexplicable wisdom. We have only to remember the boy Samuel and the boy David to understand why the looked-for Messiah was to come as a little child.

The passages in which the prophets articulated the national dream were inevitably taken over by the followers of Jesus as divinely inspired portraits of him. They are quoted in the New Testament as proof of his authentic mission. It is well for us here, however, to remember that this body of prophecy was, for devout Jews, perhaps their most precious spiritual possession. So long as the hope was not realized, it was their chief inspiration. Paradoxically but very naturally they would resent the pretension of any member of their race that he was the Messiah, arrived at last.

Since Jesus was born into a Messiah-expectant world, I might have begun this book with an account of the Messianic hope. But a common difficulty in understanding the life of Jesus results from our habit of separating the Christian era sharply from all that went before. With the birth of Christ, we assume, the Mosaic tradition stopped, or it should have stopped. Why should the ancient world keep on expecting a Messiah after the Messiah was here? We know very well that a neat partitioning of history is absurd, yet even intelligent people persist in making the Messianic hope either identify itself with Jesus or evaporate entirely. It is well to remind ourselves, as the drama of the mature life of Jesus unfolds, that thousands of men and women who could not accept him as their Messiah continued to hope for the promised Anointed. The clash between his teaching and the orthodox Jewish doctrine was a clash between two contemporary ways of thought, his being very new and as yet enjoying only feeble support. To see the situation clearly helps us to realize the difficulty of his achievement and the strange power of his ideas, once set forth, to make their own way.

We might remind ourselves of some important passages in which the old prophets spoke of the Messiah. In Isaiah, chapter 9, occur verses which the followers of Jesus always associate with him:

"The people that walked in darkness have seen a great light: they that dwell in the land of the shadow of death, upon them hath the light shined. . . . For unto us a child is born, unto us a son is given: and the government shall be upon his shoulder: and his name shall be called Wonderful, Counsellor, The mighty God, The everlasting Father, The Prince of Peace. Of the increase of his government and peace there shall be no end, upon the throne of David, and upon his kingdom, to order it, and to establish it with judgment and with justice from henceforth even for ever."

In Micah, chapter 5, occurs the prophecy that the Messiah would be born in Bethlehem:

"But thou, Bethlehem Ephratah, though thou be little among the thousands of Judah, yet out of thee shall he come forth unto me that is to be ruler in Israel; whose goings forth have been from of old, from everlasting."

In Malachi, chapter 3, the prophecy—as the followers of Jesus thought—referred not only to the Messiah but to his forerunner, John the Baptist:

"Behold, I will send my messenger, and he shall prepare the way before me: and the Lord, whom ye seek, shall suddenly come to his temple, even the messenger of the covenant, whom ye delight in: behold, he shall come, saith the Lord of hosts. But who may abide the day of his coming? and who shall stand when he appeareth? for he is like a refiner's fire, and like fullers' soap: and he shall sit as a refiner and purifier of silver: and he shall purify the sons of Levi, and purge them as gold and silver, that they may offer unto the Lord an offering in righteousness.

"Then shall the offering of Judah and Jerusalem be pleasant unto the Lord, as in the days of old, and as in former years. And I will come near to you to judgment; and I will be a swift witness against the sorcerers, and against the adulterers, and against false swearers, and against those that oppress the hireling in his wages, the widow, and the fatherless, and that turn aside the stranger from his right, and fear not me, saith the Lord of hosts."

These words and similar passages were rooted in the memory of Jesus from his childhood. It was this kind of prophecy to which his mother had encouraged him to look for his destiny. He knew well that lofty though the ancient vision was, it was still an earthly hope. The Messiah was to bring about, as we said, a golden age, or as the Jewish people would say, a kingdom of God, but that kingdom was to be achieved in this world. We cannot remind ourselves too often that in one sense Jesus never departed from this ideal; the prayer which he gave to his disciples asks that God's kingdom may come on earth as it is in heaven; in the Sermon on the Mount and in the parables—that is, in the central body of his teachings—the life which he shows us how to lead is the life here. If he had postponed the kingdom of God to some future existence, it would have been easier to see the difference between his conception of the kingdom and the Jewish hope, and consequently it would be easier to understand why he seemed to many Jews not the true Messiah. But since he kept much of the old dream and stated it in the old terms, many were puzzled and still are, to find the difference. The heart of the matter is in the contrast between the temporary and the eternal here on earth, between a life which measures itself by temporary values and a life which chooses the values which are forever.

The distinction becomes clearer to us as Jesus continued to teach. Perhaps it became clearer also to him. At the beginning and until the end he was a lover of this life, a lover of his fellow man, a lover of the good things to be found in this world. He could have become easily enough a seeker after earthly power. I doubt if the angry threats in the old prophecies against the enemies of God were at all distasteful to his temperament. Had it been his destiny to wreak divine vengeance on earth, there was an element in his human nature which could have found satisfaction in the work. But with the gradually accumulating vision which is possible to us in our human limitations, he chose to translate temporary values into eternal ones, and to combat the negative principle of evil with the positive force of love. For our comfort we notice that he too found this ideal difficult. In what he says and occasionally in what he does, he is not always consistent. Those who are interested only in the divine aspect of his personality try to persuade themselves that the life recorded in the Gospels had nothing in it but such perfection as is possible only for Almighty God himself, but it is more truly reverent, more truly devout, to see in this human record, not an exhibition of a goodness to which no human being could possibly attain, but rather the drama of our common humanity, of our human spirit set in the human body, in the midst of times and seasons but with eternity in our heart, living from day to day, asking each day for our daily bread, and yet striving here and now to live eternally.

2

WHEN ancient prophets spoke of a Messiah, they imagined him as a king. If their hopes were moderate, his kingdom was to consist of a restored Israel; in more exalted moods they foretold that he would be king of the whole earth. Zechariah, in chapter 14, says, "The Lord shall be king over all the earth: in that day shall there be one Lord, and his name one." Isaiah, chapter 52, celebrates the Messiah and his kingdom at greater length: "How beautiful upon the mountains are the feet of him that bringeth good tidings, that publisheth peace; that bringeth good tidings of good, that publisheth salvation; that saith unto Zion, Thy God reigneth! Thy watchmen shall lift up the voice: with the voice together shall they sing: for they shall see eye to eye, when the Lord shall bring again Zion.

"Break forth into joy, sing together, ye waste places of Jerusalem: for the Lord hath comforted his people; he hath redeemed Jerusalem. The Lord hath made bare his holy arm in the eyes of all the nations; and all the ends of the earth shall see the salvation of our God."

Prophecies of the Messiah's kingdom have great emotional uplift but they are not clear; apparently the kingdom is to be like other earthly kingdoms except that it will be unconquerable and it will endure, yet at moments a dark shadow is introduced among the most lyrical hopes. The Messiah, when he came, would be the ideal man, and the kingdom, since a perfect man would organize it, would be flawless, but unless all the inhabitants of the kingdom reached the same degree of perfection as their leader, would his rule be satisfactory to him or to them? The prophets raised the question without solving it. Jesus was to supply the inescapable answer, the frank admission that the kingdom of God would be perfect when every member of it was perfect, even as the king was perfect.

The prophet Isaiah followed the song of hope just quoted with an eloquent lamentation; he foresaw what would happen to a Messiah who prescribed perfection for those not ready for it: "He is despised and rejected of men; a man of sorrows, and acquainted with grief; and we hid as it were our faces from him; he was despised, and we esteemed him not.

"Surely he hath borne our griefs, and carried our sorrows: yet we did esteem him stricken, smitten of God, and afflicted. But he was wounded for our transgressions, he was bruised for our iniquities: the chastisement of our peace was upon him; and with his stripes we are healed.

"All we like sheep have gone astray; we have turned everyone to his own way; and the Lord hath laid on him the iniquity of us all.

"He was oppressed, and he was afflicted, yet he opened not his mouth; he is brought as a lamb to the slaughter, and as a sheep before her shearers is dumb, so he openeth not his mouth.

"He was taken from prison and from judgment: and who shall declare his generation? for he was cut off out of the land of the living: for the transgression of my people was he stricken."

These contrasting passages and similar quotations from other prophets haunted the followers of Jesus after the Crucifixion, when they considered the divine loveliness of the kingdom he had tried to bring on earth, and the cruel reward of the attempt. Yet the ancient prophets did not anticipate the kingdom of heaven as Jesus conceived of it, nor could they foretell the sequence which brought him to the cross.

He was determined to free his thinking from all that was accidental or temporary. This resolution pressed home would lead to a terrible sincerity. Since mankind is for the most part entangled in temporary and accidental values, he would seem to most of his fellows, not their Messiah, but their deadly enemy. In self-preservation they would kill him.

The terrible sincerity had motion in it, the least answerable form of logic. Jehovah had been to the Jews a father, but on the whole a parent to be feared. In the character of Jesus there was no place for fear. To him God was infinite goodness, the creator of goodness and beauty, the loving father who wished his children, all of them without exception, to have life in abundance, to live to the utmost in all their capacities, to live boldly, even at the risk of failure. Since the eternal Father had placed man in this temporary world, and had mated each immortal soul with a temporary and accidental body, man even at his wisest would make mistakes, and even at his noblest might slip for a moment and fall into sin. But those who did their best, God would forgive and comfort.

The conception of God as a loving rather than an angry father carried with it plain obligations for his children. We must love each other exactly as God loves us. This doctrine seems harmless if we do not examine it closely. When we are told to love our neighbor, we reflect that we live in a good neighborhood, and our immediate neighbors, after all, are fortunately few. But we get into trouble the moment we face the question whether we are really imitating the love of God if we set limits to the love of neighbors. To love our fellow man means to love all our fellow men. If we love all our fellow men, the primitive instincts of narrow or accidental loyalty will be undermined. It is natural to feel that the place where we have found happiness is the best place to live, and that other men, living elsewhere, are inferior or out of luck. Here we have the basis of narrow patriotism. If we love the people with whom we grew up, it is natural to feel that they, our race, our language, our habits, have special and exclusive merits. If we love our parents—and what decent soul does not?—it is natural to make of our home a shrine, and of our family a sacred clan with ourselves in the midst, isolated by pious conceit.

The brotherhood of man, if put into practice, would disrupt conventional patriotism, conventional family relations, the conventional attitude of children to parents. The teaching of Jesus broke the news to the world that a man who sincerely tries to illustrate in his conduct the love of God, may appear to disrupt society—society being organized on a strictly temporal and accidental basis. There is nothing permanent in national patriotism; when territories are divided or added, men can shrink or enlarge their patriotism almost overnight. There is nothing permanent in our so-called traditional ways of living; a new invention or an economic change may end an old habit or introduce a new one. Children do not choose their parents, nor in a sense do parents choose their children. Families are not equally united, nor can the members of all households be equally loyal to each other. Only the spiritual values are eternal. The love of the heavenly Father for his children is all-embracing, and it endures. The first duty of man is to love all men.

In the brief years of his ministry Jesus illustrated in a dozen ways this simple but difficult conception of the kingdom of God. We say carelessly that his people rejected him because he offered them an entirely spiritual kingdom rather than the prospect of earthly power, and to some extent this is true, but popular resentment would not have been strong enough to cause his death if he had merely disappointed a political ambition. He did far more than that. By his interpretation of divine love he undermined patriotism, he diminished the authority of parents, he made political questions seem insignificant, he attacked formal religion. All these matters, around which human pieties accumulate, he brushed aside as temporary and accidental. To be sure, he visited the temple and he attended the synagogue, but he was as likely as not to criticize what was going on there, or to tell the congregation what he thought of them, and apparently he enjoyed shattering the rules made by priestly edict or social convention. He would dine in the house of any man whom he happened to like, and he liked a queer assortment of people, without regard to their religion, their color, or their race. He seemed to think beggars were picturesque, but so were the rich. A reasonable philosopher might say a word in favor of poverty, or a sensible man might envy wealth, but this dangerous fellow hobnobbed with poverty without praising it, and enjoyed a rich man's dinner while feeling from some points of view sorry for him.

The theory of the kingdom of God as Jesus defined it must be gathered from passages in the Gospel here and there. It is presented clearly and fully in no one place. Perhaps it was too subtle or too complicated for his disciples. Or perhaps it was so clear that it frightened them. No one could enter into the kingdom who did not love God. Those who loved God would love all men. To love all men, it would be necessary to rise above prejudice, ignorance, selfishness, whatever is temporary and accidental. The kingdom will come on earth when we begin here and now to live eternally. But it is much easier to live in time.

vii

The Twelve Companions

THE NAMES of the Twelve are given, with certain variations, in the Gospels according to St. Matthew, St. Mark, and St. Luke, and in The Acts of the Apostles. In all the lists Simon Peter comes first, and Judas Iscariot last. The leadership of Peter is obvious, and so is the ignominy of the traitor. The suggestion has been made that Judas always earned, and got, the lowest rating in the group, and that he was embittered by failure.

If each of the four lists is divided into groups of four, the persons in each group appear to be always the same, though they are not always named in the same order. A comparison of the lists, therefore, clears away one or two apparent contradictions. But before we make this comparison we should put side by side for a moment two passages which tell how the first group of apostles were selected. In St. Matthew, chapter 4, we read: "Jesus, walking by the sea of Galilee, saw two brethren, Simon called Peter, and Andrew his brother, casting a net into the sea: for they were fishers. And he saith unto them, Follow me, and I will make you fishers of men. And they straightway left their nets, and followed him. And going on from thence, he saw other two brethren, James the son of Zebedee, and John his brother, in a ship with Zebedee their father, mending their nets; and he called them. And they immediately left the ship and their father, and followed him."

Practically the same account is given by St. Mark, chapter 1, with the significant little difference that James and John "left their father Zebedee in the ship with the hired servants," a detail which suggests for Zebedee an economic condition above that of an ordinary fisherman. But neither St. Matthew nor St. Mark provides information about these converts before Jesus walked by the sea and called them.

St. John, one of the sons of Zebedee, could tell the story in full (chapter 1). Simon Peter and Andrew were the sons of Jona. Like the sons of Zebedee, they lived in Bethsaida. All four were associated in their daily work, and all four were preoccupied with the coming of the Messiah and his kingdom. Andrew and John, one of each family, were disciples of the Baptist; perhaps Peter and James were also. Though St. John does not name himself, it is not doubted that he was the other disciple with Andrew who at a word from the Baptist followed Jesus.

"The next day after John stood, and two of his disciples; and looking upon Jesus as he walked, he saith, Behold the Lamb of God! And the two disciples heard him speak, and they followed Jesus.

"Then Jesus turned and saw them following, and saith unto them, What seek ye? They said unto him, Rabbi, (which is to say, being interpreted, Master) where dwellest thou? He saith unto them, Come and see. They came and saw where he dwelt, and abode with him that day: for it was about the tenth hour [almost night].

"One of the two which heard John speak, and followed him, was Andrew, Simon Peter's brother. He first findeth his own brother Simon, and saith unto him, We have found the Messias, which is, being interpreted, the Christ. And he brought him to Jesus. And when Jesus beheld him, he said, Thou art Simon the son of Jona: thou shalt be called Cephas, which is by interpretation, A stone.

"The day following Jesus would go forth into Galilee, and findeth Philip, and saith unto him, Follow me. Now Philip was of Bethsaida, the city of Andrew and Peter.

"Philip findeth Nathanael, and saith unto him, We have found him, of whom Moses in the law, and the prophets, did write, Jesus of Nazareth, the son of Joseph. And Nathanael said unto him, Can there any good thing come out of Nazareth? Philip saith unto him, Come and see.

"Jesus saw Nathanael coming to him, and saith of him, Behold an Israelite indeed, in whom is no guile! Nathanael saith unto him, Whence knowest thou me? Jesus answered and said unto him, Before that Philip called thee, when thou wast under the fig tree, I saw thee. Nathanael answered and saith unto him, Rabbi, thou art the Son of God; thou art the King of Israel."

St. John's account seems at first to contradict St. Matthew's, but it merely completes and explains it. When Jesus walked by the sea and told the sons of Jona and the sons of Zebedee to follow him, they were already his disciples, waiting for the signal to begin their work. St. John reports their first sight of him, and the overwhelming effect of his personality.

Let us now look for a moment at the complete lists of the Twelve.

In St. Matthew, chapter 10, it stands—

Simon, who is called Peter, and Andrew his brother; James the son of Zebedee, and John his brother;

Philip, and Bartholomew; Thomas, and Matthew the publican;

James the son of Alphæus, and Lebbæus, whose surname was Thaddæus; Simon the Canaanite, and Judas Iscariot, who also betrayed him.

St. Mark, chapter 3, gives the list—

Simon surnamed Peter; and James the son of Zebedee, and John the brother of James; and he surnamed them Boanerges, which is, The sons of thunder: and Andrew,

And Philip, and Bartholomew, and Matthew, and Thomas,

And James the son of Alphæus, and Thaddæus, and Simon the Canaanite, and Judas Iscariot, which also betrayed him.

St. Luke, chapter 6, gives the list—

Simon, whom he also named Peter, and Andrew his brother, James and John,

Philip and Bartholomew, Matthew and Thomas,

James the son of Alphæus, and Simon called Zelotes, and Judas the brother of James, and Judas Iscariot, which also was the traitor.

In The Acts of the Apostles, chapter 1, in the account of the meeting which elected a successor to Judas Iscariot, the names of the eleven are given—

Peter, and James, and John, and Andrew,

Philip, and Thomas, Bartholomew, and Matthew,

James the son of Alphæus, and Simon Zelotes, and Judas the brother of James.

At the meeting which these eleven attended, Matthias was chosen to make up again the full number of apostles, but his election is outside our story, and need not detain us here.

Four names in the original list invite comment at once. James the son of Alphæus was apparently the brother of Matthew, the son of Alphæus. Lebbæus, whose surname was Thaddæus, was apparently the same person as Judas the brother of James. It has been thought that Judas was the son of James rather than his brother. Lebbæus and Thaddæus are epithets, both meaning "warm-hearted." The name Judas was so common that it needed always another name for distinction. Bartholomew, a name describing ancestry, is identified with Nathanael. Simon the Canaanite is Simon Zelotes. Cananite, misspelled Canaanite, means "zealous," which is also the meaning of Zelotes.

2

s o m e readers have been astonished that so far as we can gather from the Gospel record, the majority of the apostles play minor parts in the story of Jesus. Peter was outstanding among the Twelve, and three or four others are mentioned in various scenes, but the group as a whole were simply disciples learning from their teacher, caring for his wants so far as they could, protecting him so far as he would let them. We ought not to expect from them at that time anything more. In their later careers they caused themselves to be widely remembered, if in some cases dimly and only in legend, but Jesus, it would seem, chose them as a typical group rather than to illustrate in every case a brilliant type of leadership. So far as we know, they were all young. They differed greatly in talents and in character. Several of them were by nature timid, and one was a traitor. For the brief years of the ministry they were the companions of Jesus, his daily associates. Like other men, he had to make the best of whatever life afforded.

Peter, the Prince of the Apostles, was from the beginning a marvelous character. Jesus gave him at sight the nickname of Cephas, Aramaic for "rock." The name Peter is the Greek translation of the word. Steadfast loyalty was the essence of his character. In the terrible hours before the Crucifixion he, for one moment, did tell a lie; he denied to the Roman soldiers that he had ever known Jesus. But this episode, far from discrediting Peter unduly, illustrates a profound doctrine of Jesus, then and now too often misunderstood.

Jesus taught that the children of God should imitate and practice the love which their heavenly Father showed to them; they should love to the utmost, beyond any limit; if at any point their love should come to an end, they would not be worthy of the kingdom of heaven. Time and again Jesus applied this test: Is there a limit to your love? He told the rich young man to sell all he had and give the money to the poor, and though the young man wished to follow Jesus, he could not bring himself to part with his investments. The comment of Jesus was that nothing is impossible with God, implying that the young man after all might develop the capacity for unbounded love.

In another place still more famous Jesus said, He who loveth father or mother more than me is not worthy of me. This does not mean that he discouraged us from loving our parents, but it does very specifically mean, what we all know to be true, that many a parent, unintentionally or unconsciously, interferes with the life which a child should lead. Then as now men and women, through mistaken piety, put devotion to parents ahead of devotion to the important career for which they were born; they sacrificed their destiny because perhaps they couldn't follow it without leaving home, and some older person in the household was unwilling to be left behind. Then as now the elder generation was sometimes selfish, or at least willing that life should slow down for their convenience. Jesus invariably takes the viewpoint of the young, and he insists on their duty to live their appointed lives—appointed by the wisdom of providence, not of parents. He who has the vision of the kingdom of heaven and yet cannot seek the kingdom because his mother, or his aunt, or someone else in the family asks him to stay home, is not worthy of the kingdom.

Peter serves in the Gospels as the most powerful illustration of this doctrine. Whatever we have given our hearts to, we should seek without holding back; we cannot go part way, we cannot pause at any stage, for any reason, without peril to our soul. "No man having put his hand to the plough and looking back is fit for the kingdom of God." Yet each of us has his weakness, often without suspecting it, and Simon Peter, whose courage was beyond question, for one moment became a coward. He recovered himself and made amends by redoubled service and unstinted devotion. The apparently severe sayings of Jesus about the unworthiness of those who turn back or falter, should be read always with an implication of merciful understanding; in the story of Jesus himself, there are moments of hesitation, even of self-doubt, and if there were not, he would not be human like the rest of us. He understood Peter as he understood the rich young man. He told us that if anything, even dutiful affection, keeps us from the work which heaven assigns to us, we are in a sense lost souls, but he also hopes we may see clearly at last, and he reminds us constantly that a full life is rich in blessed second chances.

As we have noted, Simon Peter came from Bethsaida. He was married, though nothing is known about his wife except that she once had a fever. He must have been extremely warm-hearted, not to say hot-blooded, and in speech he was impetuous. Recognizing his leadership, the other apostles fell into the habit of letting him do the talking, and when Jesus spoke to them, more often than not he addressed himself to Peter. He was with Jesus in all the important events of his life. He accompanied him to Gethsemane, and must have expected trouble, since he went armed with a sword. When Judas appeared with the Roman band, Peter drew his sword and sliced an ear off one of the soldiers.

The part that he played in the early history of the Church is told in The Acts of the Apostles. With characteristic vehemence he first advocated the admission of Gentiles into the Christian fellowship, and later, changing his mind, he wanted to reserve the kingdom of God to the Jewish people. He was not a great thinker, nor perhaps a great statesman; in these respects Paul was by far his superior. But Peter was endowed with the heroic ardent temper which could understand the doctrine of passion and infinite love. The opinions in which the Church decided not to follow him are now forgotten as of no account, and only his great leadership is remembered.

St. John liked to think that he was the disciple whom Jesus particularly loved, and in some sense the claim may be justified, but the Gospel record shows that Jesus turned instinctively to Peter for support, perhaps in dark moments for encouragement. He was the apostle who in the greatness of his nature came closest to the Master.

The closing part of his ministry he spent in Rome, where he suffered martyrdom under Nero. Legend has it that he died on Vatican Hill, and that St. Constantine built a church over his tomb—which church was replaced by St. Peter's. There is a further legend that the form of his martyrdom was crucifixion, and that by his own request, he was crucified head-downwards, in final atonement for his denial of Jesus.

His brother Andrew resembled him in courage and generosity but not, so far as we know, in impetuousness. Although he was one of the Twelve, Andrew was willing to remain somewhat in the background. But he proved like Peter a heroic missionary, and in various parts of the earth we still come upon reminders of him. His name is Greek, meaning "manly." That he was like his brother, an effective orator, may be doubted, and there is no ground for supposing that like Paul he had extraordinary talents as an organizer. But he certainly had unlimited enterprise, and wherever his mission took him, he seems to have left a deep mark by the sincerity and the intensity of his faith. He carried the Gospel through Asia Minor, through Macedonia, through Southern Russia, and ultimately into Greece, where he was martyred by crucifixion. The cross on which he died, now called the St. Andrew's cross, was shaped like the letter X. He is the patron saint of Russia and also of Scotland, as the St. Andrew's cross in the Union Jack bears witness. At what age he died is not known.

James, one of the sons of Zebedee, perhaps the elder, was the missionary of Jesus to Spain, and is the patron saint of that country. He left no writings and his only memorial is his vast work. He was martyred by Herod Agrippa, as we learn from a passage in The Acts of the Apostles, chapter 12, which indicates that he had returned from Spain. "Now about that time Herod the King stretched forth his hands to vex certain of the church. And he killed James the brother of John with the sword."

St. John, the other son of Zebedee and one of the earliest disciples, as we have seen, and the author not only of the fourth Gospel but of three Epistles and of The Revelation, is supposed to have lived to a great age, chiefly at Ephesus. At some time in his life he was exiled to the island of Patmos, as he tells us in The Revelation, and he paid a visit to Rome. The vagueness of the records about him is puzzling when we consider the significance of his career and the lofty place he occupies in the Christian tradition. He enjoyed the confidence and the close friendship of the Virgin Mary as well as of Jesus, and it was to him that Jesus on the cross confided the care of his mother. He was present with Mary at the meeting of the apostles which chose a successor to Judas. From then on, the details of his life are obscure.

Tradition says he was the author of the fourth Gospel, and there is, in my opinion, small reason to doubt that the tradition was correct. The spiritual insights of this Gospel are penetrating, and as we say with self-flattery, modern. St. John understood, not only the psychology of belief, but also the psychology of skepticism. In the midst of his rhapsodic expression of faith, he does justice to the unbeliever, observing him accurately. Of all the glimpses he gives us into the mind and the soul, none is more often remembered than Pilate's weary question, when Jesus said he had come into the world to bear witness to the truth. Pilate asked, "What is truth?"

St. John had literary genius of the first order. Apparently he had also an interest in other contemporary philosophies, especially in some of the more spiritual Greek thinkers. The doctrine of love, central in the teaching of Jesus, he translated into the terms of his own character. Though in his youth he may have been one of the sons of thunder, in his old age he seems to have become gentleness itself. There is a tradition that he barely escaped martyrdom at Rome, and that a church was dedicated to him in honor of this miracle. It was of him that Jesus said to Peter, "If I will that he tarry till I come, what is that to thee?" From these words sprang the legend that St. John was to live until the second coming of the Lord.

We know little about Philip, but that little suggests a personality of considerable charm. Like the sons of Jona and Zebedee, he lived in Bethsaida, and like them he was prepared for the teaching of Jesus by his own fervent hope for a Messiah. We have seen how he brought Nathanael to Jesus. Tradition made him the disciple who, when called, asked permission first to go and bury his father—to whom Jesus answered, "Let the dead bury their dead," St. Luke, chapter 9. In St. John's account of the feeding of the five thousand, it is to Philip that Jesus says, "Whence shall we buy bread, that these may eat?" And it was Philip who said to Jesus, with a simplicity which was not displeasing, "Lord, show us the father, and it sufficeth us." It was to him, as we learn from the Gospel according to St. John, that the Greeks at Jerusalem applied for an introduction to the prophet who had just raised Lazarus from the dead: "There were certain Greeks among them that came up to worship at the feast; the same came therefore to Philip, which was of Bethsaida of Galilee, and desired him, saying, Sir, we would see Jesus. Philip cometh and telleth Andrew: and again Andrew and Philip tell Jesus." (St. John, chapter 12.)

It is said that Philip was married, and had two daughters, also that he was martyred at Hierapolis, in Phrygia, and his two beautiful daughters with him. The three were buried in a row, Philip in the center, a daughter on each side. The symmetry of this legend has roused doubts. Another legend, less attractive, says he died peacefully of old age.

Thomas, sometimes called Didymus, "doubting Thomas," the apostle who believed what he saw but found it hard to believe what he heard, was a Galilean fisherman. His name means "twin," and Didymus is a Greek translation. Unsuccessful attempts have been made to identify some other apostle as his brother. The caution for which he is famous went hand in hand with great ardor and courage. The legend of his skepticism is based on an episode after the Resurrection, but an exclamation of his in the same episode is cherished among the absolute expressions of Christian faith. "Thomas, one of the twelve, called Didymus, was not with them when Jesus came. The other disciples therefore said unto him, We have seen the Lord. But he said unto them, Except I shall see in his hands the print of the nails, and put my finger into the print of the nails, and thrust my hand into his side, I will not believe.

"And after eight days again his disciples were within, and Thomas with them: then came Jesus, the doors being shut, and stood in the midst, and said, Peace be unto you. Then saith he to Thomas, Reach hither thy finger, and behold my hands; and reach hither thy hand, and thrust it into my side: and be not faithless, but believing. And Thomas answered and said unto him, My Lord and my God." (St. John, chapter 20.)

There is an apocryphal Gospel of Thomas, and an apocryphal

collection of incidents called the Acts of Thomas; neither work furnishes reliable information. From the mass of legends, however, tradition has accepted as least doubtful the report that Thomas earned the title of "Missionary to the Indies"; that he carried the Gospel to Mesopotamia, Parthia, and India; that he traveled further than any other of the Twelve, and preached in more languages. Tradition would probably accept, if it could, the story that he reached the land from which the Wise Men came, and that he arrived in time to convert Gaspar, Melchior, and Balthasar. It is to be regretted that legend here forgets to tell us the precise country in which the Magi made their home. Historians still transmit without prejudice, neither approving nor disapproving, the rumor that Thomas died a martyr, pierced with a heathen lance. We recall that he had asked to see the mark of the lance in the side of the risen Jesus. Popular legends always lean strongly toward poetic justice.

Bartholomew, identified with Nathanael, the friend of Philip, was as his name indicates the son of Tholmai. Nothing else is known about him, but he has his place in legend. It is said that he preached the Gospel in northern India, which may very well be true—also that he suffered martyrdom in Armenia. One account says that he was flayed alive, another that he was crucified, a third that he was beheaded—and a fourth suggests that he was killed by all three methods, the flaying and the crucifixion being preliminary tortures.

St. Matthew, or Levi, the publican of Capernaum, the son of Alphæus, was the author of the first Gospel. In chapter 9 he tells the incident of his calling to be an apostle. St. Mark, chapter 2, tells the story with slight variations, but St. Luke, chapter 5, gives the fullest account.

"And after these things he went forth, and saw a publican, named Levi, sitting at the receipt of custom: and he said unto him, Follow me. And he left all, rose up, and followed him. And Levi made him a great feast in his own house: and there was a great company of publicans and of others that sat down with them. But their scribes and Pharisees murmured against his disciples, saying, Why do ye eat and drink with publicans and sinners?"

The Latin word *publicanus* means "state employee," and for the Jews in the time of Jesus it had a dark meaning, reminding them of the subjugated condition of their country. Rome taxed her provinces heavily, and by a vicious method. The collection was farmed out to wealthy Romans, who were supposed to get in the money with only a reasonable profit to themselves, but they gouged their victims, and in Palestine they employed natives of each locality to do the actual collecting. The Jew who consented to be an agent for this graft was naturally detested and despised as one of the worst of sinners.

From his version of the Gospel it is easy to believe that Matthew the publican had been deeply troubled in conscience before he met Jesus. More than any other Evangelist he refers to the Old Testament; in his self-reproach perhaps he had been turning to the ancient Law for help and light. He gives the fullest account we have of the teaching of Jesus, often laying a pathetic emphasis on questions of justice connected with money.

Though we are not told so, we imagine that Jesus, before bidding Matthew to follow him, had met the unhappy publican several times, knew his frame of mind, and had formed a well-considered opinion of his character. We can believe also that the feast which Matthew prepared in his own house for Jesus, expressed only a part of his gratitude for moral rescue. Since he was leaving his well-paid post in the tax department, he may have spent on the fine dinner for such a large company all the money he had.

St. Matthew did most of his missionary work in Judæa, where his preaching formed the basis of the Gospel version which bears his name. James the son of Alphæus was almost certainly his brother, and in his later years he apparently was associated with Thomas, traveling in Parthia and in Ethiopia. In one of these countries, according to legend, he was martyred, but another tradition says he died of old age.

The four apostles named in the third group seem to have contributed least, and for that reason, no doubt, they were always placed last. Little if anything is known about their lives, though Judas Iscariot is immortalized in infamy. James the son of Alphæus, called James the less, to distinguish him from the son of Zebedee, was, as we have just said, St. Matthew's brother. He was probably the author of the General Epistle called by his name, and he was also, perhaps, the first bishop of Jerusalem. Jude, nicknamed Lebbæus or Thaddæus, was martyred in Persia, if tradition may be trusted. With him Simon Zelotes is always associated; in the Christian calendar Simon and Jude are remembered on the same day. Jude is reported to have suffered martyrdom in Persia.

3

MATTHEW, Mark, Luke and John. Of the four Evangelists only the first and the fourth were among the twelve apostles. St. Mark and St. Luke, however, may conveniently be included in this account of the men who handed on the teaching of Jesus.

St. Mark's full name was John Mark. His mother's name was Mary, and she was a sister of Barnabas. In the epistle to the Colossians, chapter 4, Paul speaks of "Marcus, sister's son to Barnabas."

St. Mark was closely associated with both Peter and Paul. It was to the house of St. Mark's mother in Jerusalem that Peter came after his release from Herod's prison. The incident is told in The Acts of the Apostles, chapter 12.

"He came to the house of Mary the mother of John, whose surname was Mark; where many were gathered together praying. And as Peter knocked at the door of the gate, a damsel came to hearken, named Rhoda. And when she knew Peter's voice, she opened not the gate for gladness, but ran in, and told how Peter stood before the gate."

Nothing more is told of the damsel named Rhoda, but we notice that she had a Greek name, and she knew Peter's voice well enough to recognize it instantly. The company at prayer were presumably a little congregation of Jews and Gentiles to whom Peter had ministered and preached, devoted followers and friends, grieving and supplicating for their imprisoned leader. The graphic detail, that the maiden Rhoda was so excited by Peter's voice that she ran to tell the others before letting him in, is characteristic of St. Mark.

He tells a short but brilliant story in a swift, hard-hitting manner, with such vividness that the scenes are to a high degree lifelike. Since the narrative moves fast and with bold strokes, we need not wonder that much which can be found in St. Matthew or St. Luke is here omitted, but we may wonder that there is no account of the birth or early history of Jesus, and no report of the Sermon on the Mount. On the other hand St. Mark more than any other Evangelist gives us words actually used by Jesus—*Boanerges*, for example, "Sons of thunder," the name he gave to the sons of Zebedee; *Talitha cumi*, "Damsel, I say unto thee, arise," spoken to the daughter of Jairus; *Ephphatha*, "be opened," the healing word to the deaf man.

St. Luke, as his name suggests, was a Greek. He was a physician; according to some accounts, a ship's doctor. Perhaps we should not dismiss too lightly the legend that he was also a painter, and that he left several portraits of the Virgin Mary. He was the author not only of the third Gospel but of The Acts of the Apostles, the great story of the early missionary work of the Church, as carried on principally by Peter and Paul. The association between Paul and St. Luke was obviously so close that it is easy to believe the tradition which makes St. Luke one of Paul's first converts. Clearly he was a well-educated man, with unusual literary gifts. His version of the Gospel and St. John's, however they may differ otherwise, are pre-eminently beautiful and moving, one rich in poetry, the other in philosophy. It is thought that St. Luke had the material for his account of Jesus directly from the Virgin herself. The book is indeed a biography, an orderly presentation of an entire life, not a compilation of traditions made by various and unknown hands, but a work designed and finished by one person and acknowledged by him, and preserved to us practically as he wrote it.

St. Luke introduces The Acts of the Apostles with these words: "The former treatise have I made, O Theophilus, of all that Jesus began both to do and teach." The treatise referred to was the version of the Gospel which we are now discussing. Theophilus was, like St. Luke, a Gentile, a Greek, presumably a convert, but somewhat perplexed by the discrepancies between the various accounts of Jesus at that time circulating. St. Luke wanted to give his friends the facts as clearly and as accurately as possible. He states his purpose in the introduction to his Gospel; he had a quite modern weakness for introductions:

"Forasmuch as many have taken in hand to set forth in order a declaration of those things which are most surely believed among us, even as they delivered them unto us, which from the beginning were eyewitnesses, and ministers of the word; it seemed good to me also, having had perfect understanding of all things from the very first, to write unto thee in order, most excellent Theophilus, that thou mightest know the certainty of those things, wherein thou hast been instructed."

It is evident at once that St. Luke believes he has his material well in hand, and that he intends to report the life of Jesus clearly and fully. As we read on we see that he is a good observer, and that he looks not only for surface detail but for underlying cause and effect. It is easy to believe he was a scientist. His thorough and accurate way of describing what he saw, furnishes those hints from which scholars have deduced the little that is known about him. The legend that he was a ship's doctor rests on the fact that he recounts nautical experiences with vividness, but not by the terms a sailor would use. Telling the journeys of Paul, in The Acts of the Apostles, he refers to the persons in the mission sometimes as "we," sometimes as "they." Assuming that "we" indicates his presence, we are fairly certain which sections of which expeditions he shared with Paul, at what stopping places he left the company, and where he rejoined it. If he is more frequently at the apostle's side, as time goes on, we think not only of their friendship but of Paul's years and declining health, and of the service a good physician could render.

4

ALL the apostles but one were Galileans. Judas Iscariot came from Judæa, where orthodoxy was intrenched. This fact may explain his story. His father Simon was called, like him, Iscariot. The name probably means that he was born in the town of Kerioth. Under what circumstances Jesus selected him for a disciple, we do not know. He "had the bag," or was the treasurer for the Twelve, and St. John, who tells us most about him, suggests that he was disliked by the others. St. John also gives us our only full-length picture of him before the betrayal:

"Then Jesus six days before the passover came to Bethany, where Lazarus was which had been dead, whom he raised from the dead. There they made him a supper, and Martha served, but Lazarus was one of them that sat at the table with him. Then took Mary a pound of ointment of spikenard, very costly, and anointed the feet of Jesus, and wiped his feet with her hair; and the house was filled with the odour of the ointment.

"Then said one of his disciples, Judas Iscariot, Simon's son, which should betray him, Why was not this ointment sold for three hundred pence, and given to the poor? This he said, not that he cared for the poor, but because he was a thief, and had the bag, and bare what was put therein. Then said Jesus, Let her alone: against the day of my burying hath she kept this." (St. John, chapter 12.)

"Bare what was put therein," should be translated "bare away," or pilfered. St. John here accuses Judas of dishonest greed for money, thus offering a motive for the rest of the story, which we might as well consider at once. The Last Supper being ended, "the devil having now put into the heart of Judas Iscariot, Simon's son, to betray him . . . Jesus was troubled in spirit, and testified, and said, Verily, verily, I say unto you, that one of you shall betray me. Then the disciples looked one on another, doubting of whom he spake. Now there was leaning on Jesus' bosom one of his disciples, whom Jesus loved. Simon Peter therefore beckoned to him, that he should ask who it should be of whom he spake. He then lying on Jesus' breast saith unto him, Lord, who is it? Jesus answered, He it is, to whom I shall give a sop, when I have dipped it. And when he had dipped the sop, he gave it to Judas Iscariot, the son of Simon. And after the sop Satan entered into him. Then said Jesus unto him, That thou doest, do quickly. Now no man at the table knew for what intent he spake this unto him. For some of them thought, because Judas had the bag, that Jesus had said unto him, Buy those things that we have need of against the feast; or, that he should give something to the poor. He then having received the sop went immediately out; and it was night." (St. John, chapter 13.)

St. Matthew's Gospel continues from this point: "Judas Iscariot went unto the chief priests, and said unto them, What will ye give me, and I will deliver him unto you? And they covenanted with him for thirty pieces of silver." (St. Matthew, chapter 26.)

While Jesus was speaking to his faithful disciples, in the garden of Gethsemane, "Judas, one of the twelve, came, and with him a great multitude with swords and staves, from the chief priests and elders of the people. Now he that betrayed him gave them a sign, saying, Whomsoever I shall kiss, that same is he: hold him fast. And forthwith he came to Jesus, and said, Hail, master; and kissed him. And Jesus said unto him, Friend, wherefore art thou come?"

"When the morning was come, all the chief priests and elders of the people took counsel against Jesus to put him to death; and when they had bound him, they led him away, and delivered him to Pontius Pilate the governor. Then Judas, which had betrayed him, when he saw that he was condemned, repented himself, and brought again the thirty pieces of silver to the chief priests and elders, saying, I have sinned in that I have betrayed the innocent blood. And they said, What is that to us? See thou to that. And he cast down the pieces of silver in the temple, and departed, and went and hanged himself. And the chief priests took the silver pieces, and said, It is not lawful for to put them into the treasury, because it is the price of blood. And they took counsel, and bought with them the potter's field, to bury strangers in. Wherefore that field was called, The field of blood, unto this day." (St. Matthew, chapter 27.)

Here is one of the great stories of the world, and it is not complete. How can we explain the conduct of Judas? If he was at any time to any extent attracted by the character of Jesus, can we readily believe that he sold his master for thirty pieces of silver? From the time when Jesus lived until now, men have tried to solve the puzzle, either because of a natural interest in a mystery, or for a more thoughtful reason, because the human story of Jesus is not entirely clear unless we know or guess at the story of Judas.

One of the guesses is that Judas loved Jesus and wanted his good opinion; Jesus sent him to town with thirty pieces of silver to buy food for the Twelve; Judas through some form of carelessness lost the money; he was offered thirty pieces of silver if he would say where Jesus could be found; he thought the lost money had been replaced by the mercy of heaven, and closed the deal, not knowing what was really involved. In this explanation of his conduct there are variations; one version says he lost the money by gambling, another says that his sister stole it. The sister is a useful invention. An old English ballad, in a thirteenth-century manuscript, says that she didn't believe in Jesus, that she tried to undermine her brother's faith, and that she stole the thirty pieces of silver when Judas unwisely dropped in at her home for a short nap.

There is also a legend, even less convincing, that Judas always took a rake-off on contributions to the common fund, and for that reason he had said that the ointment should have been turned into cash. He estimated its value at three hundred pence. The thirty pieces of silver would have been approximately his usual commission.

Whatever value these stories may have, they fail to explain

the remorse and suicide of Judas, and the plain words of Jesus at the Last Supper. If Judas was a cheap grafter and the disciples knew it, why was he allowed to remain among them? Besides— here's a question which may seem far afield—how did he come to be in touch with the high priests, having access to them at his convenience? The high priests were Annas and Caiaphas, who prudently winked at the goings on of Herod and Herodias, who looked the other way while John the Baptist was murdered, but who resolved for good and sufficient reasons of their own that Jesus must die. Was Judas involved in their plans?

I offer my own guess for what it may be worth. I believe there are three principal clues to the drama which began with the baptism at the hands of John, and ended on Calvary. One is in the character and teaching of Jesus himself; truth so thorough and so deep-cutting would rouse enemies, sooner or later. The second clue is in Annas and Caiaphas, particularly the latter, who seems to have had a strong instinct for self-preservation. The third clue is in Judas Iscariot.

An apocryphal legend makes him the nephew of Caiaphas. He certainly was of the tribe of Judah. He had little in common with Galileans. Far from being a petty thief, he was, I believe, a man of austere life, with a fanatical sense of duty. Though the high priests did nothing to save the Baptist, there is no doubt that they kept their eye on him. The Gospels tell us that they kept a hostile and steady eye on Jesus. For a while they merely wished to know what he was doing; later they saw that he must be suppressed. Judas, I believe, was their spy, their paid informer, from the moment he joined the Twelve. The others, suspecting something wrong, disliked him, and St. John voices their strong prejudices. Jesus, I believe, knew what part the man was playing, and at the Last Supper, in that cryptic speech, told him that he knew. It was too late for Judas to turn back; he went straight to the high priests and arranged for them to take Jesus. Why hadn't he told them earlier? I follow the legend that he had come to love Jesus. Beginning as a conscientious spy for the sake of his religion as he understood it, he had come under the charm of this strange person, and had been willing to postpone his arrest. The Gospels, as I read, leave us free to believe that he did not foresee death for Jesus—imprisonment, perhaps, but nothing worse. He was one of those whose love of God goes part way, who follow no loyalty through to the end, who spare themselves even the discomfort of seeing in advance the consequences of their actions.

The more profoundly the teaching of Jesus is understood, the harder it is to put out of our thought the mysterious tragedy of Judas Iscariot. He is the one soul in the Christian legend for whom, in all logic, there would seem to be no mercy; yet Jesus told us to love our fellows without exception, to love our enemies, to bless them that hate us. The disciples of Jesus never, so far as we know, forgave Judas, and we don't hold it against them, but we'd like to know that Jesus forgave, and we wonder whether the angry Evangelists didn't perhaps suppress somewhere in the story the extension of eternal love even to the traitor.

Since the Gospels are here silent, additions to the story have been invented, from century to century, in order that Judas at last might find forgiveness and peace. These fabrications are for the most part no better than the ancient apocryphal books to which I have referred and from which I have occasionally, and skeptically, quoted. But I prize highly *The Ballad of Judas Iscariot*, written in the nineteenth century by Robert William Buchanan (1841-1901). Buchanan was in his normal condition a second-rate poet and a worse critic, and once he achieved simultaneously his lowest descent in taste and his top mark in publicity by accusing Dante Gabriel Rossetti of indecency in his sonnet sequence, *The House of Life*, written, as everyone including Buchanan knew, in tribute to Rossetti's wife during that lady's fatal illness. Rossetti's grief would have been morbid enough without Buchanan, but the charge that these sincere and touching outpourings belonged to the fleshly school of poetry, unhinged his reason temporarily. Buchanan has the punishment he earned: he is remembered for this absurd and shocking mistake, and his one masterpiece is overlooked.

I recall it here, not because it throws light on the story of Judas, but because it is an inspired interpretation of the character and the teaching of Jesus. When Judas committed suicide, the ballad says, his soul wandered through the universe, seeking in vain a place to rest. Hell would not take it in, the elements disliked to touch it, the sun refused to shine on it; it was cast out from all creation—yet it could not die.

At last, in a nameless region of darkness, the soul of Judas saw a light, miles away. He crawled nearer; the light came from a cabin on a ghostly moor. He crawled nearer, though his hunted spirit was all but spent; the light came from a window. He crawled nearer and clung to the sill; inside there was a table, and Jesus at the head of it, with the Eleven around him.

> 'Twas the Bridegroom sat at the table-head,
> And the lights burnt bright and clear—
> "Oh, who is that," the Bridegroom said,
> "Whose weary feet I hear?"
>
> 'Twas one looked from the lighted hall,
> And answered soft and slow,
> "It is a wolf runs up and down
> With a black track in the snow."
>
> The Bridegroom sat in his robe of white,
> Sat at the table-head—
> "Oh, who is that who moans without?"
> The blessed Bridegroom said.
>
> 'Twas one looked from the lighted hall,
> And answered fierce and low,
> " 'Tis the soul of Judas Iscariot
> Gliding to and fro."
>
> 'Twas the soul of Judas Iscariot
> Did hush itself and stand,

And saw the Bridegroom at the door
  With a light in his hand.

.   .   .   .

'Twas the Bridegroom stood at the open door,
  And beckon'd, smiling sweet;
'Twas the soul of Judas Iscariot
  Stole in, and fell at his feet.

"The Holy Supper is spread within,
  And the many candles shine,
And I have waited long for thee
  Before I poured the wine."

viii

The Beatitudes and the Maledictions

HERE are two versions of the Sermon on the Mount, one in St. Matthew's Gospel, beginning with chapter 5, verse 3, the other in St. Luke's Gospel, beginning with chapter 6, verse 20. The version in St. Matthew is fuller and much better known, but the version in St. Luke may be more important. Many of the doctrines in the Sermon appear in the Gospel according to St. Mark, but not in the orderly arrangement of St. Luke, still less with the completeness of St. Matthew.

St. Matthew and St. Luke begin the Sermon with the Beatitudes. A comparison of the two texts is startling. They offer us very different Beatitudes. And the preface to one set of Beatitudes contrasts sharply with the other. St. Matthew begins: "And seeing the multitudes, he went up into a mountain: and when he was set, his disciples came unto him: and he opened his mouth, and taught them, saying . . ." St. Luke says that Jesus "went out into a mountain to pray, and continued all night in prayer to God. And when it was day, he called unto him his disciples: and of them he chose twelve, whom also he named apostles." Having given the list of names, St. Luke continues: "And he came down with them, and stood in the plain, and the company of his disciples, and a great multitude of people out of all Judæa and Jerusalem, and from the sea coast of Tyre and Sidon, which came to hear him, and to be healed of their diseases; and they that were vexed with unclean spirits: and they were healed. And the whole multitude sought to touch him: for there went virtue out of him, and healed them all. And he lifted up his eyes on his disciples, and said . . ."

Now what did he say? One discourse, which many of us know well, is the Sermon on the Mount; the other, which comparatively few of us have studied, is the Sermon on the Plain. The first is very beautiful, very comforting, and not likely to disturb any congregation of Christians. The second is beautiful, but it is challenging rather than comforting, and preachers who are considerate of their congregations leave it alone. Never in my life have I heard it discussed from any pulpit. I can understand why not. It probably is the doctrine of Jesus as he taught it, unsoftened and undiluted.

Here are the Beatitudes of St. Matthew:

"Blessed are the poor in spirit: for their's is the kingdom of heaven."

"Blessed are they that mourn: for they shall be comforted."

"Blessed are the meek: for they shall inherit the earth."

"Blessed are they which do hunger and thirst after righteousness: for they shall be filled."

"Blessed are the merciful: for they shall obtain mercy."

"Blessed are the pure in heart: for they shall see God."

"Blessed are the peacemakers: for they shall be called the children of God."

"Blessed are they which are persecuted for righteousness' sake: for their's is the kingdom of heaven."

"Blessed are ye, when men shall revile you, and persecute you, and shall say all manner of evil against you falsely, for my sake. Rejoice, and be exceeding glad: for great is your reward in heaven: for so persecuted they the prophets which were before you."

Here are St. Luke's Beatitudes, from the Sermon on the Plain:

"Blessed be ye poor: for your's is the kingdom of God."

"Blessed are ye that hunger now: for ye shall be filled."

"Blessed are ye that weep now: for ye shall laugh."

"Blessed are ye, when men shall hate you, and when they shall separate you from their company, and shall reproach you, and cast out your name as evil, for the Son of man's sake. Rejoice ye in that day, and leap for joy: for, behold, your reward is great in heaven: for in the like manner did their fathers unto the prophets."

In both versions there is the special comfort for the disciples, by way of conclusion, but otherwise there is far less resemblance than we should expect. St. Matthew gives seven Beatitudes in addition to the general conclusion; St. Luke gives only three. Neither Evangelist, so far as we know, was present when the Sermon was given; we are barred, therefore, from saying that they heard the same words but because of temperamental differences, heard them differently. According to his own account St. Matthew was not a follower of Jesus until some time after the Sermon, and St. Luke was not a follower until Paul converted him. In all likelihood he never saw Jesus.

Yet his account may be the correct one, and I believe it is. If the tradition is true, that he had his information about the life of Jesus from the Virgin Mary herself, it seems reasonable that he should have learned much about the teachings of Jesus from the same source, as well as from the apostles and disciples whom he had opportunity to consult, and since he had a superior mind, he probably gives us an exceptionally intelligent report. If the ideas of Jesus were revolutionary, St. Luke would not on that account edit or suppress them. Neither of course would St. Matthew, not intentionally, but he was a businessman, and he was trained in mental habits which Jesus sought to change. Prosperity, as Francis Bacon remarked, is the blessing of the Old Testament; adversity is the blessing of the New. St. Matthew manages to incorporate into his Beatitudes a substantial promise of prosperity—or to be more precise, he avoids the prospect of too much adversity. Did he find it difficult to say, "Blessed are the poor"? According to St. Luke, that was the first Beatitude, but St. Matthew makes it "Blessed are the poor in spirit." I have before me at the moment a commentary by an eminent divine, in which I read the assurance that even the very rich may be poor in spirit.

It is not my understanding that Jesus ever attacked wealth as such, but he did praise poverty as an ideal. It is misleading to say that he was either for capitalism or against it; systems of finance, like political systems, he refused to discuss. Those who call him anti-capitalistic usually cite his words to the rich young man, "Go and sell that thou hast, and give to the poor." But the rich young man could not sell his property unless there was another rich man to buy. These are all temporary questions, but poverty as Jesus advocated it is a permanent philosophy of life, the philosophy of a Francis of Assisi, the philosophy which more than one country is now contemplating, however unwillingly, as likely to yield the only program by which peace and justice can be secured. If all the wealth in the world were distributed with approximate evenness, destitution would be avoided, but we should all be poor. This result is arrived at under any economic system. At the present moment some democratic peoples are sharing with their friends all that they have, and though this generosity is far from the complete and universal love of man which Jesus advocated, it bids fair to result in poverty. This condition, according to the Beatitude in St. Luke, is ideal. Properly used, it becomes the gateway to the kingdom of heaven.

"Blessed be ye poor," "Blessed are ye that hunger," "Blessed are ye that weep." St. Matthew softens this hard doctrine by transposing it into "Blessed are the poor in spirit," "Blessed are they which do hunger and thirst after righteousness," "Blessed are they that mourn." He adds four Beatitudes, among the most beautiful sayings of Jesus, but all avoiding the issue raised by the other three. "Blessed are the meek," "Blessed are the merciful," "Blessed are the pure in heart," "Blessed are the peacemakers."

The saying that the meek are blessed and that they shall inherit the earth, has been a stumbling block for many readers. The word meek does not adequately render the meaning. The Greek word from which it is translated implies an active attitude to life, not a passive. The Beatitude does not intend to say that those shall inherit the earth who are timid, shrinking, submissive, or resigned. Meekness here describes an outward manner which is the result of inward self-discipline. In Aristotle's *Nicomachean Ethics* meekness is described as temperance, which with this philosopher is always the active virtue of self-control over the passions. Jesus is saying that they shall inherit the earth who have strong passions and gentle manners. The French translate this Beatitude as *Heureux les débonnaires*, Blessed are the debonair. Here certainly is no praise of the retired life nor of poverty, but rather a rule for worldly success.

"Blessed are the pure in heart," is a description of life here quite as much as a promise of life hereafter. Those whose hearts are pure are in a condition to see truth clearly, to see it now before they enter another world. I pause to make this comment because among the many forms which the realism of Jesus takes, one of the most interesting is his insistence that eternal truths are true now. This is another way of saying that the beginning of immortality need not be, perhaps cannot be, postponed until after death. Some insight into whatever is divine must be gained at the earliest possible moment, and the preparatory discipline leading to this insight is an utterly pure love. Here again the Beatitude may seem unrelated to any theory of prosperity or of poverty; the contemplation of truth is an end in itself, and so is purity of heart. But purity of heart comes first, and of our own choice we may aspire to it.

These four extra Beatitudes in St. Matthew which are not found in St. Luke, might all be stated as happy consequences of the self-disciplined life implied in poverty, hunger, and tears. They would seem properly placed if they were added to St. Luke's Beatitudes. I find myself inclined to believe that the original condition of the Beatitudes as they came to St. Matthew was practically as if these four happy blessings followed close upon St. Luke's austere benedictions. Transmitted by some temperament far less uncompromising than that of Jesus, the three crucial blessings became in St. Matthew's version upholstered and filled out to a point where they ceased to be either dangerous or discouraging. Perhaps the history of Christianity would have been different if the first Beatitude from the lips of Jesus had always been quoted in plain words, not to be dodged—"Blessed are the poor."

2

I T is probable that whenever Jesus presented a list of great virtues, he accompanied it with a list of contrasting vices or faults; and when he named blessings, he defined them by their opposites, in a series of woes and curses. St. Luke gives us, along with the Beatitudes, the Woes, St. Matthew leaves the Woes out. Many commentators, embarrassed by St. Luke's text, try to soften it into closer harmony with St. Matthew's comparatively comfortable report; they tell us, for example, that the Woes express regret rather than denunciation, articulate divine pity rather than divine wrath. But I cannot understand how plain words can thus be twisted, nor how honest readers can ignore the practical experience of life which is the basis for the clear statements.

"Woe unto you that are rich! for ye have received your consolation."

"Woe unto you that are full! for ye shall hunger."

"Woe unto you that laugh now! for ye shall mourn and weep."

"Woe unto you, when all men shall speak well of you! for so did their fathers to the false prophets." (St. Luke, chapter 6.)

Here is that insistence on compensation, on the ups and downs of life, which we glanced at in a previous chapter. Woe to the rich because they shall be poor; blessed are the poor because they shall be rich. When we consider from whom these words come, we may be shocked into protest: Is there no moral relation between a man's character and his fortunes? Do the rich become poor only because they have been rich? Do the poor become rich only because they have been poor? But Jesus says, here and elsewhere, that though character ought to dictate human fortunes, it does nothing of the kind. In this human life good men sometimes fail and bad men sometimes succeed, and he who is neither good nor bad, together with the saint and the villain, must make his way through changes of fortune which seem to follow no other principle than this, that those who are up will come down, and those who are down will rise. Jesus stated this idea so frequently that we have a wide choice of illustrations, but perhaps the best is the parable of Dives and Lazarus.

"There was a certain rich man, which was clothed in purple and fine linen, and fared sumptuously every day: and there was a certain beggar named Lazarus, which was laid at his gate, full of sores, and desiring to be fed with the crumbs which fell from the rich man's table: moreover the dogs came and licked his sores."

Notice that the rich man is accused of no wrong-doing, and the beggar is credited with no particular virtue. The contrast is not between their moral conditions, but between the circumstances of their lives.

"And it came to pass, that the beggar died, and was carried by the angels into Abraham's bosom: the rich man also died, and was buried; and in hell he lift up his eyes, being in torments, and seeth Abraham afar off, and Lazarus in his bosom."

No reason is given so far why the rich man went to the torments of hell, nor why Lazarus was comforted.

"And he cried and said, Father Abraham, have mercy on me, and send Lazarus, that he may dip the tip of his finger in water, and cool my tongue; for I am tormented in this flame. But Abraham said, Son, remember that thou in thy lifetime receivedst thy good things, and likewise Lazarus evil things: but now he is comforted, and thou art tormented. And beside all this, between us and you there is a great gulf fixed: so that they which would pass from hence to you cannot; neither can they pass to us, that would come from thence. Then he said, I pray thee therefore, father, that thou wouldest send him to my father's house: for I have five brethren; that he may testify unto them, lest they also come into this place of torment. Abraham saith unto him, They have Moses and the prophets; let them hear them. And he said, Nay, father Abraham: but if one went unto them from the dead, they will repent. And he said unto him, If they hear not

Moses and the prophets, neither will they be persuaded, though one rose from the dead." (St. Luke, chapter 16.)

Here again the insistence is on the wisdom to be gained and practiced within the limits of human experience; the brothers who will not heed the plain teaching of this life can learn nothing from messages out of a world they have not yet seen. But the immediate point in this parable is the moral detachment of the characters from their fate. Abraham does not pretend that the rich man deserves to be in torment, nor that the poor man has done anything to earn eternal bliss; he merely insists that good fortune is bound to turn into bad, and bad fortune into good, this being a prime condition of life. If it were otherwise, this mortal existence would have the enduring qualities of eternity.

If we now look back to the Woes or the Beatitudes of St. Luke, we may recognize in them more easily this characteristic doctrine of compensation. "Blessed are ye that hunger now: for ye shall be filled." "Blessed are ye that weep now: for ye shall laugh." But the doctrine is less clear in the diluted version, "Blessed are they which do hunger and thirst after righteousness: for they shall be filled." Did Lazarus hunger and thirst after righteousness? Or did he win peace in Abraham's bosom merely because he hungered and thirsted?

I should be sorry not to make this point from every angle clear. Jesus began his great sermon with the statement of certain earthly or temporary principles which are illustrated in this world by the experience of good and bad people alike. Outward fortune is subject to change. No matter how well we may have deserved worldly success, it will not stay with us. The conclusion drawn by those who take a long view, is that it is better to be poor with the probability of some day being rich, than to be rich with the probability of some day being poor. So far as the essential man is concerned, riches and poverty are alike accidental and temporary. If you meet a friend on the street and can tell from his bearing or from his way of greeting you that he has just made or lost some money, is there not a defect in his character? The values we prize are those which do not change.

Therefore they cannot be the values which we call earthly. If we were to lay aside, of our own will, all that fortune has the power to take away from us, we should be stripped at once of many things, but the essentials would remain. The Beatitude of St. Luke would immediately become so spiritual that St. Matthew's version in comparison would seem wordy. We should no longer be content to say, "Blessed are the poor in spirit"; we should crave the fuller statement, "Blessed be ye poor."

3

IN the Sermon on the Plain St. Luke follows the Beatitudes and the Woes by a series of admonitions which apply the doctrine of compensation to a variety of problems in our human conduct. The wise soul will try never to be in debt to the universe, because the debt must some day be paid. Rather, make sure that life owes something to us, for this debt also will be paid. We are fortunate or blessed if we are poor now; later our wealth will come. By this logic, the wise soul will wish not to be in debt to other men; rather let them be in debt to him. "Love your enemies, do good to them which hate you, bless them that curse you, and pray for them which despitefully use you. And unto him that smiteth thee on the one cheek offer also the other; and him that taketh away thy cloke forbid not to take thy coat also. Give to every man that asketh of thee; and of him that taketh away thy goods ask them not again." If we all lived simultaneously on this principle, there would be an immense rivalry to see who could put his fellows most in his debt. This would be the only rivalry permitted in the kingdom of God.

The second half of the Sermon on the Plain transfers this homely and profound wisdom to the realm of the spirit. "Judge not, and ye shall not be judged: condemn not, and ye shall not be condemned: forgive, and ye shall be forgiven: give, and it shall be given unto you; good measure, pressed down, and shaken together, and running over, shall men give into your bosom. For with the same measure that ye mete withal it shall be measured to you again." Here Jesus is drawing upon the kind of wisdom which nowadays we like to call psychological. He is considering spiritual truths of a kind which have practical value here and now, and which can be tried out daily. It is not mere optimistic encouragement to good living but a plain statement of fact to say that generosity of mind and heart begets a similar generosity in those around us, that courage in ourselves begets courage in others, that all great qualities are contagious and kindling. The promise is that those who give without stint and without hope of reward, shall receive in the same measure pressed down, and shaken together, and running over. In the larger implication the promise is that a society in which men practice this unselfish love will not divide itself into givers and receivers, but since goodness is contagious and kindling, will become an immediate example of the kingdom.

The Sermon on the Plain takes this doctrine just two steps further. The generosity of heart which will kindle generosity in other men, and so will bring about the kingdom of God, must be a natural generosity, perhaps an acquired habit, but so firmly acquired that it has become instinctive. No one in the kingdom will nudge himself into good behavior. "Every tree is known by his own fruit. For of thorns men do not gather figs, nor of a bramble bush gather they grapes. A good man out of the good treasure of his heart bringeth forth that which is good; and an evil man out of the evil treasure of his heart bringeth forth that which is evil."

The final point of the Sermon has to do with the now familiar contrast between eternal and temporary values. All these truths, including the laws of change and compensation in earthly life, are true forever. We either make truth part of ourselves, strengthening our souls with elements of eternity, or we postpone truth for later consideration, and forget to consider it, and so become prisoners of time. We are like a man who built a house and dug deep and laid the foundation on a rock—or we are like a man who without a foundation built a house on sand.

ix

The Parables

FOR THE essential teachings of Jesus many people go to the Sermon on the Mount, as reported by St. Matthew, but the parables are a more reliable source, and far more illuminating. There is nothing original in sermons as a literary form; they are not to be distinguished from secular lectures, and one of the defects of all lectures is that the hearer can interpret as he chooses. But the little pictures of life by which Jesus liked best to convey his doctrine, have a common meaning for us all. They are susceptible of individual interpretations, as life itself is, but they contain a core of experience as immune to challenge as the fact of birth, or of death, or of hunger. The doctrines expounded in a homily might easily be misunderstood or imperfectly heard; the story in a parable is easy to grasp, easy to remember, and easy to repeat, and so long as the plot is clear, the meaning must be.

There is nothing in literature quite like the parables of Jesus. He created the form, and though attempts are made to imitate him, the form remains his alone. Attempts are also made to define the form in terms of the fable or the apologue, the anecdote or the short story; but every reader feels instinctively that the quality of parables is absent from these other kinds of writing. It has been said that a parable is an allegory, an extended metaphor, but obviously a parable is nothing of the kind. An allegory is an artificial story intended to parallel life. Most fables are allegories; Red Ridinghood and the wolf set up a warning for us against actual pitfalls and villainies. But the parables of Jesus are not synthetic plots, invented to throw light on experience; they are direct quotations from experience; they are samples of life itself. The man who fell among thieves, the Prodigal Son, the woman who lost the piece of silver, the sower who went forth to sow, were real people, perhaps known to Jesus and recognized by his hearers as he spoke. In the parables he was teaching through poetry; he let the story do the teaching. Add a moral if you wish; Shakespeare tagged a salutary lesson to the end of *Romeo and Juliet;* he pointed out that the young people died because the old people quarreled. But the story by itself makes a point, and when we give the play nowadays we usually omit the superfluous moralizing. Once or twice the disciples asked what the parable meant, and Jesus told them, adding for their encouragement or perhaps by way of irony that they of all people should have the inside of it. But few of us now, two thousand years after these perfect stories were composed, need help to get at the gist.

From the parables taken as a whole we may learn something of the life of Jesus, and much of his interest in all that he saw and heard. These stories have to do with a range of experience, with many kinds of work and responsibility, of failure and success, of worry and joy. Only an observing person could have gathered this material, and he must have had unlimited curiosity and sympathy. Some of the episodes may have been recalled out of the home in which he grew up, others may have occurred at gatherings like the wedding at Cana, others he may have studied among the wealthier people in the Galilean towns, or he may have heard them as news of the great folk in Jerusalem. Taken all together, as told by one man, they show an extraordinary grasp of life, such as we might expect of a master dramatist. Even more than keenness and breadth of vision, they express affection for the characters who in these brief scenes act out their unforgettable parts.

The teachings of Jesus involved few principles, and his parables therefore, however rich the material out of which they are made, dealt with only a few themes. The general purpose was to describe the kingdom of heaven, and how it might be brought on earth. One group of parables portrays the conditions in which the work of the kingdom must be done. Evil shares with good this world of time, and it is the first mark of wisdom in good men to take into account realistically all the conditions of life, unfavorable as well as favorable. The growth of the kingdom will be slow, and those who hope to see it must be patient. They work for the kingdom in time, but the kingdom itself is for eternity.

The kingdom is for those who love God utterly, and those who love God utterly must have unbounded love for all men. The admonition to love our neighbor as ourselves must be properly understood; some men love even themselves in a half-hearted fashion, with no zest for their own abilities, no pride in achievement. The true citizen of the kingdom sets no limit to his love of all whom God has made, but love pressed home in this fashion raises problems of justice, attaches importance to humility, condemns blindness or callousness, casualness or unawareness. Those who have eyes are expected to use them—and there are many kinds of sight. We should love our neighbor as ourselves, and loving ourselves, in the teaching of Jesus, means keeping every faculty alive and disciplined and alert, so that no life can pass us unheeded.

2

T H E earliest parables were told, it seems, at the dramatic moment described in the Gospel according to St. Matthew, beginning at the 38th verse of chapter 12 and extending through chapter 13. Certain of the Pharisees and scribes, bitterly hostile, started to heckle Jesus in public, requesting a sign from him to prove that he was the authentic Messiah. He struck back at them hard, with a violence they could not forgive. He called them an evil and adulterous generation, far worse than the inhabitants of Nineveh, to whom Jonah was sent, for whereas Nineveh when it heard Jonah did repent, the scribes and Pharisees were apparently beyond saving. It was the angry Jesus who spoke:

"When the unclean spirit is gone out of a man, he walketh through dry places, seeking rest, and findeth none. Then he saith, I will return into my house from whence I came out; and when he is come, he findeth it empty, swept, and garnished. Then goeth he, and taketh with him seven other spirits more wicked than himself, and they enter in and dwell there: and the last state of that man is worse than the first. Even so shall it be also unto this wicked generation."

At this point, when the tension was greatest, the mother and the brothers of Jesus wished him to come away. They, quite as clearly as the disciples in the crowd, saw that he was challenging an implacable foe. Someone interrupted him to say that his mother and his brothers waited outside and wished to speak with him. The famous reply of Jesus need not be misunderstood if we keep in mind the whole scene, the scribes and the Pharisees stalking him, ready to jump, and the disciples standing by, a little confused, perhaps frightened. If he had walked away toward the place where his mother waited, his enemies would have said he too had lost courage. He stayed where he was, saying, "Who is my mother? and who are my brethren? And he stretched forth his hand toward his disciples, and said, Behold my mother and my brethren! For whosoever shall do the will of my Father which is in heaven, the same is my brother, and sister, and mother."

These words conclude chapter 12. Though we are not told so, we assume that he went to his mother, and though he could not assure her that he would abandon the course to which he was committed, it may be that her loving apprehension moved him to this extent, that he was willing to express his convictions in terms less likely to start a riot. In this atmosphere of danger and suppressed excitement the first parables were spoken. A large crowd milled around him on the Galilean shore, and not all of them were friendly. With a few disciples he got into a small boat, rowed out a short distance, and from that pulpit told them a story:

"Behold, a sower went forth to sow; and when he sowed, some seeds fell by the way side, and the fowls came and devoured them up: some fell upon stony places, where they had not much earth: and forthwith they sprung up, because they had no deepness of earth: and when the sun was up, they were scorched; and because they had no root, they withered away. And some fell among thorns; and the thorns sprung up, and choked them: but other fell into good ground, and brought forth fruit, some an hundredfold, some sixtyfold, some thirtyfold."

His disciples came and asked him why he now spoke in parables, from which we conclude that he had not so spoken before. He stated the meaning of the story, though interpretation would hardly seem necessary, but perhaps he was making clear once for all this new method of teaching; most of the other parables are allowed to explain themselves. St. Matthew, St. Mark and St. Luke give the story of the Sower in almost the same words, and follow it with the same commentary, but St. Matthew alone gives the parable of the Tares, which obviously should accompany the Sower.

"Another parable put he forth unto them, saying, The kingdom of heaven is likened unto a man which sowed good seed in his field: but while men slept, his enemy came and sowed tares among the wheat, and went his way. But when the blade was sprung up, and brought forth fruit, then appeared the tares also. So the servants of the householder came and said unto him, Sir, didst not thou sow good seed in thy field? from whence then hath it tares? He said unto them, An enemy hath done this. The servants said unto him, Wilt thou then that we go and gather them up? But he said, Nay; lest while ye gather up the tares, ye root up also the wheat with them. Let both grow together until the harvest: and in the time of harvest I will say to the reapers, Gather ye together first the tares, and bind them in bundles to burn them: but gather the wheat into my barn."

Here are two realistic accounts of the world in which we are to build the kingdom of God. The good seed will not always fall on good ground; that condition must be accepted with patience. Furthermore, even though the ground is favorable, there are forces at work against the kingdom, and for them too patience is needed. The poor soil is an accident of nature, but tares are the work of an active enemy. Those who listened to the parable were only too well acquainted with the mean trick it describes. There was no easier way for a farmer to satisfy a grudge. The tares, or darnel, would look like wheat until the crop was fairly grown, and the unfortunate owner of the field would congratulate himself on his plentiful harvest, or he might receive and innocently accept the compliments of the vicious fellow who had done the mischief.

St. Matthew reports two brief parables, and then tells us that the disciples brought the discussion back to the tares by asking for an explanation of the metaphor. It is difficult for us now to see what puzzled them. They might have asked instead for a comment on the two little stories which intervened, but perhaps they were still thinking of the tares, and did not hear what was said about mustard seed and leaven.

"Another parable put he forth unto them, saying, The kingdom of heaven is like to a grain of mustard seed, which a man took, and sowed in his field: which indeed is the least of all seeds: but when it is grown, it is the greatest among herbs, and becometh a tree, so that the birds of the air come and lodge in the branches thereof."

"Another parable spake he unto them; The kingdom of heaven is like unto leaven, which a woman took, and hid in three measures of meal, till the whole was leavened."

With these two parables should be placed a third, recorded in St. Mark's Gospel, chapter 4. "So is the kingdom of God, as if a man should cast seed into the ground; and should sleep and rise, night and day, and the seed should spring and grow up, he knoweth not how. For the earth bringeth forth fruit of herself; first the blade, then the ear, after that the full corn in the ear.

But when the fruit is brought forth, immediately he putteth in the sickle, because the harvest is come."

These three parables serve as encouragements after the story of the Sower and the kind of soil he must sow in and the story of the tares sown by an enemy. In spite of hard conditions the kingdom will come at last, since like the mustard seed it contains the principle of infinite growth, and like yeast it spreads its influence thoroughly, and time is its secret friend. In all three stories the good seed is harvested at last, but the farmer must wait. After the planting there is need of patience and faith.

The imagery employed in these early parables is universal and the meaning is easy to get at, but the two which come next in St. Matthew's account are simple only in appearance. Jesus told them to the disciples in private, after the crowd had dispersed. Both stories, with a slight variation, set forth his central teaching that love for God and desire for the kingdom must be to the utmost, without limit.

"The kingdom of heaven is like unto treasure hid in a field; the which when a man hath found, he hideth, and for joy thereof goeth and selleth all that he hath, and buyeth that field." It is possible to come on the kingdom of heaven as it were by accident, when we are not looking for it, as we might discover a vein of gold in another man's land. He who knows the value of the discovery will keep it secret until he has bought the land, and to make the purchase he will sell everything he has. The heart of the parable is in that last point; in the purchase of the kingdom nothing whatever can be held back. We should not fail to observe in passing the characteristic willingness of Jesus to illustrate a spiritual truth by a worldly experience. Those who listened to the parable were acquainted with the kind of shrewdness which would buy the field in haste before the owner could learn he was selling it too cheap. To find here a metaphor of the desire for righteousness was original, to say the least, and rather startling, but Jesus never hesitates to use a realistic image. He here makes his point that those who seek the kingdom with clean hearts should be at least as eager in the quest as the traders in material goods, who know a bargain when they see it.

One man stumbles on treasure in his neighbor's field; another goes far in deliberate search for it. "The kingdom of heaven is like unto a merchant man, seeking goodly pearls: who, when he had found one pearl of great price, went and sold all that he had, and bought it." Whether or not the treasure is found by intention, whether its full price is asked or whether it is a bargain, we must give for it all that we have.

Since these two parables are told to the disciples rather than to the general public, perhaps Jesus was concerned over different degrees of loyalty among his followers. If we do not attend closely to the story which the Gospels tell, we easily think of the apostles as all in the same measure zealous for their leader and his cause, but Judas was a tragic exception, perhaps from the first, and it may be that others were now and then lukewarm. These two parables illuminate at once passages otherwise difficult, in which Jesus insists on a devotion which tolerates no rival loyalties.

The cluster of remarkable stories in St. Matthew's Gospel, chapter 13, ends with the parable of the Drag-net, which perhaps should come earlier, with the account of the Sower and of the Tares, since like them it stresses the mixture of good and evil in this earthly life. "The kingdom of heaven is like unto a net, that was cast into the sea, and gathered of every kind: which, when it was full, they drew to shore, and sat down, and gathered the good into vessels, but cast the bad away. So shall it be at the end of the world: the angels shall come forth, and sever the wicked from among the just, and shall cast them into the furnace of fire: there shall be wailing and gnashing of teeth."

3

T H E parables in this chapter of St. Matthew which deal with a love without limit, refer to the love of man toward God. In the Gospel according to St. Luke, chapters 14, 15, and 19, there are a similar cluster of stories dealing with God's boundless love for man. The first of these stories tells of the great supper.

"A certain man made a great supper, and bade many: and sent his servant at supper time to say to them that were bidden, Come; for all things are now ready. And they all with one consent began to make excuse. The first said unto him, I have bought a piece of ground, and I must needs go and see it: I pray thee have me excused. And another said, I have bought five yoke of oxen, and I go to prove them: I pray thee have me excused. And another said, I have married a wife, and therefore I cannot come. So that servant came, and shewed his lord these things. Then the master of the house being angry said to his servant, Go out quickly into the streets and lanes of the city, and bring in hither the poor, and the maimed, and the halt, and the blind. And the servant said, Lord, it is done as thou hast commanded, and yet there is room. And the lord said unto the servant, Go out into the highways and hedges, and compel them to come in, that my house may be filled. For I say unto you, That none of those men which were bidden shall taste of my supper."

This parable is remarkable for its little pictures of human nature, the reluctance to receive true benefits, the preoccupation with temporal affairs, the failure to appreciate what is important. But the host who prepares the supper is determined to have guests at the feast, even though those he first invited declined to come. When after invitations of the most generous and inclusive sort, there are still empty places at his table, he tells his servant to go out into the highways and compel them to come in, whether or not they wish to. This command is sometimes misread as the steppingstone to a cruel inquisition. The intention of the story, however, is simply to set forth a love which refuses to be discouraged or defeated.

The parable of the Lost Sheep and the parable of the Lost Piece of Silver say the same thing in a different way. Only one sheep out of a hundred was lost, only one piece of money out of ten, but immediately what was lost had an extraordinary value.

The loss of the sheep may not have been the owner's fault, since sheep like to stray, but the piece of silver must have been dropped or mislaid through carelessness. In either case the search is unwearying, and when the lost is found the neighbors are called in to rejoice. In both parables this joy in the return is the essence of the story.

"What man of you, having an hundred sheep, if he lose one of them, doth not leave the ninety and nine in the wilderness, and go after that which is lost, until he find it? And when he hath found it, he layeth it on his shoulders, rejoicing. And when he cometh home, he calleth together his friends and neighbours, saying unto them, Rejoice with me; for I have found my sheep which was lost. I say unto you, that likewise joy shall be in heaven over one sinner that repenteth, more than over ninety and nine just persons, which need no repentance."

The earliest parables, we may remind ourselves, were spoken to the multitude by the seashore, after the heckling tactics of the Pharisees and the sharp reply of Jesus. The parables which we are now considering are introduced, in the Gospel of St. Luke, chapter 15, with these words: "Then drew near unto him all the publicans and sinners for to hear him. And the Pharisees and scribes murmured, saying, This man receiveth sinners, and eateth with them. And he spake this parable unto them, saying, What man of you, having an hundred sheep, if he lose one of them, . . ."

The publicans and sinners doubtless knew that the battle was joined between Jesus and the strait-laced Pharisees; this new prophet, who invited a publican to be one of his followers, was becoming the idol and the champion of the social outcasts. The Pharisees followed relentlessly, tracking him down, watching for the unguarded moment when an ill-advised word might expose him to prosecution and perhaps to destruction. The parables which he now spoke were addressed to both parts of his audience. To the publicans and to all who in their hearts were conscious of sin, he said nothing which would make sin excusable, but he described the grandeur of God's love, which goes after the child who has lost his way, and brings him home. To the Pharisees he conveyed a rebuke all the more stinging because it was public; he suggested that although sin is to be shunned, God does not shun the sinner, and over the sinner who repents there is joy in heaven. Then why not dine with Matthew the publican, when the collector of unjust taxes gives up his shameful occupation? By love all men are drawn toward each other, and toward God; by respectability, the legalistic substitute for love, the Pharisees separate themselves from God and from other men.

"Either what woman having ten pieces of silver, if she lose one piece, doth not light a candle, and sweep the house, and seek diligently till she find it? And when she hath found it, she calleth her friends and her neighbours together, saying, Rejoice with me; for I have found the piece which I had lost. Likewise, I say unto you, there is joy in the presence of the angels of God over one sinner that repenteth."

The owner of the sheep asked the friends and neighbors to rejoice with him because he had found the sheep which was lost. The woman asked her neighbors to rejoice because she had found the piece which she had lost. The slight change in statement makes the difference between these two brief but great parables. The sheep had strayed; the woman had lost the piece of money.

St. Luke immediately proceeds to one of the most famous of all parables, the story of the Prodigal Son. The literary climax here is carefully planned. The sheep owner lost one sheep out of a hundred; the loss of the woman is far greater in proportion— one out of ten; the loss of the father was one son out of two. Since St. Luke was an artist in storytelling rather than a philosopher, he may have sacrificed something for the fine emphasis obtained by the rising proportion of the loss, but something also would have been gained if he had inserted, after the parable of the Lost Sheep, the parable of the Pounds. St. Matthew, chapter 25, tells it in the better-known version as the parable of the Talents, but for our purposes the two versions are identical. A man who has occasion to travel into a far country leaves some money with his servants, and when he returns he asks for an accounting. In one version there are ten servants, to each of whom one pound has been entrusted. In the other version there are three servants, to one of whom five talents had been given, to the second two talents, and to the third one talent. From that point on the parable of the Pounds is completely swallowed up in the story of the talents. The first of the ten servants has invested his one pound and gained ten pounds, the second, investing one pound, has gained five pounds, the third brings his pound wrapped up in a napkin, having been afraid to invest it. What became of the other seven out of ten servants, we are not told. In the parable of the Talents, the first servant has doubled his five talents, the second has doubled his two talents, and the third brings his talent as he received it, unused. In both versions the first and the second servant are praised for having done their best, but the third is utterly cursed for being afraid to take a risk. By implication no one really loves God who is afraid to live.

Do you ask why I think this parable of the Talents should come before the story of the Prodigal Son? Because, unless the two parables are taken together, one difficult question in the story of the talents is left unanswered. The man who took no risk gave as his excuse that his master was harsh, and if he had lost the talent, it would have gone hard with him. Unless his point is fairly met, the condemnation he received seems a little unjust. By all means, let us say that true love of God implies a readiness to live bravely, but since evil shares this world with good and the likelihood of misfortune is great, there ought to be some hint of what will happen to us in case we lose the only talent we have.

That hint, as I understand, is given in the story of the Prodigal Son. The boy had the zest of life in him and his father gladly gave him his inheritance and let him go into the world to see what he could do with himself. Apparently he had no great talent; the best part of him was at first his courage and later his recognition of failure, but he probably saw little of the world, and even in riotous terms had no very good time. He wasted his substance, spent his little fortune without getting anything in return for it. But his father received him with joy. He had been lost to the home, he had come back. I think we ought to understand that his father approved of him, and why. The father's opinion is very important. He, rather than the prodigal or his careful brother, is the hero of the story. He understood both his sons, and for good reason loved the prodigal best.

The parable is easy to misread. Unless we are alert to all the circumstances, we may think the younger son took his inheritance, turned his back on his home, spent his money in drunkenness and debauchery, and then came whining back, looking for food; whereas the elder brother, having asked his father for nothing, and having received nothing, stayed home and worked loyally. If these had been the facts, the elder brother with justice might have complained that his father was unjust in preparing a banquet for the returning ne'er-do-well.

But this is not the story. The younger son said, "Father, give me the portion of goods that falleth to me. And he divided unto them his living." In other words, they both received, then and there, the inheritance which would have come to them at their father's death. The elder brother had exactly the same amount of money as the younger, and he still had it, wrapped up in a napkin like the unused talent, when the younger brother came home. One of his complaints to his father was, as you remember, "Thou never gavest me a kid, that I might make merry with my friends." The parable supplies no evidence that the elder brother ever spent a penny on his friends, nor that he had any friends. The younger brother, on the other hand, did find friends in that far country he went to, and he spent his money on them. He "took his journey into a far country, and there wasted his substance with riotous living." A literal translation would read, "and there scattered his substance, living unsafely"—that is, without thrift. He was unwise, of course, and the friends he made were of small account, but his impulse was generous, the impulse which Jesus approved, the impulse to live.

The elder brother seems to have had a dirty mind. He continued his complaint, "As soon as this thy son was come, which hath devoured thy living with harlots, thou hast killed for him the fatted calf." Apparently the elder son could not imagine a good time in a foreign country without harlots. His mind is not only mean but tricky; he says his brother has devoured his father's living. What the brother imprudently wasted was an outright gift, his own to do with as he chose, and the elder brother had received exactly the same. To be sure, he had not lost a penny of it, but he had not risked a penny, either. In the parable of the Talents, the investors always win. No doubt the Prodigal Son hoped his way of life would be profitable. Though he lost, we like him, as his father did, for making the venture.

In my boyhood I read a story, designed for children, in which one of the characters says, "Imitate the elder son, not the prodigal. Be faithful to your home, to your people, to your duty." I applaud the virtue of loyalty, but I think it was a mistake to offer the elder son as a bright example. Jesus shows us, in this parable, how a father can love the child who has left home, as youth has the right to do; if he falls into difficulties, where should he go for help but to that same father who backed the trial flight? The elder son is prudent and respectable, but he is the family liability.

Well though this parable is known, I put the text here, for immediate reading after what has been said.

"A certain man had two sons: and the younger of them said to his father, Father, give me the portion of goods that falleth to me. And he divided unto them his living. And not many days after the younger son gathered all together, and took his journey into a far country, and there wasted his substance with riotous living. And when he had spent all, there arose a mighty famine in that land; and he began to be in want. And he went and joined himself to a citizen of that country; and he sent him into his fields to feed swine. And he would fain have filled his belly with the husks that the swine did eat: and no man gave unto him. And when he came to himself, he said, How many hired servants of my father's have bread enough and to spare, and I perish with hunger! I will arise and go to my father, and will say unto him,

Father, I have sinned against heaven, and before thee, and am no more worthy to be called thy son: make me as one of thy hired servants. And he arose, and came to his father. But when he was yet a great way off, his father saw him, and had compassion, and ran, and fell on his neck, and kissed him. And the son said unto him, Father, I have sinned against heaven, and in thy sight, and am no more worthy to be called thy son. But the father said to his servants, Bring forth the best robe, and put it on him; and put a ring on his hand, and shoes on his feet: and bring hither the fatted calf, and kill it; and let us eat, and be merry: for this my son was dead, and is alive again; he was lost, and is found. And they began to be merry. Now his elder son was in the field: and as he came and drew nigh to the house, he heard music and dancing. And he called one of the servants, and asked what these things meant. And he said unto him, Thy brother is come; and thy father hath killed the fatted calf, because he hath received him safe and sound. And he was angry, and would not go in: therefore came his father out, and intreated him. And he answering said to his father, Lo, these many years do I serve thee, neither transgressed I at any time thy commandment: and yet thou never gavest me a kid, that I might make merry with my friends: but as soon as this thy son was come, which hath devoured thy living with harlots, thou hast killed for him the fatted calf. And he said unto him, Son, thou art ever with me, and all that I have is thine. It was meet that we should make merry, and be glad: for this thy brother was dead, and is alive again; and was lost, and is found."

4

T H E sequence of parables in St. Matthew's Gospel and the sequence in St. Luke's are sufficient to illustrate the remarkable type of story which Jesus used in his teaching. All the other parables invite comment, but we have the opportunity here to discuss only the most significant. The doctrine of love for all men, love without limit, involved, as we said, problems of justice and implied certain other virtues, such as humility and sensitiveness to the welfare of our neighbors. If the organization of society in the time of Jesus, as in our own day, seems in certain respects cruel, it was not that men then any more than now were heartless; the reason was and is that any system simple enough to be logical, must disregard the innumerable variations and fine shadings in life, life being not logical at all. If justice is defined, as in practice it usually is, as the enforcement of law, justice will be cruel, and by the same definition of justice mercy will seem unfair. Jesus made this point frequently, and nowhere with more power than in the parable of the Laborers in the Vineyard.

This parable begins with chapter 20 of St. Matthew's Gospel, but in the end of the preceding chapter Peter says to Jesus, "Behold, we have forsaken all, and followed thee; what shall we have therefore?" Jesus replies that those who have given complete devotion to the cause shall be rewarded an hundredfold. He adds, however, that many that are first shall be last, and the last shall be first. The parable then makes clear that cryptic remark.

"For the kingdom of heaven is like unto a man that is an householder, which went out early in the morning to hire labourers into his vineyard. And when he had agreed with the labourers for a penny a day, he sent them into his vineyard. And he went out about the third hour, and saw others standing idle in the marketplace, and said unto them; Go ye also into the vineyard, and whatsoever is right I will give you. And they went their way. Again he went out about the sixth and ninth hour, and did likewise. And about the eleventh hour he went out, and found others standing idle, and saith unto them, Why stand ye here all the day idle? They say unto him, Because no man hath hired us. He saith unto them, Go ye also into the vineyard; and whatsoever is right, that shall ye receive. So when even was come, the lord of the vineyard saith unto his steward, Call the labourers, and give them their hire, beginning from the last unto the first. And when they came that were hired about the eleventh hour, they received every man a penny. But when the first came, they supposed that they should have received more; and they likewise received every man a penny. And when they had received it, they murmured against the goodman of the house, saying, These last have wrought but one hour, and thou hast made them equal unto us, which have borne the burden and heat of the day. But he answered one of them, and said, Friend, I do thee no wrong: didst not thou agree with me for a penny? Take that thine is, and go thy way: I will give unto this last, even as unto thee. Is it not lawful for me to do what I will with mine own? Is thine eye evil, because I am good? So the last shall be first, and the first last."

This parable has troubled many people. The man went into the market place and hired laborers to work in his vineyard. They agreed to work for a penny a day. Later he came back for more laborers and still more laborers, and engaged them on a vague promise to settle fairly. When the working day was nearing its end he returned to the market place for the last time, and said to the remaining laborers, "Why stand ye here all the day idle?" They answered, "Because no man hath hired us." He told them to go into the vineyard and their pay would be whatever was right.

At the end of the day he paid them all off, beginning with those whom he had hired last. They received each a full penny. The others received the same sum, no matter at what hour they had been hired. Those who had started earliest in the day complained, but the vineyard owner replied that he had paid the sum agreed, and if he chose to pay the same amount to those who had worked fewer hours, he had a right to give away his money as he chose.

At first this disposition of the problem may be no more satisfying to the reader than it was to the discontented workmen, but the parable becomes clearer if we see that its theme is unemployment. All the workmen were in the market place at the beginning of the day, eager to be engaged. Those chosen first were the lucky ones. Those chosen last spent most of the day worrying. The parable leaves us free to imagine that there were still other laborers waiting in the market place who found no employment at all. The same wages went to all alike because of their equal willingness to work, their equal right to work. What seems in the parable at first an injustice, becomes on second thought a foreshadowing of unemployment insurance. The point of the story lies in the reply of the workmen at the end of the day, that though they had been ready, no man had hired them.

Jesus thought of sin as a form of debt. In one version of the Lord's Prayer, St. Matthew, chapter 6, we say, "Forgive us our debts, as we forgive our debtors." In another version, St. Luke, chapter 11, we say, "Forgive us our sins; for we also forgive every one that is indebted to us." The ideas of debt and sin are here interchangeable. Whatever disturbs the order of life, or puts life out of balance, is an offense which can be righted only by a repayment. Strict justice asks that the debt be paid in full, but love or mercy, which is a form of love, lends and asks nothing in return.

In St. Matthew's Gospel, chapter 18, we are told that Simon Peter came to Jesus with the question, "How oft shall my brother sin against me, and I forgive him? till seven times?" Jesus answered, "I say not unto thee, Until seven times: but, Until seventy times seven"—that is, for an indefinite or even for an infinite number of times. By way of illustration he immediately told the parable of the Unmerciful Servant.

"Therefore is the kingdom of heaven likened unto a certain king, which would take account of his servants. And when he had begun to reckon, one was brought unto him, which owed him ten thousand talents. But forasmuch as he had not to pay, his lord commanded him to be sold, and his wife, and children, and all that he had, and payment to be made. The servant therefore fell down, and worshipped him, saying, Lord, have patience with me, and I will pay thee all. Then the lord of that servant was moved with compassion, and loosed him, and forgave him the debt. But the same servant went out, and found one of his fellow-servants, which owed him an hundred pence: and he laid hands on him, and took him by the throat, saying, Pay me that thou owest. And his fellow-servant fell down at his feet, and besought him, saying, Have patience with me, and I will pay thee all. And he would not: but went and cast him into prison, till he should pay the debt. So when his fellow-servants saw what was done, they were very sorry, and came and told unto their lord all that was done. Then his lord, after that he had called him, said unto him, O thou wicked servant, I forgave thee all that debt, because thou desiredst me: shouldest not thou also have had compassion on thy fellow-servant, even as I had pity on thee? And his lord was wroth, and delivered him to the tormentors, till he should pay all that was due unto him. So likewise shall my heavenly Father do also unto you, if ye from your hearts forgive not every one his brother their trespasses."

It would have been bad enough if the servant had pressed his debtor for payment in order to make good his own debt to the lord, but that is not what the story says. The lord did not extend the time of payment; he was not merely helping the servant to collect whatever was owing to him; the debt was wiped out once for all. The doctrine is that the servant should have practiced this same mercy. Carried out to the end, the doctrine is that no debt should be collected. No wonder the pillars of established society began their plotting to put Jesus out of the way! The older law had taught that the sins or debts of the fathers are visited upon the children unto the third or fourth generation, but Jesus preferred to remind us of the mercy showered upon us all our days. If we pay the penalty of some mistakes, perhaps they are repeated mistakes. For most of our errors life exacts no penalty. But when we ourselves refuse to practice mercy, we become outcasts from the heavenly love.

The doctrine is easy to argue against, but experience does not contradict it. No form of the teaching that love should be unbounded, is more revolutionary. If put into practice it would disrupt society as we know it. It is perhaps the severest test of our agreement or disagreement with the mission of Jesus. He was more than willing that society as we know it should be disrupted. He never identified that society with the kingdom of God.

This doctrine of debt is treated again in the parable of the Good Samaritan. Once more the meaning is made clearer by the conversation which precedes it. In the Gospel according to St. Luke, chapter 10, we read that a certain lawyer, one of the enemies of Jesus, tried to ask a question he could not answer. "Master, what shall I do to inherit eternal life?" Jesus countered by asking what was written in the law. The lawyer replied, "Thou shalt love the Lord thy God with all thy heart, and with all thy soul, and with all thy strength, and with all thy mind; and thy neighbour as thyself." Jesus said, "Thou hast answered right: this do, and thou shalt live." But the lawyer, willing to justify himself, as St. Luke tells us, asked again, "And who is my neighbour?"

That little clause, "willing to justify himself," is interesting. Apparently the lawyer, even while quoting the great commandment to love, became a little conscience-stricken. He was engaged at the moment in trying to trap Jesus into some disaster. It was not a very neighborly act. He seems to have had no doubt that he loved God, but he knew he did not love Jesus, and he would have been glad to define "neighbour" so as to leave Jesus out. It should be noted that in his thought a neighbor was someone toward whom he had a duty. He was to be the neighbor's benefactor. It had not occurred to him that the neighbor might prove a benefactor to him, and that he might end in the neighbor's debt. Jesus frames the parable to prick the lawyer's conscience. The man who falls among thieves is an orthodox Jew, like the lawyer himself. The good neighbor who comes to the rescue is a man from Samaria, one of those whom a correct Jew would hold in contempt. When the victim of the robbers was lying in the gutter, two eminently respectable people came along the road and passed him by, not perhaps because they consciously wished to avoid a responsibility, but because they were not alert or sensitive to the needs of those around them. When the Samaritan has saved the injured man and has provided for his comfort, Jesus turns to the lawyer with the embarrassing question, "Which now of these three, thinkest thou, was neighbour unto him that fell among the thieves?" The lawyer cannot bring himself to say it was the Samaritan. He says, "He that shewed mercy on him." The conception of neighbor had been changed from the passive receiving of benefits to the active conferring of them. The concluding remark of Jesus is striking. The lawyer had asked what he must do to inherit eternal life, but in the discussion which followed perhaps he forgot his own question. At the end of the parable he is making a definition of neighborliness, rather than seeking an immediate program for himself. But as soon as he says, "He that shewed mercy on him," Jesus brings him back to the original question, with the words, "Go, and do thou likewise."

"A certain man went down from Jerusalem to Jericho, and fell among thieves, which stripped him of his raiment, and wounded him, and departed, leaving him half dead. And by chance there came down a certain priest that way: and when he saw him, he passed by on the other side. And likewise a Levite, when he was at the place, came and looked on him, and passed by on the other side. But a certain Samaritan, as he journeyed, came where he was: and when he saw him, he had compassion on him, and went to him, and bound up his wounds, pouring in oil and wine, and set him on his own beast, and brought him to an inn, and took care of him. And on the morrow when he departed, he took out two pence, and gave them to the host, and said unto him, Take care of him; and whatsoever thou spendest more, when I come again, I will repay thee. Which now of these three, thinkest thou, was neighbour unto him that fell among the thieves? And he said, He that shewed mercy on him. Then said Jesus unto him, Go, and do thou likewise."

It would perhaps be instructive to consider side by side a well-known parable which owes its fame perhaps to its beautiful simplicity, and an equally well-known parable which to some readers is the hardest of all to understand. I refer to the parable of the Pharisee and the Publican, and the parable of the Unjust Steward.

The first story was told to illustrate true humility. "He spake this parable unto certain which trusted in themselves that they were righteous, and despised others." (St. Luke, chapter 18.) To consider ourselves in any respect superior is to create a form of debt; we have taken credit from our neighbor and appropriated it for our own use, quite as much as though we had borrowed money. Jesus advises us after we have performed our duty in every detail to think of ourselves as unprofitable servants. To think otherwise would be conceit, and conceit is a form of trespass.

In this story of the two men praying, we must be careful not to assume that the Pharisee was unrighteous. We should accept the boasts in his prayer as the literal truth. Similarly, we should understand that the publican was probably guilty, as he said. Accepting the facts as correct in each case, we are asked to give our attention to the difference in their attitude. According to himself, the Pharisee owes nothing to anybody, neither to God nor to man. According to his own confession, the publican is hopelessly in debt and can ask nothing but mercy. Yet his attitude, Jesus teaches, is the right one for normal man, not that normal man is a hopeless sinner, but that humility is a condition of true love. A love which boasts or which condescends is not love, but on the contrary, a kind of hostility.

"Two men went up into the temple to pray; the one a Pharisee, and the other a publican. The Pharisee stood and prayed thus with himself, God, I thank thee, that I am not as other men are, extortioners, unjust, adulterers, or even as this publican. I fast twice in the week, I give tithes of all that I possess. And the publican, standing afar off, would not lift up so much as his eyes unto heaven, but smote upon his breast, saying, God be merciful to me a sinner. I tell you, this man went down to his house justified rather than the other: for every one that exalteth himself shall be abased; and he that humbleth himself shall be exalted."

The parable of the Unjust Steward is told in St. Luke's Gospel, chapter 16. It follows immediately after the story of the Prodigal Son. There could be no stranger contrast. A certain rich man had a steward who cheated him. Without arguing the case, the employer told the fellow that he was discharged, and demanded his account books. The steward, desperately plotting to make for himself a good berth somewhere, called in all those who owed anything to the rich man, and revised their bills downward. It was a final act of dishonesty at the employer's expense, and it made all the debtors dishonest men, but it also made them forget that they still owed something to the rich man, and it made them conscious that they owed something to the steward. He intended later to draw on this questionable credit.

What on earth does this parable mean? The comment of Jesus is even more perplexing than the story itself. He says, "The children of this world are in their generation wiser than the children of light." He adds sarcastically that we had better make friends of the mammon of unrighteousness, so that when we fail, they may receive us into everlasting habitations. The cause of our perplexity is that here, as in some other places which we have noticed, Jesus represents the conditions of this life realistically, strictly as they are. In the story of the unjust steward he reminds us how a certain kind of man behaves, not how he should behave. Having set up that realistic picture, which his hearers would condemn as heartily as his readers now, he points out that even this rascal had more thought for the future than most good people. The steward should have been faithful, but even in his dishonesty he had a kind of wisdom. If the parable of the Prodigal Son illustrates, as I think it does, the approval of Jesus for the man who ventures his one talent, even though he loses it, then the parable of the Unjust Steward may be a further comment on the same theme; the children of light who do not look to the future resemble too closely the man who buried his talent in a napkin, or the elder son who had his inheritance but never made use of it. They might learn something even from the unjust steward and his scheming.

"There was a certain rich man, which had a steward; and the same was accused unto him that he had wasted his goods. And he called him, and said unto him, How is it that I hear this of thee? give an account of thy stewardship; for thou mayest be no longer steward. Then the steward said within himself, What shall I do? for my lord taketh away from me the stewardship: I cannot dig; to beg I am ashamed. I am resolved what to do, that, when I am put out of the stewardship, they may receive me into their houses. So he called every one of his lord's debtors unto him, and said unto the first, How much owest thou unto my lord? And he said, An hundred measures of oil. And he said unto him, Take thy bill, and sit down quickly, and write fifty. Then said he to another, And how much owest thou? And he said, An hundred measures of wheat. And he said unto him, Take thy bill, and write fourscore. And the lord commended the un-just steward, because he had done wisely: for the children of this world are in their generation wiser than the children of light. And I say unto you, Make to yourselves friends of the mammon of unrighteousness; that, when ye fail, they may receive you into everlasting habitations."

We have considered the parable of Dives and Lazarus in an earlier chapter. The interpretation which I have given will to many readers be unwelcome; they would prefer to say that the story teaches the duty of awareness and sensitiveness, the sin of the rich man being that he could enjoy his wealth even though a miserable beggar lay at his door. It may be that this is what the parable meant to say, but I am not convinced that it says it. When Dives asks Abraham for comfort, Abraham does not men-tion any failure to be sympathetic, any disregard for the misfor-tunes of others; he says merely that Dives was fortunate on earth and now he has his turn at misfortune, and Lazarus, having had his bad luck first, now enjoys good luck. Since no other lesson is directly conveyed, and since what is stated constitutes a rather unusual philosophy, I accept this philosophy as the meaning of the parable. But there is no question that in the story of the good Samaritan, and in other places, Jesus taught plainly the duty of awareness, of keen sensitiveness to the condition in which our fellows are living.

He makes the best-remembered statement of this doctrine in

his account of the Last Judgment. This imaginative picture is not usually called a parable, but I see no reason for calling it anything else. It follows the parable of the Talents, in the Gospel according to St. Matthew, chapter 25. It is not intended to be a description of a far-off day of judgment nor of life after death; it is a dramatic way of criticizing our conduct here and now. Just as we use or misuse our talents, so we either are wide awake to the needs of those around us, or we are deaf and blind. In both parables the condemnation has a severity which we are not usually supposed to find in the teaching of Jesus. The man who declined to risk his one talent, is practically annihilated; those who were not sensitive to want and suffering around them are cast into hell. There is a curious severity also, as we noticed before, in the designation of the good and the wicked as sheep and goats; we cannot help asking how the goats could have been anything but goats, or the sheep anything but sheep. Does Jesus mean that all our fortune, even the proportion of goodness and badness in us, is fated? I cannot believe that this was his meaning, yet this is what the parable seems to imply. Its central doctrine, however, is beyond challenge; those who are lovers of mankind are lovers of God, and those who love mankind do not need to be told, through any special instructions, what at any moment their neighbor stands in need of.

This passage, remarkable even among the most eloquent words of Jesus for its moving power, is a fitting conclusion to any discussion of the parables. It serves as reminder that the little stories which he used to drive home his truths, are masterpieces. Are we shocked at the suggestion that Jesus was a great artist, a superb storyteller, a born dramatist? Literature furnishes no close parallels and no rivals to these perfect compositions. They can be explained by no study of previous authors. The lessons they convey seem to come, not indirectly through images of life, but from immediate contact with life itself. They are life, speaking. Of no story can this be said more truly than of the majestic account of the final winnowing of the good from the bad.

"When the Son of man shall come in his glory, and all the

holy angels with him, then shall he sit upon the throne of his glory: and before him shall be gathered all nations: and he shall separate them one from another, as a shepherd divideth his sheep from the goats: and he shall set the sheep on his right hand, but the goats on the left. Then shall the King say unto them on his right hand, Come, ye blessed of my Father, inherit the kingdom prepared for you from the foundation of the world: for I was an hungred, and ye gave me meat: I was thirsty, and ye gave me drink: I was a stranger, and ye took me in: naked, and ye clothed me: I was sick, and ye visited me: I was in prison, and ye came unto me. Then shall the righteous answer him, saying, Lord, when saw we thee an hungred, and fed thee? or thirsty, and gave thee drink? When saw we thee a stranger, and took thee in? or naked, and clothed thee? Or when saw we thee sick, or in prison, and came unto thee? And the King shall answer and say unto them, Verily I say unto you, Inasmuch as ye have done it unto one of the least of these my brethren, ye have done it unto me. Then shall he say also unto them on the left hand, Depart from me, ye cursed, into everlasting fire, prepared for the devil and his angels: for I was an hungred, and ye gave me no meat: I was thirsty, and ye gave me no drink: I was a stranger, and ye took me not in: naked, and ye clothed me not: sick, and in prison, and ye visited me not. Then shall they also answer him, saying, Lord, when saw we thee an hungred, or athirst, or a stranger, or naked, or sick, or in prison, and did not minister unto thee? Then shall he answer them, saying, Verily I say unto you, Inasmuch as ye did it not to one of the least of these, ye did it not to me. And these shall go away into everlasting punishment: but the righteous into life eternal."

X

The Miracles

JESUS taught through parables, but it seems that the multitude were far more impressed by his miracles. He did not welcome their admiration when it was based on mere astonishment, as in most cases it was. Whether or not he had all the powers, or made use of all the powers, which the Gospels attribute to him, no miracle would logically prove the spiritual truths which he taught. To bring a dead man to life would be a fabulous achievement, but it would not reinforce the doctrine that we should love God utterly and love our neighbor as ourself. To be able to turn water into wine would be a great convenience, especially at a large party where the wine had given out, but it would teach nothing about the duty to be just in all our dealings, or to be humble toward God and man. To multiply the loaves and fishes in order that the hungry might on one occasion be fed, would be a feat less astonishing than troubling, especially if it were used as evidence that Jesus was the son of God. If he could feed the hungry so easily, and if it was legitimate for him on one occasion to suspend natural laws. why are those laws not suspended whenever hunger recurs?

To tell the life of Jesus or to read intelligently any account of it, we must decide what to do with those episodes in the story which the Gospels call indiscriminately miracles. Certainly they were in any case works of wonder, and some of them undoubtedly occurred, but we are not likely to agree on which ones. In the multitudes who listened to Jesus there doubtless were many who by temperament shut their eyes to what was human in him and looked eagerly for something superhuman. Among the apostles there seems to have been little agreement as to certain miracles, considerable agreement as to others. St. John is the only Evangelist who reports the turning of water into wine, and he alone tells the story of Lazarus, the brother of Martha and Mary. In this latter case we have a real problem, since what is called the raising of Lazarus from the dead was for Jesus a crucial incident; the populace was so excited over it and their enthusiasm for Jesus was so fanned by it, that the high priests resolved then and there to put him to death. I do not believe that Jesus raised Lazarus from the dead, nor that he ever said he did or ever intended to deceive his followers. He certainly brought Lazarus back to health, but just what happened, we are not likely to know, since our only source of information is the Gospel according to St. John, and the account there, as we may see in a moment, is confused.

It is easy to accept, with certain reservations, practically all the miracles of healing, whether they were concerned with the casting out of evil spirits, or as we should say, with the restoration of sanity—or whether they involved the restoring of the nerves of arms and legs, or of any other part of the body. The power of mind and will is so great and as yet so little explored, that it would be extreme rashness to say a great natural healer could not, by the therapy of his own abundant vitality, bring certain cripples quickly to a condition where they could get up from their bed and walk.

Jesus had this vitality and used it, but always with a certain reluctance. The question has been asked thousands of times, why, if he had the power, he did not use it constantly. The answer is that he conceived of his mission as another kind of healing. He might have spent all his days curing sick bodies, but he knew that at the end of life he would take his healing with him, and the sicknesses would remain. There is evidence that he sometimes was torn between the wish to get on with his great mission and the pleas of those near him for immediate aid. He seems to have denied none of these requests, but they interrupted his work, less by using up his time than by diverting attention from his doctrine.

The incident of Lazarus, told in St. John's Gospel, chapter 11, illustrates the point I here would make. The Evangelist seems to have reported some of the words of Jesus with a high degree of accuracy, and there is nothing in those words that compels us to believe Lazarus was literally dead. But it is evident also that the Evangelist himself believed that Lazarus died and was brought back to life by divine intervention.

"Now a certain man was sick, named Lazarus, of Bethany, the town of Mary and her sister Martha. (It was that Mary which anointed the Lord with ointment, and wiped his feet with her hair, whose brother Lazarus was sick.) Therefore his sisters sent unto him, saying, Lord, behold, he whom thou lovest is sick. When Jesus heard that, he said, This sickness is not unto death, but for the glory of God, that the Son of God might be glorified thereby. Now Jesus loved Martha, and her sister, and Lazarus. When he had heard therefore that he was sick, he abode two days still in the same place where he was. Then after that saith he to his disciples, Let us go into Judæa again. His disciples say unto him, Master, the Jews of late sought to stone thee; and goest thou thither again? Jesus answered, Are there not twelve hours in the day? If any man walk in the day, he stumbleth not, because he seeth the light of this world. But if a man walk in the night, he stumbleth, because there is no light in him. These things said he: and after that he saith unto them, Our friend Lazarus sleepeth; but I go, that I may awake him out of sleep. Then said his disciples, Lord, if he sleep, he shall do well. Howbeit Jesus spake of his death: but they thought that he had spoken of taking of rest in sleep. Then said Jesus unto them plainly, Lazarus is dead. And I am glad for your sakes that I was not there, to the intent ye may believe; nevertheless let us go unto him. Then said Thomas, which is called Didymus, unto his fellow-disciples, Let us also go, that we may die with him. Then when Jesus came, he found that he had lain in the grave four days already. Now Bethany was nigh unto Jerusalem, about fifteen furlongs off: and many of the Jews came to Martha and Mary to comfort them concerning their brother. Then Martha, as soon as she heard that Jesus was coming, went and met him: but Mary sat still in the house. Then said Martha unto Jesus, Lord, if thou hadst been here, my brother had not died. But I know, that even now, whatsoever thou wilt ask of God, God will give it thee. Jesus saith unto her, Thy brother shall rise again. Martha said unto him, I know that he shall rise again in the resurrection at the last day. Jesus said unto her, I am the resurrection, and the life: he that believeth in me, though he were dead, yet shall he live: and whosoever liveth and believeth in me shall never die. Believest thou this? She saith unto him, Yea, Lord: I believe that thou art the Christ, the Son of God, which should come into the world. And when she had so said, she went her way, and called Mary her sister secretly, saying, The Master is come, and calleth for thee. As soon as she heard that, she arose quickly, and came unto him. Now Jesus was not yet come into the town, but was in that place where Martha met him. The Jews then which were with her in the house, and comforted her, when they saw Mary, that she rose up hastily and went out, followed her, saying, She goeth unto the grave to weep there. Then when Mary was come where Jesus was, and saw him, she fell down at his feet, saying unto him, Lord, if thou hadst been here, my brother had not died. When Jesus therefore saw her weeping, and the Jews also weeping which came with her, he groaned in the spirit, and was troubled, and said, Where have ye laid him? They said unto him, Lord, come and see. Jesus wept. Then said the Jews, Behold how he loved him! And some of them said, Could not this man, which opened the eyes of the blind, have caused that even this man should not have died? Jesus therefore again groaning in himself cometh to the grave. It was a cave, and a stone lay upon it. Jesus said, Take ye away the stone. Martha, the sister of him that was dead, saith unto him, Lord, by this time he stinketh: for he hath been dead four days. Jesus saith unto her. Said I not unto thee, that, if thou wouldest believe, thou shouldest see the glory of God? Then they took away the stone from the place where the dead was laid. And Jesus lifted up his eyes, and said, Father, I thank thee that thou hast heard me. And I knew that thou hearest me always: but because of the people which stand by I said it, that they may believe that thou hast sent me. And when he thus had spoken, he cried with a loud voice, Lazarus, come forth. And he that was dead came forth, bound hand and foot with graveclothes: and his face was bound about with a napkin. Jesus saith unto them, Loose him, and let him go."

When I said that the Evangelist seems to have reported some of the words of Jesus accurately, I referred to his statement that Lazarus was not dead but sleeping. Evidently the disciples understood him to mean, literally, that he was in some sort of deep slumber or trance. The Evangelist immediately explains that Jesus meant death, not sleep, but the story has in it elements which suggest that the episode had already become a miracle by tradition, whatever the original facts were. Two passages in the text I cannot believe. When Jesus told Lazarus to come forth, Lazarus got to his feet and walked out of the cave, though we are told he was bound hand and foot in the grave clothes. This would be almost as great a miracle as the raising from the dead. After Lazarus had glided or floated out of the cave, Jesus said to the bystanders, "Loose him, and let him go."

The other passage which seems to me incredible is the prayer which Jesus made out loud, before he told Lazarus to come forth. In the prayer he thanks God for hearing him, says that God always hears him, and explains to God why he told Martha she would see God's glory; he made that promise because a crowd was standing by, who were sure to hear, and the words, together with the miracle which he now intended to execute, would induce them to believe in him.

After what Jesus had told his disciples about the nature of prayer, and after his frequently demonstrated reluctance to astonish people into believing, it is incredible that he should have uttered these words. I go so far as to say it would be a reflection on the intelligence of Jesus, of his audience then, of Gospel-readers now, to ask us to believe that in this prayer he informed not only the Almighty but the bystanders of his calculated intention to make converts by a public demonstration of super-human power. It is much easier for me to believe the tradition that St. John, when he wrote his version of the Gospel, was an old man, a very old man indeed, and that he was using incidents in the life of Jesus, not in the interest of biographical accuracy, but to illustrate a doctrine. There are phrases in the scene at the grave of Lazarus which are echoes from the story of the Resurrection. Jesus said, for example, "Take ye away the stone"; Mary Magdalene, coming early to the sepulcher of Jesus, saw the stone taken away from the sepulcher. Yet however we may question this account of the miracle, there is no doubt that something remarkable occurred, some unhoped-for recovery of the sick man which vastly increased the reputation of Jesus as a merciful healer. It increased also the enmity of the Pharisees to him. Whether or not it helped his followers to an understanding of his teachings, is another matter. His whole life was a miracle, but the incidents in it, according to the doctrine of the Incarnation, belonged to human experience. If ever he had exerted, during his years on earth, powers of such supernatural quality that no human being can hope to share them, then the Incarnation would have been incomplete; if he had refused to submit to our limitations, then he would not have taken upon him our nature, and the life he lived among men would not have been altogether an example for us, since we could not in every respect imitate it.

2

A N Y attentive reader of the Gospels must have noticed the number of incidents in which Jesus performs miracles of healing by a mere word. Some of those incidents, like the raising of Lazarus from the dead, are for people like myself, both incredible and undesirable. I have just given my reasons; I should like to emphasize them. I believe that Jesus was an incarnation of the Divine. Other religions than Christianity contain legends of gods or goddesses who made visits to earth disguised as mortals, but those visits were often for frivolous or unworthy purposes. The Christian doctrine that God, man's Creator, came to earth to live as man, to show man how to live, to become man's Saviour, is a remarkable conception, remarkable not only for its nobility but for its warm humanness. Here for the first time was revealed a God of love, a sympathetic and friendly God; the help which Jesus gave to the sick, to the lame, especially to those with unhappy minds, was friendly help. Perhaps he was never more truly a healer, never more truly a miracle worker, than when he was teaching and practicing the forgiveness of sin. In his parables and in those moments of his life when he dealt face to face with sinners, his concern was plainly with the health of the soul. He wished the sinner to give up his sin, but he also wished the sinner not to be ruined by a wrong way of remembering sin. I use the word sin here in a range of meanings, as it was used in the parables, to include debts and anything else that creates a sense of obligation.

Perhaps the commonest disease of the sick minds which Jesus cured, was worry. We are accustomed to say that our modern life exposes us to nervous diseases, and the chief cause of various forms of collapse is our inability to relax. No doubt the pressure of a complex civilization is great, but the pressure of earlier civilization was quite great enough to break down the human being who allowed himself to become, as we say, too tense. With us, as with the men and women in old times, one of the greatest pressures came from conscience. The memory of error, intended or unintended, may easily turn itself into morbidness, even to such extreme forms of morbidness as cannot be distinguished from insanity. There is no release from this pressure except through hope, or through the prospect of a second chance, or through any one of the many forms of comfort summed up in that word "forgiveness." Those who have something in their past which they regret, and which it is now too late to repair or correct, understand what is said here. If Jesus speaks often of sin, it is not because he is brooding on the capacity of mankind for ill-doing; it is because he knew that most of us suffer for the mistakes we have made, and our suffering, since it is morbid, is unprofitable. Apoplexy can be brought on by worry; brooding on our sins may literally cripple us at last. The only effective comfort for souls in such distress is a kind of forgiveness which will release them from their past, and enable them to live again.

In the Gospel according to St. Mark, chapter 2, we read the story of the man whom Jesus healed of the palsy. The episode is remembered for the energy and the faith of the man's friends, four of whom brought him on a stretcher, and when they couldn't reach Jesus through the crowd they lifted off part of the roof and lowered the invalid in front of Jesus, who astonished the bystanders by saying, "Son, thy sins be forgiven thee." Some hostile critics asked at once what power he had to forgive sins. Jesus replied with the question, whether it was easier to say, "Thy sins be forgiven thee," or "Arise, and take up thy bed, and walk." Then, in order to show that he had power, and that the two expressions were interchangeable, he told the palsied man to get up, take his bed, and go home. Immediately the man was cured. If you ask how, the answer is, by something in the speech, the manner, the personality of Jesus, which released the man . from his worries and regrets. We are not told what brought on his nervous collapse, and it is not worth guessing about. The point is that true forgiveness has to do with the future rather than with the past; it releases from the pressure of morbid fears and regrets, and invites to a new and healthier life. It would be tragic indeed if we were skeptical about miracles of this kind.

Since this is the type of cure which Jesus constantly performed, it is well to have the episode before us as St. Mark tells it, with the vivid details of the crowded house at Capernaum, the pathetic eagerness of the sick man and his friends, the heart-breaking skepticism of the hostile scribes, who then as now would rather have a cure not performed than performed in what to them was an unorthodox way. "Again he entered into Capernaum, after some days; and it was noised that he was in the house. And straightway many were gathered together, insomuch that there was no room to receive them, no, not so much as about the door: and he preached the word unto them. And they come unto him, bringing one sick of the palsy, which was borne of four. And when they could not come nigh unto him for the press, they uncovered the roof where he was: and when they had broken it up, they let down the bed wherein the sick of the palsy lay. When Jesus saw their faith, he said unto the sick of the palsy, Son, thy sins be forgiven thee. But there were certain of the scribes sitting there, and reasoning in their hearts, Why doth this man thus speak blasphemies? who can forgive sins but God only? And immediately when Jesus perceived in his spirit that they so reasoned within themselves, he said unto them, Why reason ye these things in your hearts? Whether is it easier to say to the sick of the palsy, Thy sins be forgiven thee; or to say, Arise, and take up thy bed, and walk? But that ye may know that the Son of man hath power on earth to forgive sins, (he saith to the sick of the palsy,) I say unto thee, Arise, and take up thy bed, and go thy way into thine house. And immediately he arose, took up the bed, and went forth before them all."

3

I T should be noted that the friends of the palsied man had faith. In many of the cures which Jesus performed, the faith of those around the sick person was extraordinary. There is no reason to think that this circumstance was accidental or insignificant. I have tried to indicate that in the teaching of Jesus, sin and lack of health are not unconnected. Terms such as faith, repentance, or love, which we are sometimes inclined to take in a general or vague sense, are to him always the names of real forces. We approach his doctrine, however gropingly, when we talk of mental healing, or of the importance of being "in the right frame of mind"; but with him the words stand always for something quite simple and definite. The heavenly Father, of whose love for man Jesus taught us, was God the Creator; he created the world because he loved to create, and afterwards he loved the world which he had created, and he wished his children to be like him, creative in their love. Perhaps it is sometimes difficult for us, hearing this oft-repeated doctrine of Jesus, and attaching to every word from his lips august and reverent overtones, to remember that what he said is literally true. He invited his hearers to measure the truth by their own experience, and we can do the same. We know that affection is health-giving, not only to those who are sick but to those who are sound. We know that the presence of friends who wish the sick to get well, contributes something to the recovery. On the other hand we know that an atmosphere of indifference or hostility reduces the vitality of even the strongest, and may even cause the death of the weak. Love for our neighbor, then, is not simply a spiritual luxury, a grace of the soul; it is a heavy responsibility. From everyone about us whom we do not love, we withhold life. To withdraw faith, to cease to believe in a man, is the first step toward destroying him.

Perhaps no parable illustrates the therapeutic value of affection and faith more than the story of the Centurion and his servant. St. Matthew and St. Luke both tell the incident, but St. Luke's version (chapter 7) is fuller, and contains details which we should be sorry to miss. The Centurion was of course a Roman soldier who commanded a hundred men. He must have had a remarkable character, this particular Centurion, to be popular in Capernaum, where he was stationed in the military garrison. The troops were there to keep the Jews in subjection. But this Centurion was a great soul, with many of the virtues which Jesus urged upon his followers. There had been need of a local synagogue, and the Centurion had donated the building, not because he was ready to embrace the Jewish religion, but because he profoundly admired the character of this people whom Rome had overcome only by force of arms in warfare. The Roman character at its best had extraordinary grandeur, and this Centurion, charged with keeping peace among a people who would resent his presence, had the largeness of mind to recognize the quality of the Jewish spirit. Evidently he treated his servants as members of his family, and when one of them, of whom he was particularly fond, fell desperately ill, he asked the elders of the Capernaum synagogue to ask Jesus to come and cure him.

The elders were in a difficult position. The Centurion had befriended their congregation; how could they refuse his request? Evidently he supposed they were on terms of intimate accord with Jesus, as with the newest prophet of their people; how could he guess that their sympathies might be with Annas and Caiaphas, with the Pharisees and the scribes? When they brought the Centurion's plea to Jesus, he went at once. But as soon as the Centurion knew he was at hand, he sent word that it would not be necessary for Jesus to take so much trouble, and he explained why. His faith in a well-ordered universe was one reason why the servant got well. And this man, full of the creative, health-giving love, was a Gentile, as Jesus points out.

"He entered into Capernaum. And a certain centurion's servant, who was dear unto him, was sick, and ready to die. And when he heard of Jesus, he sent unto him the elders of the Jews, beseeching him that he would come and heal his servant. And when they came to Jesus, they besought him instantly, saying, That he was worthy for whom he should do this: for he loveth our nation, and he hath built us a synagogue. Then Jesus went with them. And when he was now not far from the house, the centurion sent friends to him, saying unto him, Lord, trouble not thyself: for I am not worthy that thou shouldest enter under my roof: wherefore neither thought I myself worthy to come unto thee: but say in a word, and my servant shall be healed. For I also am a man set under authority, having under me soldiers, and I say unto one, Go, and he goeth; and to another, Come, and he cometh; and to my servant, Do this, and he doeth it. When Jesus heard these things, he marvelled at him, and turned him about, and said unto the people that followed him, I say unto you, I have not found so great faith, no, not in Israel. And they that were sent, returning to the house, found the servant whole that had been sick."

The Centurion evidently had a military mind. He conceived of all authority as transmitted through various grades, as in an army, from the commander-in-chief down to the non-commissioned officer. We need not smile at his simplicity. The church has found no better model of spiritual discipline than that furnished by the life of the soldier, the knight-errant, the Crusader. Jesus came himself in answer to the Centurion's call, there being no substitute for him to send, but the Centurion shows complete understanding of the psychology upon which all discipline and all authority rest. A commander-in-chief has the power to enforce his orders, but if he has to enforce them, he lacks true authority, which is a moral force operating even in his absence, even in the absence of his subordinates. To the Centurion God was a Commander-in-chief, not tangibly present in Capernaum at the moment, but represented by this prophet. Jesus had but to speak the word, and the servant would be healed.

4

THROUGHOUT the Gospels the miracles are frequently called Signs and Wonders. The healing of the palsied man is a Sign, and so was the healing of the Centurion's servant. The turning of water into wine and the raising of Lazarus were Wonders. A Wonder was a work of astonishment. It was intended to surprise and amaze. For greater effect, it was usually reported as occurring in an atmosphere of incredulity. The sisters of Lazarus and the disciples who accompanied Jesus, had no faith whatever that Lazarus would ever again appear among them as a living man. In the case of the water turned into wine, the performance was so unexpected and so successful that perhaps the astonishment did not quite come off; there is little evidence that any of those present except Jesus, his mother, and the servants, knew what had happened.

I have made it clear that I do not believe in the Wonders. They were no novelties, either in ancient religious legends or in secular poetry. The ancient world was very weak in science, chiefly because antiquity liked magic for its own sake, liked to be astonished, liked to be entertained and baffled, as by sleight-of-hand. The apocryphal legends of Jesus in his boyhood are full of magic, they fairly reek with it; for that very reason the early Church rejected those particular writings, since the teaching of Jesus did not rest on that kind of demonstration, and could only be discredited by it. How large a mass of unworthy material they deleted from the earliest legends, we too easily forget. Because there was so much to throw out, they left in more, perhaps, than they intended. The Wonders are grand stories, if literature is what we are after, but they are parasitic growths upon the true life of Jesus. He himself lost no opportunity of warning us that faith does not follow from a Wonder, but rather from the sight of truth, and from the love of it. "If they hear not Moses and the prophets, neither will they be persuaded, though one rose from the dead."

A Sign is a work of healing which indicates the presence of God. A Sign is a work which is possible only where faith and love are present. Those miracles which had the effect of restoring health and of making life more abundant, were Signs, often if not always the result of a collaboration in faith and love. It is not difficult to believe in Signs.

There can be no astonishment from a Sign, since that kind of miracle is wished for, prayed for, made the object of faith. It neither surprises nor amazes, but it excites to gratitude. At least, that is the effect on those who really desire the presence of God. The scribes and Pharisees asked Jesus for a sign that he was the Messiah, practically defying him to convince them. But what they were expecting was a Wonder, a work of astonishment.

xi

The Lord's Prayer

WE LEARN from the Gospels that Jesus on more than one occasion talked to his disciples about the nature of prayer. The purpose of prayer, he told them, is not to inform our heavenly Father of our needs; he knows what we need before we ask. There would be something of insult and indignity in treating God as a source of supplies, to whom we had to send in our daily order. Jesus taught that prayer is an exercise in self-examination. Our petitions should be chosen for the purpose of searching out our own heart. So long as we can say them sincerely, all is well with us. If at any time our praying becomes perfunctory, or any particular petition becomes hard to say, we should look to ourselves.

We learn from St. Luke, chapter 11, that once when Jesus was praying in a certain place, his disciples waited until his prayer was ended, and then said to him, "Lord, teach us to pray, as John also taught his disciples." It is supposed that John the Baptist trained his disciples to imitate the Pharisees in praying three times a day, at the third hour, the sixth, and the ninth, using prayers from the Jewish manual of private devotion. The question which the disciples of Jesus now asked, had probably nothing to do with the profound nature of prayer; they wished to know what prayers to repeat, and when to repeat them. That they intended no more than this is implied in St. Matthew's account of the incident. He omits the detail that their question was prompted by seeing Jesus at prayer, and he incorporates the reply of Jesus in his version of the Sermon on the Mount; but by putting his version side by side with St. Luke's, we can see that Jesus did not wish his disciples to pray on any particular schedule, nor to imitate the Pharisees in the ostentation of their prayers, nor to trust in the number of times they prayed. "When thou prayest, thou shalt not be as the hypocrites are: for they love to pray standing in the synagogues and in the corners of the streets, that they may be seen of men. Verily I say unto you, They have their reward. But thou, when thou prayest, enter into thy closet, and when thou hast shut thy door, pray to thy Father which is in secret; and thy Father which seeth in secret shall reward thee openly. But when ye pray, use not vain repetitions, as the heathen do: for they think that they shall be heard for their much speaking. Be not ye therefore like unto them: for your Father knoweth what things ye have need of, before ye ask him." (St. Matthew, chapter 6.)

Here follows immediately in St. Matthew's account the pattern which Jesus offered of all prayer. "After this manner therefore pray ye: Our Father which art in heaven, Hallowed be thy name. Thy kingdom come. Thy will be done in earth, as it is in heaven. Give us this day our daily bread. And forgive us our debts, as we forgive our debtors. And lead us not into temptation, but deliver us from evil: For thine is the kingdom, and the power, and the glory, for ever. Amen."

This prayer is remarkable for the importance of its petitions and for the small number of them. Nothing is asked which has merely a temporary value, and nothing is asked which does not involve the will. This was not explained to me when I was taught the prayer as a child. I thought the first clause merely stated a fact—Our Father which art in heaven. In the three petitions which immediately follow, I thought I was giving my consent rather than asking for anything—Hallowed be thy name, Thy kingdom come, Thy will be done in earth, as it is in heaven. At that point, as I understood, the prayer began. I thought I was asking for daily bread, for forgiveness of my debts or trespasses and for protection against evil. The prayer then closed, I was quite sure, with a respectful statement about God's kingdom, and his power, and his glory forever.

But prayer, as Jesus taught, is an exercise of the will, and to this extent a self-examination, that if we do not care sufficiently to put our will into everything we ask, we are not sincere in our praying. The Lord's Prayer begins with an ascription, a form of address. We are making our petition to a heavenly rather than an earthly father, but even in this ascription there is an opportunity for us to exert our will; we wish our heavenly Father's name to be hallowed, or revered; we wish his kingdom to come; we wish his will to be carried out in earth, as it is in heaven. With these words the first part of the prayer ends. We have as yet asked nothing for ourselves; in no true prayer should we be to any degree selfish. In all humility we have offered our individual will in co-operation with the divinely ordered universe. Since man first noticed the stars and left us any comment on them, the heavens have stood symbolically for obedience and order. The stars keep to their courses no matter how wandering they may seem to be; sun and moon divide the day and the night, not in an even balance of light and darkness, but according to the law of their own rhythm. Sun, moon and stars revere or keep hallowed the name of their creator; the morning stars sang together in his honor, and to those who are attuned to the celestial music, they are singing still, but on earth, as the prayer admits there is as yet no such divine order. To man has been granted freedom of will, which means freedom to choose between good and evil. Perhaps, as the story of the garden of Eden would have us believe, the knowledge of good and evil came from the devil himself. Perhaps man would have been happier if he had continued to know only how to do the will of his heavenly Father. But since human life is what it is, we pray and work for the reestablishment on earth of the broken order.

The few petitions which apparently refer only to us who are making the prayer, have a wider meaning than at first we may realize. "Give us this day our daily bread." The repetition in "this day" and "daily" has seemed to some people a difficulty; to others the fact that we ask God to give us whatever sustenance we need, seems to excuse us from the responsibility of feeding ourselves. Neither point ought to detain us. We work for our daily bread, but our work must be in collaboration with certain natural laws, which we can use and to that extent can control, but which we cannot alter. The wheat must be planted by us; it will grow steadily and silently, as fast as the sunlight, the weather, and the soil permit. When the bread is made at last, it is indeed our daily bread, our staff of life, but it is granted to us not once for all but daily. There must be fresh preparations of the flour, fresh bakings.

No doubt the expression "daily bread" is to be understood symbolically as meaning all the things essential to our life. The prayer trains us to realize that the gift of life is conditional upon our co-operating efforts and that the gift is renewed daily. It is the manna which dropped from heaven, but which had to be gathered each morning, and only so much could be gathered as was sufficient for the day.

If by bread we are to understand all that sustains life, then in these simple words we are asking for the opportunity and the right to do the work which produces our daily bread. We are asking also for the economic conditions which are necessary if we and our neighbors alike are to get at whatever is essential to our living. There is evidence enough in the parables that Jesus was indifferent to the conventional discussion of economic questions, though he must have been acquainted with those questions, since they perplexed men in his day as in ours. But he seems to have thought it useless to seek economic justice by regulating our condition as it were from the outside. He said plainly that those who have more wealth than their fellows have a greater responsibility and will find it harder to get into the kingdom of heaven; yet he refuses to say that the rich are shut out. Strong as his sympathy is for the poor, he refuses to say that a man who deserves our pity is necessarily on that account good or useful.

What he does say, is that those men are blessed who do the work which produces more life for them and for others. The workers in the vineyard who were engaged in the last hour received as much as those who labored through the whole day, but their wage was a kind of consolation for their misfortune in not having had the opportunity to work earlier. The laborers who did the full day's task were the blessed ones.

From what has been said about the definition of sin and debt in the teaching of Jesus, we should be able to understand without difficulty the petition for forgiveness, in the same measure as we forgive others. Here the implication of our personal will is clear indeed. We cannot ask for any release from conscience or from unhappy memory, unless we are ready on our part to release others from the same torment. It is not by accident that the forgiveness of sins follows the reference to daily bread. Bread symbolizes whatever sustains the health of the body. In order that the mind may be healthy, all transgressions, errors, and debts must be forgiven. The petition for bread and the petition for the wiping out of whatever troubles accompany it, constitute together a prayer for health.

"Lead us not into temptation, but deliver us from evil." Another translation reads: "Deliver us from the evil one." The meaning is the same, no matter which version is adopted. If any petition in this prayer were simply a request that the heavenly Father would do something for us, then this particular request would mean that we admit God's power to test us as he tried out poor Job, but we hope he will not put us to any such proof, since we doubt that we have Job's endurance. If this interpretation were adopted, many of us might be disturbed at the notion that God would tempt us to do evil or would turn us over to Satan as he turned Job over, almost by way of experiment to decide a wager. But if in these petitions some effort of the will is involved, the meaning is quite otherwise. We are asking not that our heavenly Father will refrain from exposing us to unnecessary risk, but that we shall avoid the risk ourselves. We sometimes hear men of the most conspicuous probity say that a wise merchant hedges himself around with safeguards, not to protect himself from being cheated, but to make sure that he cannot cheat others. This wisdom is entirely in the spirit of the prayer that we be not led into temptation. The kind of risk or danger which is here referred to, comes by way of what might be called a natural pitfall; we do not ourselves plan it, nor is it plotted against us. Yet in this human life evil is sometimes aggressive. A bad neighbor, an enemy, even a misguided friend may set a trap for us or push us into it. "Deliver us from evil." That is, if aggressive wickedness is for a moment too strong for us, we not only ask the heavenly Father to lend a helping hand, but we promise to do our best to get out of the trap at once.

If we enjoy—and first of all, if we earn—the daily bread which sustains life; if we obtain that release from our own wrong-doings and our own error—and if we grant to others that release —which restores and sustains the health of the soul; if we subject our peace of mind to no moral risk, and if we escape all forms of malice that deliberately would upset our peace; if we are careful not to imperil the peace of others, or if when they stumble we are quick to lift them up—then the name of our heavenly Father will be revered, his kingdom will be on its way, his will, the divine order, will be obeyed by men on earth as it is obeyed in heaven by the bodies of light.

2

I N ancient literature few images are used more often as metaphors of life than bread and wine. It is not remarkable, then, that Jesus in his teaching spoke of the sower, of the grain growing silently, of the grapes which are not gathered from bramble bushes, but from the true vine. But the total number of his references to the seed, to planting and reaping, to loaves of bread, is unusually large, and they sum themselves up in the most famous petition of the Lord's Prayer. We are conscious of praying, not simply for daily bread, but for an order of life which he had described by a broad extension of the metaphor.

He used the growing wheat, for example, to illustrate the difference between the shortness and the length of time, and the larger difference between time and eternity, as both can be recognized here and now. We cannot hurry the seasons. The seed will grow as fast as the sun and the weather permit, and having done our part in the original planting, we must have patience. Again, the seed which we sow this season, came from last year's harvest. All living things owe their existence to some form of continuity, and as soon as we try to imagine this continuity from its beginning to its end, we leave the world of time and of finite things. To explain the origin of the loaf of bread on our table today, we should have to explain the origin of life itself.

Doubtless we speculate little about the infinite beginnings of bread, but we do put our minds on the problem of next year's food supply, on the still more remote yet pressing problem of our children's food supply long after we may be dead and in our graves. This is what Joseph taught Pharaoh when he advised storehouses for the wheat in the plentiful years, so that Egypt might not starve in the lean years. Growing things extend our notions of time, first to embrace a future beyond our own lives, and then to embrace the concept of eternity. The most obvious idea connected with food—a sensation before it is even an idea— is hunger. In immediate experience hunger is temporary, and so are its satisfactions, but soon we find ourselves speaking of a hunger for beauty, a hunger for justice, a hunger for truth. Jesus speaks of those who hunger and thirst after righteousness. Hunger has become, in this expression, the right attitude toward righteousness, an attitude as eternal as righteousness itself.

When Jesus tells us that in this life one sows and another reaps, he employs a metaphor of continuity, but he is also speaking of faith. Our daily bread is the product of long-continued faith. We use the word perhaps more often than we understand it. There are two aspects of faith, one looking to the future, the other to the past, and it would be difficult to say which aspect is more important. If we keep faith with a friend, we are continuing something out of the past, and for the moment we attach to the past a large importance. "Honour thy father and thy mother, that thy days may be long in the land." Here is the kind of faith which for the moment has regard to the past, to the roots rather than to the blossom and fruit. The promise in this commandment does look toward the future, but only in part. Those who honor their father and their mother extend their own lives backward through many generations until their days have been long in the land. This is peculiarly true, as we all know, of the farmer who works the fields which his father worked before him and perhaps his grandfather. In old and settled countries, the cultivation of the soil becomes a religion of piety. Every corner of every field, every fence or gate, is associated with long memories, and touching the soil under his feet, the farmer in memory is brought nearer to those who worked there as he now is working. Those who plant the seed of life-giving food and who bring the grain to harvest, are proverbially conservative. Faith as they understand the word, means almost the same thing as loyalty.

In the other sense the word is bound up with the idea of trust or confidence. The element of loyalty is in it too, since confidence in the future is properly based on the experience of the past. When experience is long enough, it begins to embrace eternal principles, and as soon as we can believe that our knowledge is valid not only for a moment or for a number of moments but for all time, we are warranted in our faith. Here again we shall have to be patient. The further we reach into the future with our confidence based on experience, the longer we shall have to wait to see our faith justified. When we pray, "Give us this day our daily bread," we are accepting the need of patience. We shall need sustenance always, and when we are gone, our children will need it, but by faith we live from day to day, knowing that this year's harvest will yield not only this year's food but seed for next year.

Our daily bread implies, then, a continuity from the remote

past into the remote future, yet the bread is to be earned daily. Asking for food, we accept the order of life which is possible only if we work—we are promising to work—we are asking for the privilege of working. Some of our modern attitudes toward work are completely absent from the teaching of Jesus. He never speaks of wresting a living from the soil any more than of wresting it from other men. He insists, first and last, that work is either a collaboration, or else it is a form of conflict, of robbery, of war. When we want food from the soil, we must permit and even encourage the soil to produce the food in its own way, and we must wait until the soil is ready. Our part is to a remarkable degree only a form of assisting nature to do better what nature would manage somehow to do anyway. Even without us the wheat would produce its seed, the seeds would fall into the ground, and there would be more wheat. The wheat would not by itself produce the loaves of bread; here we collaborate. We also encourage the soil to yield more plentifully, and we train the wheat to produce more fruitful seeds. But we have created nothing; we merely have aided nature by obeying its laws and by collaborating in its work. If we are not willing to collaborate, we can rob the soil or loot it; for a season or two we can take out more than we put in. In the end, however, we must pay for our violence. Those who in their haste wrest a living from the soil, incur a great debt.

Jesus taught the same truth as regards the work we do for our fellows. It is possible to wrest a living from other men, but this is robbery. Only now after two thousand years does human society begin to agree on this point with Jesus. Less than a century ago, the institution of slavery flourished in lands which prided themselves on their worship of Jesus. Only today, and only in parts of our society, are men and women convinced that a form of slavery persists wherever one man wrests his living from another. When we take out of the soil more than we put back, we loot the soil. When we take from the neighbor who works with us more in labor than we pay for, we rob him. Perhaps we are putting ourselves in the proper frame of mind for robbery when we accustom him to the idea that we are in some degree his superior, and that he is our servant, or even our employee. If I understand the teaching of Jesus, he wished to plant a serious doubt in our minds whether the servant is the inferior or the superior. Certainly any neighbor who does us a service and who does not receive from us compensation in full, is our superior, since we are in his debt. It would be better by far if we thought of all work as a partnership or collaboration. The product of work is life, or the means to life. Those who work together should share the life or the means to life which their work produces. When we say "Give us this day our daily bread," perhaps we are asking for the share that belongs to us, and for no more. Our daily bread. Perhaps the emphasis is upon the word "our."

If one man sows and another reaps, if the harvest of one year yields seed for another harvest, what is wealth? Most of us would be content to say that wealth is the result of our labor, but that definition when closely examined proves rough and inadequate. The result of our labors in one harvest is bread to sustain us for a time, and seed for another harvest and for more bread another year. Since the bread must be eaten and since the new seed must be planted, wealth is not very permanent, by our own definition. True labor surprises us by producing a living kind of wealth, something which becomes in turn life-giving. But no man would have the audacity to say that life is his private property. According to the teaching of Jesus there is a sense in which not even our soul is our own; at any time God may require it of us.

"The ground of a certain rich man brought forth plentifully: and he thought within himself, saying, What shall I do, because I have no room where to bestow my fruits? And he said, This will I do: I will pull down my barns, and build greater; and there will I bestow all my fruits and my goods. And I will say to my soul, Soul, thou hast much goods laid up for many years; take thine ease, eat, drink, and be merry. But God said unto

him, Thou fool, this night thy soul shall be required of thee."
(St. Luke, chapter 12.)

This quotation is from what is called the parable of the Rich Fool. If the man saved the wheat and did nothing with it, he was putting a stop to life. He could not eat it all himself. There were but two choices left to him: he could plant the wheat and produce more harvest, or he could share it with those who lacked food. But only a fool, Jesus is saying, would imagine that he possessed wealth, if he were only hoarding up life in some arrested state.

When we ask for our daily bread, therefore, we are praying for the kind of wealth which can be used—for health, for wisdom, for an abundance of life which can be shared with those who need it as much as we do.

Unless we are no better than the animals, food implies hospitality. The oldest of all sacraments, even among the most primitive men, is the sharing of food and drink with all who come to our door. The ancient custom may have a simple explanation: it may have arisen from the fact that where the traveler had no inn to stop at, he must carry his food with him, and when the journey was long he must ask food from homes along his road. The master of the house would offer hospitality even though it were not asked; he knew that his turn would come for making a journey, and he too would depend upon strangers for sustenance. It would have been hard to share food with an enemy, with one, for example, who had killed a kinsman of the houseowner, either in battle or in private feud. For that reason it became good manners not to ask the stranger who he was—not, at least, until he was fed. This ritual still persists. If we are reading a book when a caller interrupts, we feel no obligation whatever to give him the volume, but if we are eating and drinking, decency compels us to offer him some of the food or the drink. Even if we are not ourselves eating, we offer some hospitality, however slight.

Jesus emphasized and developed this ancient tradition. In the sharing of food he taught his disciples to recognize a primary obligation. John the Baptist taught his disciples to fast, but Jesus, by his own declaration, came among men eating and drinking, taking part in the constantly repeated ritual of hospitality. When at the end of his days he instituted the sacrament of the Lord's Supper, he was lifting into immense significance an impulse common to all men, and in some measure to all religions, an impulse which so far as we know he had encouraged all his life.

The spiritual meanings of hospitality are numerous, but the commonest of them, and the one which concerns us here, is a transposing of a purely physical act into an exchange of thought and a communion of souls. At the dinner table we may be a group of animals feeding, but our table manners disguise that fact. We do not reach for the food, or grab it. We help each other to forget we are hungry; we feel the obligation to exhibit our most attractive ideas, our best humor, our unselfish interest in the great things that are happening in the world. We raise ourselves as far as possible to that level of being on which physical or temporal values are forgotten. For the moment we try to live eternally. And to live eternally we must not live alone.

When we pray, therefore, for the bread which human labor, collaborating with the soil, the sun, and the weather, has brought from the wheat field to the table, we pray also for the perpetual communion, here in this life, of minds, and hearts, and souls, in the grace of fellowship. We are praying, that is, for the coming of the kingdom of God.

xii

Mission to the Gentiles

WHEN Jesus began his preaching and organized his group of chosen apostles, he seems to have thought of his mission as primarily for his own people. He began to visit the little towns of his own district on the shores of Galilee. Gentile traders passed through Nazareth in large numbers, but apparently he made no effort to address them. He still thought of his destiny as the restoration of David's throne, and if he interpreted that restoration in a larger sense than he had at first learned from his mother, he still was thinking in fairly narrow terms. The Gospel according to St. Matthew tells us that when he commissioned his apostles, he warned them, "Go not into the way of the Gentiles, and into any city of the Samaritans enter ye not: but go rather to the lost sheep of the house of Israel." (St. Matthew, chapter 10.) The Gospel according to St. Luke, chapter 10, reporting the commission to the disciples, sets no limit on the range of their labors. The Gentiles and the Samaritans are not mentioned. "Go your ways: behold, I send you forth as lambs among wolves. Carry neither purse, nor scrip, nor shoes: and salute no man by the way. And into whatsoever house ye enter, first say, Peace be to this house. And if the son of peace be there, your peace shall rest upon it: if not, it shall turn to you again. And in the same house remain, eating and drinking such things as they give: for the labourer is worthy of his hire. Go not from house to house. And into whatsoever city ye enter, and they receive you, eat such things as are set before you: and heal the sick that are therein, and say unto them, The kingdom of God is come nigh unto you. But into whatsoever city ye enter, and they receive you not, go your ways out into the streets of the same, and say, Even the very dust of your city, which cleaveth on us, we do wipe off against you: notwithstanding be ye sure of this, that the kingdom of God is come nigh unto you."

Gradually Jesus extended the scope of his own preaching to the Gentiles. He could not do otherwise, since some Gentiles, like the Centurion with the sick servant, made themselves his followers. Perhaps the transition between preaching exclusively to his own people and ministering equally to the Gentiles, came through his extension of the art of healing to include the forgiveness of sin. Liberating himself and his hearers from the tyranny of names, he refused to condemn all Pharisees or all publicans, or all adulteresses. The individual case must be judged by itself. After that, it was but a step to include Gentile with Jew among the children of God.

The charity which Jesus practiced seemed to his enemies subversive. It was all very well to confer peace of mind upon the sinner, but would the sin be sufficiently condemned if the sinner were encouraged merely to repent and begin again? The occasions—and they seem to have been numerous—on which Jesus forgave women whose morals were decidedly unconventional, provoked much scandal. The critics of Jesus found difficulty in understanding his logic, if he had any, since he forgave these women for different reasons. Apparently he was consistent only in this, that he always forgave.

St. John, chapter 8, tells of the woman taken in adultery who was brought to him by the scribes and Pharisees. Their purpose, of course, was to trap him. Moses in the law, they said, commanded that such a woman should be stoned. What was his opinion? No doubt a crowd had gathered about the woman and her captors; if Jesus now said that the law of Moses was correct, he would be contradicting his doctrine of mercy, and his followers would leave him. If, on the other hand, he declined to accept the ancient law, the scribes and Pharisees would have a basis for prosecuting him.

"Jesus stooped down, and with his finger wrote on the ground, as though he heard them not. So when they continued asking him, he lifted up himself, and said unto them, He that is without sin among you, let him first cast a stone at her. And again he stooped down, and wrote on the ground. And they which heard it, being convicted by their own conscience, went out one by one, beginning at the eldest, even unto the last: and Jesus was left alone, and the woman standing in the midst. When Jesus had lifted up himself, and saw none but the woman, he said unto her, Woman, where are those thine accusers? hath no man condemned thee? She said, No man, Lord. And Jesus said unto her, Neither do I condemn thee: go, and sin no more."

In this story the attention is less on the woman than on the scribes and Pharisees. Those who have themselves sinned are rebuked for presuming to judge sin in others. We have here a dramatic statement of the idea which is in the petition for forgiveness in the Lord's Prayer. But what Jesus thinks of the particular woman taken in adultery, we are not told. He tells her to sin no more; beyond that, he passes no judgment.

But in a more remarkable episode, in the Gospel according to St. Luke, chapter 7, a reason is given for the forgiveness:

"And one of the Pharisees desired him that he would eat with him. And he went into the Pharisee's house, and sat down to meat. And, behold, a woman in the city, which was a sinner, when she knew that Jesus sat at meat in the Pharisee's house, brought an alabaster box of ointment, and stood at his feet behind him weeping, and began to wash his feet with tears, and did wipe them with the hairs of her head, and kissed his feet, and anointed them with the ointment. Now when the Pharisee which had bidden him saw it, he spake within himself, saying, This man, if he were a prophet, would have known who and what manner of woman this is that toucheth him: for she is a sinner. And Jesus answering said unto him, Simon, I have somewhat to say unto thee. And he saith, Master, say on. There was a certain creditor which had two debtors: the one owed five hundred pence, and the other fifty. And when they had nothing to pay, he frankly forgave them both. Tell me therefore, which of them will love him most? Simon answered and said, I suppose that he, to whom he forgave most. And he said unto him, Thou hast rightly judged. And he turned to the woman, and said unto Simon, Seest thou this woman? I entered into thine house, thou gavest me no water for my feet: but she hath washed my feet with tears, and wiped them with the hairs of her head. Thou gavest me no kiss: but this woman since the time I came in hath not ceased to kiss my feet. My head with oil thou didst not anoint: but this woman hath anointed my feet with ointment. Wherefore I say unto thee, Her sins, which are many, are forgiven; for she loved much: but to whom little is forgiven, the same loveth little. And he said unto her, Thy sins are forgiven. And they that sat at meat with him began to say within themselves, Who is this that forgiveth sins also? And he said to the woman, Thy faith hath saved thee; go in peace."

By a strange tradition the woman in this story has been identi-fied as Mary Magdalene. The identification is so universal that in many languages women of evil life who have repented are called Magdalens. But there is not the slightest reason for this identification, and there are grounds in plenty for challenging it. The firmest ground is supplied by the very next words in St. Luke's Gospel, at the beginning of chapter 8, which tell us that Mary Magdalene was grateful to Jesus, not for the forgiveness of adultery, but for release from some mental disease. "And it came to pass afterward, that he went throughout every city and village, preaching and shewing the glad tidings of the kingdom of God: and the twelve were with him, and certain women, which had been healed of evil spirits and infirmities, Mary called Magdalene, out of whom went seven devils, and Joanna the wife of Chuza Herod's steward, and Susanna, and many others, which ministered unto him of their substance."

The woman at the dinner given by the Pharisee was not Mary

Magdalene, but a person of some notoriety whose bringing of the alabaster box might easily have embarrassed Jesus. The Pharisee who was host on this occasion was not an enemy, so far as the story indicates. He seems to have been one of the exceptions in his class, who leaned to the teaching of Jesus, yet the highly emotional, almost hysterical, tribute of the notorious woman might well have been embarrassing to him. She was not one of the invited guests. It is quite possible that she was a Gentile, one of those from the sea coast of Tyre and Sidon who were present when Jesus preached the Sermon on the Plain. They had been attracted by rumor of his healing, and this woman, if the words of Jesus are correctly reported, may have been expressing gratitude for the restoration of health in mind and heart and soul. In the Sermon he had said, "Judge not, and ye shall not be judged."

In St. Luke's Gospel the Sermon was followed immediately by the healing of the Centurion's servant and by the significant statement of Jesus that he had not found such faith in Israel. St. Matthew, in telling that incident (chapter 8), adds a still clearer tribute to the Gentiles: "I say unto you, That many shall come from the east and west, and shall sit down with Abraham, and Isaac, and Jacob, in the kingdom of heaven." When Jesus said this, had the woman already confessed her trouble, and had he taught her the way to repentance and peace of mind? Though we are told nothing more of her story, and though there is not the slightest hint who the man was for love of whom she had become known as a sinner, it is evident that Jesus had learned the circumstances before she came to the Pharisee's dinner. He was in position to know that the motive of her wrong-doing had been a great love; because she loved much, she was forgiven.

There is some confusion here in the use of the word love in two senses. Jesus says that he to whom most is forgiven will love most, love being in this case the result of the forgiveness, a form of gratitude. He also says that the woman is forgiven because she loved much, love being now not the result of forgiveness but the cause of it. The same confusion exists in the ancient Latin and Greek versions. I venture to suggest, in disagreement with the interpretation commonly followed, that Jesus could not have meant that sin, however grave, is pardoned in those who believe in him. A great love had caused her to err; merciful forgiveness had inspired a very different kind of affection.

Whether or not this woman was a Gentile, there is no doubt about the Phœnician woman, whose daughter Jesus healed. St. Matthew and St. Mark both tell this story, each supplying individual touches which are invaluable. St. Matthew, chapter 15, says, "Then Jesus went thence, [from Capernaum] and departed into the coasts of Tyre and Sidon. And, behold, a woman of Canaan came out of the same coasts, and cried unto him, saying, Have mercy on me, O Lord, thou son of David; my daughter is grievously vexed with a devil. But he answered her not a word. And his disciples came and besought him, saying, Send her away; for she crieth after us. But he answered and said, I am not sent but unto the lost sheep of the house of Israel. Then came she and worshipped him, saying, Lord, help me. But he answered and said, It is not meet to take the children's bread, and to cast it to dogs. And she said, Truth, Lord: yet the dogs eat of the crumbs which fall from their masters' table. Then Jesus answered and said unto her, O woman, great is thy faith: be it unto thee even as thou wilt. And her daughter was made whole from that very hour."

St. Matthew stresses the unwillingness of the disciples to be bothered by this importunate woman. He makes it seem also that Jesus was nothing short of discourteous to her. No explanation of his harsh manner is convincing. For the first and only time in his career, so far as we know, he had gone outside his own country, but not for the purpose of making converts. The journey into Phœnicia gave him a brief rest from the growing hostility of the scribes and Pharisees, and for the moment he apparently sought nothing but quiet. Was he nervously worn out? Did the woman annoy him, as she annoyed the disciples? If that is so, we can understand it humanly, but there is nothing to indicate that Jesus was in a state of exhaustion. He had a powerful constitution, he was extraordinarily vital, and he lived in the open air, in the sunlight. It has been said that he wished to do more for his own people before he began any considerable work among foreigners, but if he wished to avoid strangers he went about it in a strange way, when he crossed the border into Phœnicia.

Perhaps St. Mark's rendering of the episode will help us. He says less (chapter 7) about the unwillingness to hear the woman's plea, and much more about the wish for solitude, which the woman interfered with. He begins by saying that Jesus, having crossed the border, stopped at a certain house, and tried to keep his presence there a secret.

"And from thence he arose, and went into the borders of Tyre and Sidon, and entered into an house, and would have no man know it: but he could not be hid. For a certain woman, whose young daughter had an unclean spirit, heard of him, and came and fell at his feet: the woman was a Greek, a Syrophenician by nation; and she besought him that he would cast forth the devil out of her daughter. But Jesus said unto her, Let the children first be filled: for it is not meet to take the children's bread, and to cast it unto the dogs. And she answered and said unto him, Yes, Lord: yet the dogs under the table eat of the children's crumbs. And he said unto her, For this saying go thy way; the devil is gone out of thy daughter. And when she was come to her house, she found the devil gone out, and her daughter laid upon the bed."

After this episode Jesus returned to Galilee and found an unusually large number of people waiting to be cured, or bringing their sick to him for treatment. Perhaps the news of these miracles in Phœnicia had made them fear he would travel further, and they would be left without his aid.

W E cannot help wondering where the mother of Jesus was at this time, and to what extent he consulted with her about his plans. The record tells us nothing precise, but we can draw some reasonable conclusions from the fact that Mary is supposed to have taken up her residence at Capernaum, the little town which Jesus in his travels frequently visited, and from which he set out on his trip across the northern border. As she had imagined his earthly mission in his childhood, there probably were no Gentiles in the picture; he had been destined to sit on the throne of David, and his path lay toward Jerusalem, to the center of his own people. It is not difficult, however, to believe that Mary followed his career with profound sympathy as it changed and expanded from the dream she had originally cherished. All the apocryphal legends which the followers of Jesus composed about her, agree in their testimony to her extraordinary pity for all human beings and her quickness to understand those in trouble, whether the trouble had come on them through their own fault or through some unavoidable catastrophe. If there was any criticism of the ministrations to the Gentiles, it came from the group of the apostles, to whom Jesus was first of all the Messiah of his own people. Their vision broadened with time, but perhaps they realized the full scope of his work not during his lifetime but after his death. Their protests against the Phœnician woman who annoyed them by following Jesus with her petitions for her daughter, no doubt were typical of their attitude on other occasions. We can understand their point of view. They were loyal to the religion and the traditions of their people, and in their district of Galilee they felt the daily impact of heathendom in the traders and travelers who streamed down through their towns from Tyre and Sidon. With difficulty had they preserved their ancient faith unaffected by foreign influences, and Jesus had called them to a revival of the hopes and beliefs of their fathers

rather than to missionary work among the pagans who sur-
rounded their country and on occasion visited them. They must
have been not a little puzzled by his brief journey into Phœnicia
and by his willingness to respond to heathen requests for help.
Whatever the original purpose of the journey, one result was to
educate them more deeply in his universal love.

We wish the record told us what he himself thought of this
journey. If he looked for solitude in which to rest, he must have
been disappointed, but perhaps that was not his entire purpose.
He had begun his preaching and healing in the district where his
youth had been passed, on the shores of the Sea of Galilee. In
spite of his marvelous sermons and his epoch-making cures of
disease, this first mission in Galilee had been disappointing. His
audiences in Nazareth, in Capernaum, and in one or two other
places had proved hostile. He had encountered what seems to
be the oldest and most deeply rooted jealousy in the human
heart, the resentment against a neighbor whom we have known
as a modest and undistinguished companion, and who afterward
reveals himself as a person of importance, destined to honors to
which we cannot aspire. When Jesus speaks about prophets who
are appreciated anywhere except at home, he is thinking of this
kind of jealousy, the primitive resentment of the neighbors in
seeing one of the community get ahead. Was there in the group
of the apostles any evidence of this resentment? Apparently
most of them were entirely free from it, and had an unbroken
record of loyal friendship, but it may well be, as many people
have thought, that jealousy burned the heart of Judas Iscariot
to see the leader of their group winning public applause while
they, his followers, remained in the background, and he, Judas,
in particular was involved with the difficult and inglorious details of the commissary. We do not know how provision was
made for board and lodging on this trip into Phœnicia. The
people at whose house Jesus stayed must have been willing to
entertain him, but on what basis? Did Judas, the treasurer of
the group, go ahead and engage rooms for the visit? If so, did
he feel sufficiently rewarded for his efforts by the healing of

the Syrophœnician woman's daughter, an episode in which his name is not mentioned?

If the early preaching and healing in Galilee, in spite of remarkable results, was to some extent disappointing, the short trip into Phœnicia, significant though it was in implications, offered no immediate opportunity for the work Jesus felt he must do. There remained one other mission to undertake, the hardest and most dangerous, but the one which could not much longer be postponed—the mission to Jerusalem.

xiii

The Mission to Jerusalem

S T. MATTHEW, speaking of this crisis in the life of Jesus, says (chapter 16): "From that time forth began Jesus to shew unto his disciples, how that he must go unto Jerusalem, and suffer many things of the elders and chief priests and scribes, and be killed, and be raised again the third day. Then Peter took him, and began to rebuke him, saying, Be it far from thee, Lord: this shall not be unto thee. But he turned, and said unto Peter, Get thee behind me, Satan: thou art an offence unto me: for thou savourest not the things that be of God, but those that be of men." Some commentators have thought that the prophecy of the Resurrection on the third day was inserted among these words of Jesus in the early records after the Crucifixion, and that all that Jesus said at the moment to his disciples was that he must carry his preaching to Jerusalem, though he was sure to encounter there the full hostility of the scribes and Pharisees, and this mission to the great city of his people would end in his death. If it was his death he prophesied, rather than his resurrection, we can understand more readily the continuation of his speech, which was addressed to the disciples, warning them that the journey to Jerusalem would be for them too a test of the sincerity of their mission, and they must come with him only if they, like him, were prepared to die.

As usual we can profit by a comparison of the slightly different accounts; St. Luke, reporting the announcement of the mission to Jerusalem (chapter 18), makes it clear beyond question, that Jesus, drawing on ancient prophecies, foretold that he would be delivered unto the Gentiles, in other words to the Roman soldiers, and that he would be put to death and on the third day he would rise again.

"He took unto him the twelve, and said unto them, Behold, we go up to Jerusalem, and all things that are written by the prophets concerning the Son of man shall be accomplished. For he shall be delivered unto the Gentiles, and shall be mocked, and spitefully entreated, and spitted on: and they shall scourge him, and put him to death: and the third day he shall rise again. And they understood none of these things: and this saying was hid from them, neither knew they the things which were spoken."

If, as we suggested in the last chapter, there was any jealousy of Jesus on the part of Judas Iscariot or of any other apostle, Jesus now makes it clear to them all that their reward on earth would be bitter indeed and that they would all share it. In what he says to Simon Peter we can understand that a hope still lingered among the apostles for a worldly and comfortable triumph of their cause. When Peter wished that suffering and the death might remain far from his beloved leader, Jesus rebuked him as being a tempter, speaking the language of the body and of time rather than of the soul and of eternity.

The decision to go to Jerusalem was made deliberately, and the strategy upon which the decision was based was profound. Jesus at this point in his career might have avoided further conflicts with his enemies and might have survived for many years in Galilee or in Phœnicia, repeating the doctrines which he had already announced and duplicating his successful cures of disease. But by such a program he could not have spread his teaching in the world. Gradually or at some dramatic moment he realized that the doctrine of love must be driven home by his own sacrifice. Even beyond the words reported in the Gospel he must have explained this conviction of his repeatedly to the disciples, for it is clear that they went to Jerusalem expecting the things which did happen.

Here again we wish that our knowledge of what he said to his mother, and of the advice she must have given him, was more complete. Though the Gospels are silent about so much that we yearn to know, yet they establish the fact that Mary was in Jerusalem with him, and present at least for a short time at the Crucifixion. Presumably she made the journey with Jesus and the apostles, and took up residence in some friendly household, about which we have no precise information. She must have witnessed the events along the journey to Jericho and from Jericho up to Jerusalem. She must have seen the strewing of palms before her son as he rode into the city. No doubt she was as keenly aware as anyone of the unstable character of that mob, who hailed the famous prophet and worker of miracles, yet a few days later were persuaded by his enemies to call for his destruction. No account of these crowded and tragic days in Jerusalem can be complete unless it includes somewhere in the background the figure of Mary, with her watchful love, faithful still to her vision of her son's heaven-promised destiny.

2

THE journey from Galilee down to Jerusalem might be made though Samaria, the usual route, or along the banks of the river Jordan as far as Jericho, and then up the sharp incline from Jericho to Jerusalem. Apparently this was the route chosen by Jesus and his apostles and his mother. St. Luke tells us (chapter 18) that "It came to pass, that as he was come nigh unto Jericho, a certain blind man sat by the way side begging; and hearing the multitude pass by, he asked what it meant. And they told him, that Jesus of Nazareth passeth by." Evidently the little party had been greeted all along the journey by curious if not admiring crowds. Jesus was a famous man. Those who suffered from any infirmity were likely to know that he had gained his fame by his gifts of healing. This popular welcome explains the strewing of palm branches in the Jerusalem streets, the enthusiasm of the countryside being prolonged for some distance inside the city walls.

The blind man who sat begging outside of Jericho, hearing that Jesus of Nazareth passed by, called to him: "Jesus, thou son of David, have mercy on me." St. Luke says that those who went before, presumably the apostles who were at the head of the little party, told the man to be silent; but the more they rebuked him, the louder he cried, "Thou son of David, have mercy on me." At last Jesus stood still in the road and asked that the man be brought to him. Some bystanders, perhaps the very apostles who had just been discouraging him, led the man to the spot where Jesus stood. His plea had been simply for mercy. Jesus asked him, "What wilt thou that I shall do unto thee?" The man replied, "Lord, that I may receive my sight." Jesus said unto him, "Receive thy sight; thy faith hath saved thee." The man's sight returned to him, and the bystanders were astounded at the cure.

Only a few minutes later the party of travelers encountered another example of faith, another tribute to the reputation of Jesus among humble people.

"And Jesus entered and passed through Jericho. And, behold, there was a man named Zacchæus, which was the chief among the publicans, and he was rich. And he sought to see Jesus who he was; and could not for the press, because he was little of stature. And he ran before, and climbed up into a sycomore tree to see him: for he was to pass that way. And when Jesus came to the place, he looked up, and saw him, and said unto him, Zacchæus, make haste, and come down; for to day I must abide at thy house. And he made haste, and came down, and received him joyfully. And when they saw it, they all murmured, saying, That he was gone to be guest with a man that is a sinner. And Zacchæus stood, and said unto the Lord; Behold, Lord, the half of my goods I give to the poor; and if I have taken any thing from any man by false accusation, I restore him fourfold. And Jesus said unto him, This day is salvation come to this house, forsomuch as he also is a son of Abraham. For the Son of man is come to seek and to save that which was lost. And as they heard these things, he added and spake a parable, because he was nigh to Jerusalem, and because they thought that the kingdom of God should immediately appear."

The parable which Jesus told to his disciples was the parable of the Pounds, which had special meaning because of the circumstances, and because of what he had already told them about his future. The nobleman who went into a far country to receive for himself a kingship and to return, was evidently Jesus himself, the far journey was into the other world beyond the grave, and the servants entrusted with the pounds were evidently the disciples. Of particular interest when read against the background of the moment is the account of the unprofitable servant who buried his pounds in a napkin. Commentators have long agreed that here we have a portrait of Judas Iscariot. The unprofitable servant complains that his employer was an austere man who wanted to receive back more than he had given and to reap where he had not sown. Judas had occupied for some reason the lowest rank among the disciples, and the service that he had been called upon to render was arduous. He had been jealous of the friendship shown to Peter and John and some other disciples. In telling the parable, therefore, Jesus is once more warning his companions that he will probably be taken from them, and that the fortunes of the doctrine he had preached would depend upon their fidelity. For Judas there was an individual warning, perhaps a threat. There is small room for doubt that Jesus by this time was conscious of the treacherous disposition of the man. Perhaps it had made itself known on this journey from Galilee down to Jerusalem, and for that reason, perhaps, Jesus showed himself much preoccupied with his own thoughts. His habit on previous journeys had been to walk in the midst of the disciples, talking with them, but now he went on several paces ahead of them, as though he wished to be alone.

The road from Jericho to Jerusalem passed through the small village of Bethany, and the still smaller adjacent village of Bethphage. At Bethany the sisters Mary and Martha lived with their brother Lazarus, and during the eventful days at Jerusalem Jesus returned nightly to Bethany, either to the home of Lazarus or to some neighboring house. It may well be that during this time the mother of Jesus took up her residence with the family of Lazarus, and there St. John at the most tragic moment may have come to guide her to the place where her son was dying on the cross.

When Jesus and his companions came near to Bethphage and Bethany, he sent two of his disciples ahead into the village, telling them that they would find in the village street a colt which had never yet been ridden. If anyone asked why they loosed the colt and led him away, they should answer that the Lord hath need of him. The two disciples went ahead and found the colt, as Jesus had foretold, and when they began to lead the animal off, the owners protested, but the disciples said that the Lord hath need of him, and the explanation seems to have been satisfactory. On this animal Jesus rode into Jerusalem amid the welcomes of the crowd. Some cried, Who is this? and the majority shouted, This is Jesus, the prophet of Nazareth of Galilee.

Once inside the city Jesus went to the temple and created a public disturbance by driving out the merchants and the money-changers who there were doing business. Devout pilgrims came to the temple from many directions and from long distances, and it was a convenience for them to find shops where they could buy the offerings which they wished to make, but the shops had encroached upon the temple until the sacred building had become the headquarters for merchants and money-changers, and this latter class were too often expert in short-changing the simple people from the countryside. According to the tradition which seems to preserve the essential facts, Jesus made a scourge of rope-ends knotted together and drove the rascals out of the temple by main force. Since these merchants were there in the first place with the permission of the temple authorities, the action of Jesus and his statement that they had turned the house of God into a den of thieves, were not likely to ingratiate him with the high priests. He seems to have challenged them deliberately from the moment of his arrival from Jerusalem.

There was a difference of opinion among the Evangelists as to when this cleansing of the temple occurred. St. John placed it in an earlier visit to Jerusalem, at the beginning of the public ministry. St. Matthew, St. Mark, and St. Luke remembered it as occurring on the final journey to Jerusalem, as we have here reported it. The arguments for placing the incident early or late are equally illuminating, but St. John's memory in his old age was not dependable, and there is little doubt that since the other Evangelists were in agreement, they remembered the facts correctly. Had the cleansing of the temple occurred at the beginning of the ministry, the incident might have illustrated the early impetuousness of Jesus, which he learned to curb. If the incident, on the other hand, is accepted as belonging to the final visit to Jerusalem, it illustrates the challenging mood in which he made this journey, drawing the issue as sharply as possible between himself, the high priests, and the Pharisees. He knew there was one in his own company who would betray him, and that the high priests had decided that he must be put out of the way. Temporarily, at least, he had the people on his side. By judicious compromises he might have remained in Jerusalem throughout the Passover without coming to harm, but it would have been at the cost of the principles which he had taught. He preferred to illustrate his own doctrine, that a man must love truth without any limitation or holding back.

3

THE Pharisees and the temple authorities accepted in their own way the challenge which Jesus had so publicly made. Each day as he came in from Bethany where he lodged, they waited for him with some prearranged questions, hoping either to trap him in some statement for which he might be prosecuted, or to lure him into some doctrine which would offend his adherents among the crowd. The first hard question they asked was about tribute money. Most of the revolts of the Jews against the Romans had been caused by excessive and unwelcome taxation. If Jesus could be tricked into saying that the Roman levy should not be paid, he would be in trouble with the officers of the Empire. If he advised the Jews to pay the tax, he would be hated by the people. The studied compliments with which his enemies introduced the question more than justified Jesus in calling them hypocrites. He knew they were after his life. "Then went the Pharisees, and took counsel how they might entangle him in his talk. And they sent out unto him their disciples with the Herodians, saying, Master, we know that thou art true, and teachest the way of God in truth, neither carest thou for any man: for thou regardest not the person of men. Tell us therefore, What thinkest thou? Is it lawful to give tribute unto Cæsar, or not?"

The Herodians were a minor political party distinguished chiefly by their adherence to the house of Herod. They played small part in the prosecution and crucifixion of Jesus. But it was at least ironical that through them, as in other ways, the name and influence of the family of Herod should appear at the end of the life of Jesus as at the beginning.

"Jesus perceived their wickedness, and said, Why tempt ye me, ye hypocrites? Shew me the tribute money. And they brought unto him a penny. And he saith unto them, Whose is this image and superscription? They say unto him, Cæsar's. Then saith he unto them, Render therefore unto Cæsar the things which are Cæsar's; and unto God the things that are God's." (St. Matthew, chapter 22.)

The adroit answer confused them, and temporarily they left him in peace, but later in the same day the Sadducees returned with a legalistic question, the insincerity of which was obvious to all who heard them. The Pharisees believed in the resurrection of the dead, but the Sadducees did not. Their hypercritical question involved the resurrection, in which they did not believe.

"Master, Moses said, If a man die, having no children, his brother shall marry his wife, and raise up seed unto his brother.

Now there were with us seven brethren: and the first, when he had married a wife, deceased, and, having no issue, left his wife unto his brother: likewise the second also, and the third, unto the seventh. And last of all the woman died also. Therefore in the resurrection whose wife shall she be of the seven?"

The comment of Jesus on this question was far more profound than his answer to the problem of the tribute money. He told the Sadducees that they had not interpreted the Scriptures intelligently. In the resurrection there is neither marriage nor giving in marriage. But since the Sadducees did not believe in the resurrection, evidently they thought Jehovah was the God of the dead rather than of the living, for he had declared himself the God of Abraham, of Isaac, and of Jacob. Are these patriarchs dead, or do they continue to live somewhere in the universe?

There were two other incidents which may be thought of as a climax to the Jerusalem journey or as a prelude to the tragic experiences there. One was the dinner in the house of Simon the leper. "Now when Jesus was in Bethany, in the house of Simon the leper, there came unto him a woman having an alabaster box of very precious ointment, and poured it on his head, as he sat at meat. But when his disciples saw it, they had indignation, saying, To what purpose is this waste? For this ointment might have been sold for much, and given to the poor. When Jesus understood it, he said unto them, Why trouble ye the woman? for she hath wrought a good work upon me. For ye have the poor always with you, but me ye have not always. For in that she hath poured this ointment on my body, she did it for my burial. Verily I say unto you, Wheresoever this gospel shall be preached in the whole world, there shall also this, that this woman hath done, be told for a memorial of her." (St. Matthew, chapter 26.)

Nothing is known about this Simon the leper, but it is supposed that the woman with the alabaster box was Mary the sister of Martha. The similarity between this incident and the gift of the sinful woman at the dinner in the Pharisee's house, is of course obvious. There is probably no duplication here of the single episode. The episode of the woman who was a sinner was known to all the disciples and had probably been talked about among the friends of Jesus. Mary the sister of Martha brings her box of ointment in a similar tribute of affection, but no sin is implied and no need for forgiveness. The incident reveals the affection in which Jesus was held, and the cult of adoration which was growing up among those who knew him intimately and were, like the sisters of Lazarus, deeply indebted to him.

The second episode is that of the widow and her two mites, the illustration which Jesus found in the temple for his doctrine that love should be without limitation. "And he looked up, and saw the rich men casting their gifts into the treasury. And he saw also a certain poor widow casting in thither two mites. And he said, Of a truth I say unto you, that this poor widow hath cast in more than they all: for all these have of their abundance cast in unto the offerings of God: but she of her penury hath cast in all the living that she had." (St. Luke, chapter 21.)

From the words and the incidents reported of the journey to Jerusalem and of the first hours in the city, it is clear that both Jesus and his followers were conscious that he was about to illustrate his teaching by a complete sacrifice of himself, and naturally they found symbolic reflections of that coming sacrifice in the life around them. He had discovered for himself at last what his true destiny was to be, and his disciples had begun to realize it. At the beginning of his stay in Jerusalem they perhaps did not foresee clearly the tragic events which were to follow so quickly, but at least they were aware of the direction in which his mission now lay, and this new awareness must have affected the character of each one of them.

xiv

The Growth of the Revelation of Jesus

THE REALIZATION of his own nature and of the work which he was in the world to do, came to the human Jesus gradually. Like all those whose humanity he shared he learned his destiny by living it, by meeting the challenges of life one by one, as they were presented to him. Many Christians have preferred to read his story a different way, assuming that he was born with a divine foreknowledge of all he would at any time do and suffer. Such an assumption is untenable in the point of view from which this book is written—complete acceptance of the doctrine of the Incarnation. Jesus taking our nature upon him became subject to our limitations and to the common disciplines of our experience. If man ever acquires the gift of prophecy it is only after much living and much reflecting. What is told in the Gospels indicates that Jesus went through this normal process of learning, differing from other men not in his approach to experience but in what he learned about himself from it. Step by step he saw what his teaching must be, and how his powers of healing must be integrated with the doctrine, and later how both his acts and his words could have their effect only if he made a supreme sacrifice of himself; and last of all he knew that his inability to give his allegiance to any but eternal values came from the fact that he belonged to eternity, that his nature was not only human but divine. All this he learned by being true to himself from day to day.

The revelation spoke first, we may believe, in the constant reminder he had from his mother that he must be a great man to illustrate and restore the ancient glory of his people. It spoke again, with increased force, when at the age of twelve he heard the doctors in the temple, and found he could understand at least part of their wisdom—when he ventured a few simple questions of his own, and the doctors, truly wise, answered him courteously. Often indeed had his parents spoken of the temple, and now in the august and sacred place he felt at home. What was revealed to him in that accession of self-confidence we can guess.

The revelation of a man's destiny may come to him through experiences which are troubling as well as through those which are reassuring. Some critical self-examination must have preceded the acceptance of public baptism at the hands of John the Baptist. For the moment at least the decision was satisfying, and Jesus could believe his heavenly Father was well pleased with him, but the fact that John's program on further study seemed narrow, was in itself a revelation of a much broader program in the heart of Jesus, waiting for definition and expression. John's perfect world was to be built on self-denial and self-discipline, but the perfection which Jesus began to dream of could be attained only through a creative life-giving love. At what moment did the vision of such love come to Jesus? May it not have been when coming up out of the water of Jordan he thought he heard a voice from heaven saying, "This is my beloved Son." What would it mean to be the son of God the Father, of God the creator? The story of Jesus thereafter shows what he thought it meant. He would teach men the more abundant life, he would give them the health to live abundantly, he would break down by the pressure of expanding love the man-made walls which prevent the free flow and spread of the life which God intended man to have abundantly.

But the revelation at Jordan would also have for Jesus, we

must think, a tragic aspect. John did not share it with him. John, the devoted cousin, was of a temperament which could never understand the vision of complete love, yet in his grand way he acknowledged the superiority of what was beyond his grasp. "There cometh one mightier than I after me," he had said, "the latchet of whose shoes I am not worthy to stoop down and unloose." (St. Mark, chapter 1.) John followed without compromise the course which led to his death, and Jesus could not have been happy to watch in temporary safety, even though that safety was the result of greater wisdom and a more humane ideal. In a few years, almost within a few months, he was to see that his course too must be followed without compromise, and that it too would lead to a violent end. When Jesus therefore speaks to his disciples of the crucifixion which attends him in Jerusalem, we may find the reasons for that prediction, not in a peculiar and superhuman foresight, but in the revelation of his destiny which experience, in the order of the universe, makes to every man.

No doubt Jesus learned something of his mission from all the incidents which challenged him to a decision and so brought out the qualities of his nature. He was criticized for teaching, even when the critics conceded that he had taught the truth; they asked by what authority he spoke. The repeated challenge together with the repeated admission that his doctrine was sound, led inevitably to his conviction that his doctrine came direct from God rather than from an earthly source. When his disciples were blamed with him for consorting with publicans and others who were classed as sinners, or for satisfying their hunger when occasion offered on the Sabbath, his defense of them brought him into a clearly realized antagonism toward precise sticklers for ceremony or formalized ethics. And perhaps his meeting with the woman of Samaria at Jacob's well made him aware of the disembodied and spiritual quality of true worship. If he had not talked with her, and if she had not posed the question whether Jerusalem or the mountain were the place where men ought to worship, would he at that time in his career have pronounced that "the hour cometh, and now is, when the true worshippers shall worship the Father in spirit . . . God is a spirit: and they that worship him must worship him in spirit and in truth." (St. John, chapter 4.) This doctrine logically carried out would diminish the importance of all sacred places, even of the temple itself. The Gentile who worshiped in spirit and in truth would draw as near to God as the Jew. The mission of Jesus would be to the whole world.

As we said, the destiny of Jesus was molded in his own mind by the hard questions of the scribes and Pharisees. Seeing the traps they tried to spread for him, and realizing how far he was from believing the doctrine their hostility implied, he gradually took his position on ground he could sincerely defend. Whether he was disposed at any moment to articulate in intellectual terms his growing consciousness of himself, is highly improbable. If such a statement of his nature and his purposes had been possible for him to make, perhaps it would have been an error to make it; such a definition might have interrupted the growth of the revelation in him.

The progressive awareness of his own greatness and of his mission on earth came to a climax in the episode called in the Gospel the Transfiguration. Here in one tremendous moment he saw himself not in time but in eternity, and the vision so transformed his appearance that the disciples who were with him were amazed. In their profound emotion he seemed attended in person by ancient prophets who spoke to him on his death soon to occur in Jerusalem. Then the attendant figures disappeared and the disciples saw Jesus in his usual form, but never again could they forget the brief transfiguration. St. Luke tells the episode (chapter 9). "He took Peter and John and James, and went up into a mountain to pray. And as he prayed, the fashion of his countenance was altered, and his raiment was white and glistening. And, behold, there talked with him two men, which were Moses and Elias: who appeared in glory, and spake of his decease which he should accomplish at Jerusalem. But Peter and they that were with him were heavy with sleep: and when they were awake, they saw his glory, and the two men that stood with him. And it came to pass, as they departed from him, Peter said unto Jesus, Master, it is good for us to be here: and let us make three tabernacles; one for thee, and one for Moses, and one for Elias: not knowing what he said. While he thus spake, there came a cloud, and overshadowed them: and they feared as they entered into the cloud. And there came a voice out of the cloud, saying, This is my beloved Son: hear him. And when the voice was past, Jesus was found alone."

The experience described in the Transfiguration seems not entirely unlike the early wrestling with himself which constituted the temptation in the wilderness. Once more, but in a manner suitable to his greater maturity, he contemplated his relation to the Eternal and his immediate obligations in time and space. It was while he was praying that the fashion of his countenance was altered. The light which shone about him was the rapture of devout ecstasy. Perhaps at that moment he was completely reconciled to the death on the cross. He who had taught others that no true disciple ever turned back, saw as in a light from heaven that he must set the example in this as in lesser matters. It would be a failure of his mission if he should be spared the final agony. This would not be the last time that Jesus withdrew for prayer and self-communion, and perhaps the purpose would again be to contemplate the path ahead of him and to gather strength to take it. How many prophets had taught the truth but had neglected to illustrate it! They had been everything but an example, but to furnish an example was the purpose of the life of Jesus. Those others had gone to their rest and were forgotten, their teaching having died with them. "And I, if I be lifted up from the earth, will draw all men unto me." (St. John, chapter 12.)

The apostles present at the Transfiguration, Simon Peter and the two sons of Zebedee, were thrown by the experience into a sort of hallucination. At successive stages of the episode we can estimate their state of mind. They saw the change in the face of Jesus as he prayed, and their consequent emotion and enthusiasm resulted from this revelation. Next they observed a white radiance in the raiment of Jesus, and they thought they saw and heard two men temporarily with him, and these two men they took to be Moses and Elijah. This part of the story, involving the two men, came to the Evangelists apparently in different versions. St. Luke says they talked with Jesus about his approaching death; St. Matthew and St. Mark say that the men talked, but what they said to Jesus the disciples did not hear. St. John, who was present on the occasion, gives no account of it. It should be noted that Peter and his companions went into a trance, being heavy with sleep, and when they awoke the two men were on the point of disappearing. The episode has been made still more trancelike by early religious painters, who represented the two men and sometimes Jesus himself as floating in the air.

But the truth of the experience need not be lost beneath fanciful embroideries. Jesus in the ecstasy of prayer was obviously and literally of a nobler and more inspired appearance. The disciples seem to have been far more deeply impressed by this outward change than by the spiritual crisis which moved Jesus to pray, and very humanly they suggested, as soon as they were awake, the building of a monument to commemorate the occasion. In their enthusiasm they forgot the teaching that God is a spirit, to be worshiped in spirit; having had a glimpse of the light from heaven, their first impulse was to put up a commemorative shaft or tablet.

The progressive revelation of his mission continued for Jesus even after the Transfiguration, but he had seen clearly what he must do, and what remained was only a filling in of the picture, or a correction of his hopes. He would have need of prayer, from the mount of Transfiguration to the garden of Gethsemane, and always of very human prayer, asking strength to go on. Those who prefer to believe that he was sustained in his last difficult days by a superhuman resolution which never for one minute faltered, misread the story and rob him not only of his humanity but of his heroism. He chose his course and persisted in it. The high priests wished to do away with him. He could have escaped if that had been his will.

2

THE life of Jesus from the Transfiguration to the Crucifixion can be interpreted directly from the Gospel records or from the point of view suggested in a well-known episode of The Acts of the Apostles. The first interpretation, which is followed in this book, stresses the heroic character of Jesus and his voluntary decision by sacrifice to make his work as Saviour complete and enduring. The other interpretation sees in him a Saviour indeed, but primarily a victim.

The story which gave currency to this theory of Jesus as a passive victim occurs in the Acts, chapter 8. Philip, one of the apostles, going south from Jerusalem toward Gaza, fell in with a man of Ethiopia, a eunuch of great authority under Candace, queen of the Ethiopians. He had come to Jerusalem to worship and now was returning, and as he sat in his chariot he read the prophet Isaiah. Like other orientals of his time he did his reading out loud, and Philip hearing him asked if he understood what he read. The eunuch answered that he needed someone to interpret, and at his invitation Philip got into the chariot and explained the text, which was the fifty-third chapter of the prophet, beginning with the words, "He was led as a sheep to the slaughter; and like a lamb dumb before his shearer, so opened he not his mouth." The eunuch listened while Philip expounded to him the doctrine of Jesus, and afterwards he became a believer, and the text which provided the occasion of his conversion was generally accepted by other Christians besides Philip as a prophetic portrait of Jesus, even though Isaiah in this passage included several sentences which did not harmonize with what the followers of Jesus believed. The pathetic conception of the divine victim, led as a sheep to the slaughter, took root and persists to this day, often obscuring incalculably the true work and teaching of him whom Philip called his master. Yet it is strange that a group of believers who through centuries have thought of themselves as a church militant should miss the plain fact that they follow a militant leader. On his last journey to Jerusalem Jesus was carrying the war into the most hostile territory.

It was to be, however, a war not of force but of ideals. He had realized this in his youthful days when he first dreamed of saving his people, and the enemy had then seemed to be the Roman Empire; he realized it doubly now when those who opposed him were typical of elements in human nature which would oppose him forever.

Perhaps these progressive revelations were of a subtlety which baffled the disciples. At least on one occasion at the start of the journey to Jerusalem they proposed a too literal application of his new militancy. If he went south by the road along the Jordan, it was because the road through Samaria was closed to him. St. Luke tells us (chapter 9) that the journey to Jerusalem was begun shortly after the Transfiguration, and that Jesus would have preferred to go through Samaria, wishing perhaps to reassert his disregard and his disapproval of religious and racial prejudice, but the Samaritans refused to match his breadth of mind or his warmth of heart. "He stedfastly set his face to go to Jerusalem, and sent messengers before his face: and they went, and entered into a village of the Samaritans, to make ready for him. And they did not receive him, because his face was as though he would go to Jerusalem." The woman at Jacob's well had condescended to exchange words with Jesus, and the people in the Samaritan village had sold food to his disciples, because they had then been traveling north toward Galilee, but they would aid no one who was going south to Jerusalem, the seat of what might be called the rival religion.

"And when his disciples James and John saw this, they said, Lord, wilt thou that we command fire to come down from heaven, and consume them, even as Elias did?" The disciples must have been angry indeed to suggest that Jesus model his conduct on Elijah's treatment of the Samaritans in an earlier age, as is recorded in The Second Book of the Kings, chapter 1. The king of Samaria, having suffered a severe accident, sent messengers to the god Baalzebub to inquire if he would recover, and Elijah met the messengers and turned them back with the cheerless tidings that since the king consulted Baalzebub rather than Jehovah he would never recover but would surely die. Then the king sent a captain with fifty men to arrest Elijah, but Elijah called down fire from heaven upon them, and they were consumed.

To hear his followers appealing to this grim old story must have been for Jesus an additional revelation of his mission and a sharp reminder that even those who accepted his doctrine might fail to grasp his spirit. "He turned, and rebuked them, and said, Ye know not what manner of spirit ye are of. For the Son of man is not come to destroy men's lives, but to save them."

3

AFTER the arrival in Jerusalem, as St. Luke tells us toward the end of chapter 21, Jesus spent his days teaching in the temple, and at night he retired to Bethany, where presumably his mother was staying. Since his disciples were present when he taught, we may imagine him in daily contact with Judas, of whose disposition toward treachery he was already aware. What a strange joining of influences in the final days, the influence of the Virgin Mary and that of Judas Iscariot, by contrast completing the revelation of his destiny, the inevitable fate which willingly he embraced. That we have no record whatever of his talks with Mary is an abysmal loss to history. Our fancy can readily invent conventional interchanges of affection and confidence, but we should like something more; we crave a hint of the reasoned process by which Jesus perfected his program as the moment approached for carrying it out, and we should be glad to know whether his mother approved or disapproved, and on what grounds.

The treachery of Judas he might have thwarted, knowing it in advance, and thousands of people have asked why he did not protect himself and save the weak wretch from his awful sin. There is probably no answer unless we look for it in the progressive revelation of his mission, which came to a climax in the certainty that Judas would sell his master's life for thirty pieces of silver. Let us now summarize the gradual revelation step by step.

John's preaching of repentance was not enough unless the doctrine of love were added, and Jesus drew that doctrine from the ancient law, as he told the Pharisee in St. Matthew's Gospel, chapter 22. "Thou shalt love the Lord thy God with all thy heart, and with all thy soul, and with all thy mind. This is the first and great commandment. And the second is like unto it, Thou shalt love thy neighbour as thyself. On these two commandments hang all the law and the prophets." But this doctrine too was not enough unless the love of one's neighbor were defined. We have already noticed the definition in the Sermon on the Plain: "Love your enemies, do good to them which hate you, bless them that curse you, and pray for them which despitefully use you. And unto him that smiteth thee on the one cheek offer also the other; and him that taketh away thy cloke forbid not to take thy coat also."

But the love of God and of our neighbor must, he realized, go even further; it must be without any limit whatever. If father or mother detain us, if we pause to bury our dead, if having put our hand to the plow we are tempted for an instant to look back, then we are not worthy.

The great final stages of the progressive revelation taught Jesus that he must illustrate his expanded doctrine of love by living it out. Instead of protecting himself from Judas he must forgive him. Instead of placating his enemies he must go where they could get at him, and he must preach to their face the doctrines which he had taught in safety when they were not present.

Perhaps the ultimate and most important revelation was the insight that in this drama he and his enemies were symbols. If his disciples had all understood this truth the world might have been spared bitterness and distrust between Christian and Jew. Jesus saw that if he were crucified he might become as a dramatic symbol of sacrifice far more persuasive than ever he could be if he escaped the Cross. His teachings would eventually win not only over the Pharisees and the high priests who actually were involved in his death, but also over the formalists and hypocrites forever, even though they called themselves Christians, for whom the Pharisees and the scribes served as symbols. He saw it was not the Jews who would kill him, still less the Roman soldiery, but he would be slain by qualities in human nature, by self-interest and ambition, and narrow-mindedness, and by ambition and fear, and those qualities would be illustrated quite as often by his followers as by the Jewish people. Between him and other men, between his followers and other men, if he might have his way, there would be nothing but charity. The warfare in which he could be militant was a conflict not of persons but of ideas.

Who Were His Enemies?

B Y WHAT PERSONS or groups were these hostile ideas represented? Or it might be fairer to ask what persons or groups represented the ideas to which he was hostile. We can hardly remind ourselves too often that Jesus was aggressive and militant against beliefs and prejudices sanctioned by custom and embedded in human nature. To those who opposed him he seemed rightly a dangerous threat. The Pharisees were leagued with the scribes and the Sadducees against him, though ordinarily they went their separate ways, and all three groups supported the high priests, whose reason for opposing Jesus was special.

The Pharisees were not a priestly class but a patriotic group who made a cult of preserving Jewish customs and cherishing Jewish history. Their name means "the separated," and their fundamental doctrine was that their people should not mingle with the Gentiles. They resisted the influence of Greek culture and Greek religion, they would have no intermarrying with Greeks or other non-Jews, and they forbade even a casual mingling with the unorthodox in ordinary social life. They held to the doctrine of the resurrection of the dead. They did all they could to foster education and to promote the building of synagogues. In religious discipline they were strict, insisting on prayer, on fasting, and on the giving of alms; they attached excessive importance to the keeping of the Sabbath, as to the very safeguard of their faith.

There is no question that the severe discipline which the Pharisees advocated produced in some of their number an austere magnificence of character, but in most of them the austerity went hand in hand with a literal-minded formalism, and in some cases their strict observance was hard to distinguish from ostentation. It seems remarkable that any of them could have approved the teaching of Jesus in the slightest degree, yet as we have noticed it was a Pharisee who was entertaining Jesus when the sinful woman brought the box of ointment. Perhaps among the Pharisees were more than one who craved more generous ideals than their sect as a whole stood for. Jesus challenged their strict Sabbatarianism, their ostentatious way of praying, of fasting, of giving alms, and their prejudice against Gentiles and against men like the publicans who accepted employment from the Romans.

The Sadducees were a priestly cast who frequently joined with the Pharisees, although on certain points of doctrine they differed. They taught that one should do good without hope of reward, and since immortality would be a reward for a good life, they denied the possibility of a resurrection and of immortality. Since they believed in no future life, they could not teach that sin would be punished hereafter, but by way of compensation they advocated punishment in this life of the utmost severity, appealing always to precedents in the ancient law. When he could, Jesus blocked their attempts to inflict the death penalty, as in the case of the woman taken in adultery. Since he seemed to them an influence which undermined morality, and since they believed in prompt and violent punishment of wrong-doing, it was logical that they should be leaders among those who sought his death.

The scribes were the class of scholars who preserved the oral tradition of the law, and who taught it to the people. We may think of them as representing the legalistic opposition to Jesus, in return for his invariable assault upon legalism of all kinds. The scribes and Pharisees are mentioned often together because the

Pharisees depended upon them for arguments and authorities. The Sadducees and the Pharisees would collaborate less readily, because of their disagreement as to the doctrine of a future life.

2

T H E I R attitude toward Jesus is disclosed in the questions which these groups repeatedly asked of him. His attitude toward them is expressed directly in his reproaches. He disliked them even before his ministry began. Perhaps the feud between him and them began with the ministry of his cousin John, when a few Pharisees and Sadducees joined the crowds that came to the banks of Jordan, and the Baptist, recognizing them as Pharisees and Sadducees, asked what they were doing there. "O generation of vipers, who hath warned you to flee from the wrath to come?" In the ministry of Jesus the first scribe mentioned is the friendly person in St. Matthew, chapter 8, who expressed a willingness to be one of the disciples. "Master, I will follow thee whithersoever thou goest." What later became of him we are not told. In chapter 9, when Jesus said to the sick with the palsy, "Son, be of good cheer; thy sins be forgiven thee," certain of the scribes immediately raised a characteristic objection. "This man," they said, "blasphemeth."

When Jesus accepted the invitation of Matthew, the Pharisees said to the disciples, "Why eateth your Master with publicans and sinners?" When Jesus began his healing and the multitudes marveled, the Pharisees said, "He casteth out devils through the prince of the devils."

St. Matthew tells us, chapter 12, "At that time Jesus went on the sabbath day through the corn; and his disciples were an hungred, and began to pluck the ears of corn, and to eat. But when the Pharisees saw it, they said unto him, Behold, thy disciples do that which is not lawful to do upon the sabbath day. But he said unto them, Have ye not read what David did, when he was an hungred, and they that were with him; how he entered into the house of God, and did eat the shewbread, which was not lawful for him to eat, neither for them which were with him, but only for the priests? Or have ye not read in the law, how that on the sabbath days the priests in the temple profane the sabbath, and are blameless?"

The Pharisees of course would protest against what they thought was desecration of the Sabbath, but they would be doubly offended when Jesus reminded them of the liberty which David had taken with the shewbread, and of the services required of the priests in slaying the victims to be offered and in arranging the shewbread, an amount of work which, done by anyone but priests in the temple, would have seemed to the Pharisees a profanation of the Sabbath. Immediately afterwards, still in the presence of the Pharisees, Jesus saw a man with a withered hand. The pity in his face showed that he was moved to do what he could for the invalid, and the Pharisees tried again to trap him. "Is it lawful to heal on the sabbath days?" He answered the question with an appeal, not to ancient history nor to accepted custom, but to humane instincts and common sense, "What man shall there be among you, that shall have one sheep, and if it fall into a pit on the sabbath day, will he not lay hold on it, and lift it out? How much then is a man better than a sheep? Wherefore it is lawful to do well on the sabbath days."

There must have been a number of bystanders who heard Jesus confound the Pharisees by these two answers. They were not accustomed to be made ridiculous. St. Matthew says that they immediately went out and consulted among themselves how they might destroy him, but the scribes and Pharisees were both present when next they tried to embarrass Jesus. Perhaps the consultation to destroy him had resulted in a decision to call in the lawyers. "Master," they said, "we would see a sign from thee." This was an invitation to produce some miracle which would imply superhuman power and therefore authority. Of course they did not wish to be convinced nor did they expect that Jesus could produce a spectacular wonder, and understanding what was in their thought, he disposed of them by calling them hypocrites, an evil and adulterous generation. From that moment the vigor with which he attacked them leaves us marveling that he escaped their wrath as long as he did.

In chapter 15 St. Matthew says that the scribes and Pharisees brought to Jesus a criticism of his disciples for failing to observe the customs of their fathers. "Why do thy disciples transgress the tradition of the elders? for they wash not their hands when they eat bread." The offense charged against the disciples was in itself of no great consequence, but the Pharisees meant to stress the fact that those who followed Jesus were neglecting the commands of their religion. The reply that Jesus made is one of the most scathing attacks in the whole record of his crusade against the Pharisees. They could not possibly forgive him for it. He accused them bluntly of disobeying those commands of God which would seem to be also the commands of nature. The illustration which he used is easily understood after a word of explanation, but it suggests a depth of selfish hypocrisy which is incredible. Some Pharisees seem to have been guilty of what he charged, but surely not all of them. Money or property assigned to the temple as a gift could not be spent for anything but the needs of the temple. The gift thus set apart was called corban. Some Pharisees, according to Jesus, assigned their goods as corban to avoid supporting their parents, who might be in destitution. Gifts to the temple would be required in any case, and by setting apart most of one's wealth as corban, one would gain high credit as a faithful son of Israel, and at the same time one would have a valid excuse for refusing the appeals of relatives.

"God commanded, saying, Honour thy father and mother: and, He that curseth father and mother, let him die the death. But ye say, Whosoever shall say to his father or his mother, It is a gift, by whatsoever thou mightest be profited by me; and honour not his father or his mother, he shall be free. Thus have ye made the commandment of God of none effect by your tradition. Ye hypocrites, well did Esaias prophesy of you, saying, This people draweth nigh unto me with their mouth, and honoureth me with their lips; but their heart is far from me."

In St. Matthew, chapter 19, we are told of the famous question of the Pharisees concerning divorce. The Sadducees, on another occasion, as we saw, came to grief by telling Jesus about a woman who had had in succession seven husbands, and asking whose wife she would be at the Last Judgment when the dead should rise. He had disposed of this question without difficulty, since its effrontery would be obvious to all who remembered that the Sadducees believed in no resurrection. The Pharisees now spread their snare more carefully, confining their question strictly to this life. They may have heard what he had said in the Sermon on the Mount, forbidding the putting away of a wife except for the cause of fornication. Some of the Jewish scholars would not have allowed even this exception, others would have permitted divorce, and the extremely liberal disposition of Jesus toward women who had sinned, suggested the possibility of tangling him up in some aspect of this problem. "And he answered and said unto them, Have ye not read, that he which made them at the beginning made them male and female, and said, For this cause shall a man leave father and mother, and shall cleave to his wife: and they twain shall be one flesh? Wherefore they are no more twain, but one flesh. What therefore God hath joined together, let not man put asunder."

When the Pharisees asked, Why, then, if man and wife cannot be separated, did Moses tell us to give an unfaithful wife a divorce? That, said Jesus, was because of the hardness of your heart. You were not capable of entertaining a nobler doctrine.

The sequel of this exchange between Jesus and the Pharisees gave him the occasion to utter his much-prized words about children, words which are not entirely understood unless taken in connection with what went before.

As soon as the Pharisees were gone, the disciples asked whether, if wives could behave so badly, it would not be better for a man not to marry. Jesus answered that marriage was good for some men but not good for others, and the disciples drew from his words the conclusion that he did not set the usual value upon the importance of the family, to be carried on from generation to generation. When children were brought to him, that he should put his hands on them and pray, the disciples, still misunderstanding what he had said, rebuked the mothers and urged them to take the children away. "But Jesus said, Suffer little children, and forbid them not, to come unto me: for of such is the kingdom of heaven."

When the Pharisees came again with plans to entangle him in his talk, they asked whether it was lawful to give tribute to Cæsar. Their other questions were but variations of those we have already noticed. They watched Jesus for signs of weakness in the matters which to them were important; they hoped to convict him of a lack of patriotism, of carelessness in religious observance, of disloyalty to the ideals and customs of his people, of undue leniency toward the sinner and the Gentile.

If we attended only, however, to what they said to him, and neglected what he said to them, the venom in their disposition might be hard to explain. That they were narrow in their religion is clear, but the attacks of Jesus upon that narrowness would have been enough to arouse them, even if they had been far more generous. He summarized all his criticisms in one terrific indictment which St. Matthew reports in chapter 23.

"Woe unto you, scribes and Pharisees, hypocrites! for ye shut up the kingdom of heaven against men: for ye neither go in yourselves, neither suffer ye them that are entering to go in. Woe unto you, scribes and Pharisees, hypocrites! for ye devour widows' houses, and for a pretence make long prayer: therefore ye shall receive the greater damnation. Woe unto you, scribes and Pharisees, hypocrites! for ye compass sea and land to make one proselyte, and when he is made, ye make him twofold more the child of hell than yourselves. Woe unto you, ye blind guides, which say, Whosoever shall swear by the temple, it is nothing; but whosoever shall swear by the gold of the temple, he is a debtor! Ye fools and blind: for whether is greater, the gold, or the temple that sanctifieth the gold? And, Whosoever shall swear by the altar, it is nothing; but whosoever sweareth by the gift that is upon it, he is guilty. Ye fools and blind: for whether is greater, the gift, or the altar that sanctifieth the gift? Whoso therefore shall swear by the altar, sweareth by it, and by all things thereon. And whoso shall swear by the temple, sweareth by it, and by him that dwelleth therein. And he that shall swear by heaven, sweareth by the throne of God, and by him that sitteth thereon. Woe unto you, scribes and Pharisees, hypocrites! for ye pay tithe of mint and anise and cummin, and have omitted the weightier matters of the law, judgment, mercy, and faith: these ought ye to have done, and not to leave the other undone. Ye blind guides, which strain at a gnat, and swallow a camel. Woe unto you, scribes and Pharisees, hypocrites! for ye make clean the outside of the cup and of the platter, but within they are full of extortion and excess. Thou blind Pharisee, cleanse first that which is within the cup and platter, that the outside of them may be clean also. Woe unto you, scribes and Pharisees, hypocrites! for ye are like unto whited sepulchres, which indeed appear beautiful outward, but are within full of dead men's bones, and of all uncleanness. Even so ye also outwardly appear righteous unto men, but within ye are full of hypocrisy and iniquity. Woe unto you, scribes and Pharisees, hypocrites! because ye build the tombs of the prophets, and garnish the sepulchres of the righteous, and say, If we had been in the days of our fathers, we would not have been partakers with them in the blood of the prophets. Wherefore ye be witnesses unto yourselves, that ye are the children of them which killed the prophets. Fill ye up then the measure of your fathers. Ye serpents, ye generation of vipers, how can ye escape the damnation of hell?"

3

THE high priests were at all times in such close sympathy with the Pharisees and the scribes that it is no wonder they were united against Jesus, but their motives were peculiar to themselves and their class. Annas and Caiaphas, who had been in office when John the Baptist began his preaching, and had looked on while Herod sacrificed the prophet to a revengeful whim of his wife, had now a far better reason for putting Jesus to death. With Judas Iscariot they are the villains in the story. No excuse can be made for them, but the explanation of their villainy opens for us a page of ancient history.

No people ever excelled the Romans in certain kinds of political wisdom. They were true empire builders, and they knew all the methods of holding their scattered empire together. As conquerors they were ruthless, but as rulers they were singularly wise. It was never their wish that people whom they had subjugated should feel the yoke unduly. If possible they encouraged the conquered to preserve whatever institutions were dear to them, and in return they expected only that the conquered would continue their institutions for the peace and harmony of the Empire. Among the Jewish people they found a society which was held together by religious faith. That faith centered in the temple, and the high priest, though primarily a religious rather than a political figure, controlled the social organization of the whole people. For the religion of Jehovah, the Romans felt no need, but they needed the organization which had grown up in that religion; in particular they would need the high priests, if ever the Jewish people were to be brought to an amicable acceptance of the Empire, complete subjection to it being unlikely. When a patriot like Judas the Galilean revolted against Rome, the high priests were in a dangerous position; in order to retain the confidence of the imperial authorities, they had to make some pretense at putting down the rebellion, but in order to keep the allegiance of their own people, they had to side with every nationalistic impulse.

The high priest Annas had at times failed to pick his steps with sufficient shrewdness during moments of crisis, and he had therefore been removed from office, but Pilate had too much respect for his influence with the Jewish people to discard him absolutely. Annas became a sort of high priest emeritus, and his son-in-law, Caiaphas, became his official successor. But it was not the wish of Caiaphas, nor perhaps of Pilate, that any loss of prestige should attach to this change. Annas and Caiaphas ruled together, Caiaphas supplying youthful energy and decision, and Annas a natural shrewdness sharpened by long experience.

If Jesus had been only a nationalistic leader of moderate success, the high priests would have left him undisturbed. They never interfered with John the Baptist, and if John had avoided giving offense to Herod and his queen, he might have continued his preaching indefinitely so far as Annas and Caiaphas were concerned. They would have been roused positively against him only if he had created a disturbance or if he had threatened to impair their authority.

We are left in no doubt as to their reasons for hunting Jesus down. The situation is made clear in the Gospel according to St. John, chapter 11. After the raising of Lazarus, the excitement of the crowds was so great that the high priests feared they might lose their authority. This young man who attracted thousands by his teaching, and even greater numbers by his astonishing cures, might establish a new religion, even without intending to do so, or at least he might gain so much influence over the people that they would look to him instead of the high priests for guidance. If that should happen, the realistic Roman governor would expect Jesus to control the people and keep order. Jesus would occupy with the Romans the importance which the high priests must have if they were to keep their footing in the slippery world.

When Caiaphas says, therefore, that all the world is gone after this new prophet, he is warning the other priests and elders of the temple that unless they take vigorous measures, their authority will be destroyed, the confidence of Rome will be lost, and quite possibly their lives as well as their fortunes will be forfeit. The high priests maintained themselves in almost regal state, and their tastes were to say the least expensive. If this plain-living young man from Galilee could now persuade the people to go in any direction he chose, the Romans would engage him to lead his followers in the right direction, and he could be rewarded for his services at far less cost than Annas and Caiaphas.

They would have said that they were acting for the good of their whole people, but their reputation among Hebrew historians of the time was for invariable selfishness and greed. They had been ruined by their private wealth and good living, which made them callous to the misfortunes of their people. Callousness with them easily became extreme cruelty. For the sake of preserving their comfortable position in the world, they would not for a moment hesitate to take a life. They would wish it understood, however, that the execution was for the benefit of all the people. Their reputation must be saved, or at least as much of it as possible, among both the Romans and their own people. St. John says that many of the crowd which had followed Jesus to the grave of Lazarus, went away completely converted to his doctrines, of which some of them so far must have heard little. They talked readily to all the Pharisees they met, who were glad for their own purposes to hear the latest tidings of Jesus and his work, and to report quickly to the priests.

"Then gathered the chief priests and the Pharisees a council, and said, What do we? for this man doeth many miracles. If we let him thus alone, all men will believe on him: and the Romans shall come and take away both our place and nation. And one of them, named Caiaphas, being the high priest that same year, said unto them, Ye know nothing at all, nor consider that it is expedient for us, that one man should die for the people, and that the whole nation perish not."

The conclusion of his speech is perhaps not obvious at first, but from his point of view it was logical enough. The Romans wished for friendly relations between themselves and the Jews, and to that end they wished through the high priests to keep the Jewish people in order. If, however, the people at some fatal moment should get out of hand, there was no doubt what the Romans would do. In crises of that kind they turned the soldiers on the people and killed them to the last man. Now if Jesus were to be the leader of his people, Caiaphas argued, he would soon prove unequal to the task of maintaining harmony among so many discordant elements. His was not a temperament to promote respectful accord. The high priests would be deposed and ruined when he undertook this control; when he failed in the attempt, the whole people would be destroyed.

When we consider the trial of Jesus we shall see how Annas and Caiaphas clung to this argument. They did their best to persuade Pontius Pilate that Jesus was promoting revolution, that he had ambitions to displace the Roman power and make himself king. Even the mob who clamored for his death pretended to be supporters of Cæsar, anxious for the preservation of the Empire. They cried to Pilate, "If thou let this man go, thou art not Cæsar's friend."

It was entirely in character for Annas and Caiaphas, who habitually played a double part, to pretend, as the trial of Jesus proceeded, that Pilate was responsible for it, and that the issues at stake concerned the Roman Empire rather than the high priests or the Jewish people. They did not once state the undoubted grounds that the Pharisees and the scribes had for opposing Jesus and his teachings, and naturally we should not expect them to confess their private interest in getting him out of the way. But they could have said truthfully that from the moment the journey to Jerusalem began he had foreseen that his trial and condemnation were inevitable, and that he had on all occasions attacked them as hypocrites and as false leaders. If in the end he was on trial for his life, it was because he had forced the issue.

The portrait of Caiaphas is rounded out by his treatment of Jesus during the trial and by his dealings with Judas Iscariot. After the Crucifixion he continued his hostility to the teaching of Jesus. He was present and perhaps presided at the council of priests and elders and scribes which examined Peter and John, as we are told in The Acts of the Apostles, on the charge of teaching the people and preaching through Jesus the resurrection of the dead. Caiaphas was still a shrewd politician, not above packing his court. He had Pharisees present who would join him in protest against the spread of their great critic's reputation, and there were Sadducees, who would condemn any who taught the doctrine of the resurrection; but most significant of all, the council included a number of his relatives.

"And it came to pass on the morrow, that their rulers, and elders, and scribes, and Annas the high priest, and Caiaphas, and John, and Alexander, and as many as were of the kindred of the high priest, were gathered together at Jerusalem." The identity of this John and this Alexander has not been established, but they may have been two Jewish scholars of distinction at the time. Perhaps they were indeed kindred of the high priest. With the rest of the council they disposed of the case in a manner which suggests the craftiness of Caiaphas. It had been a mistake to arrest Peter and John, since no offense was charged against them, yet it was awkward to discharge them as innocent men. Therefore, having commanded Peter and John to withdraw from the council room, the high priest and his relatives conferred among themselves, saying, "What shall we do to these men?" So they called them back, and threatened them.

xvi

The Passover in Jerusalem

THE LAST VISIT of Jesus to Jerusalem coincided with the week of the Passover. Nothing is clearer than that he looked forward to his probable death during the great feast of his people which celebrated their deliverance from bondage in Egypt. The Passover was symbolic of a larger deliverance, and he intended to make it a symbol of deliverance for all men. His preoccupation with symbols at all times in his ministry was simply an aspect of his genius as a teacher. He liked to use whatever was familiar in daily life as an expression of truth on a still higher plane.

The historic ceremonies of the Passover extended over a full week, and though the Evangelists tell the events of that week with the variations natural in different temperaments and different memories, we can still follow the story with ease, if first of all we try to visualize the sequence of the commemoration. At the beginning of the week there was a formal meal at which the unleavened bread was eaten. Before this meal took place, there was a symbolic search through the house for any leaven which through oversight might remain there. This part of the custom is not mentioned in the Gospel accounts of Jesus, but it may very well have been observed by Lazarus or by Simon the leper, or by whoever was host to Jesus. After the unleavened bread had been eaten the preparations were made for the paschal feast, and these preparations necessarily took time. For each household a paschal lamb was offered at the temple, slain in the temple court and burned in the temple fire, according to the ancient rules recorded in Leviticus and in Numbers. The lamb was then taken back to the home and eaten by the family with the ceremonial red wine, mixed with water. The sacrifice of the paschal lambs began at the ninth hour, about three o'clock in the afternoon. During the Passover Jerusalem would be crowded with the faithful who had returned even from a distance to celebrate their great feast at the national shrine, and the number of paschal lambs to be sacrificed would be very great. Jewish historians writing shortly after the time of Jesus placed the figure at 270,000. The various courses of priests at the temple overtasked themselves in order to make it possible for the families to celebrate the feast without excessive delay, yet in most cases the paschal meal could not begin until well into the night.

Jesus, as we have noticed, usually returned to Bethany to sleep, and during this paschal week he seems to have spent some of the nights in the garden of Gethsemane. Since his habits were known to his apostles, Judas would be sure that after the paschal supper there would hardly be time for return to the house in Bethany, and Jesus would pass the rest of the night in the garden.

The fact should be noted that Jesus from the first planned to celebrate the paschal feast, not with Lazarus or Simon, but with his disciples. They had become his household and his family. By celebrating the feast with them, he knew he was emphasizing this fact for his own and for later times. That he had originally any intention of instituting at the supper a development of the ancient ceremony which should be a memorial of himself, has been much debated by scholars. What we may be sure of is that his sense of the great symbolic truths in his national history was never stronger than during the celebration of this Passover.

As to the sequence of events during the Passover week, the Evangelists are in essential agreement, but no one of them gives all the details. We must read them together for the whole story. St. Luke, chapter 22, says that when the feast of unleavened bread drew near, the chief priests and scribes conferred as to how they might kill Jesus, since they were afraid of the respect and affection which the people had for him. If an open attack on Jesus should precipitate a riot, the high priests would be discredited with Pilate. At this point Judas Iscariot undertook, for thirty pieces of silver, to betray Jesus in some place and at some moment when there was no crowd around him. St. Matthew, chapter 26, fills out the story by saying that the suggestion of treachery came from Judas himself, and that Judas insisted on being paid.

We are told next that when it was time to prepare for the paschal feast Jesus sent Peter and John to find a room. St. Matthew adds the explanation why Jesus wished to celebrate the feast in some strange room rather than at one of the Bethany homes. "I will keep the passover . . . with my disciples."

St. Luke's account is satisfactory as a starting point. "Then came the day of unleavened bread, when the passover must be killed. And he sent Peter and John, saying, Go and prepare us the passover, that we may eat. And they said unto him, Where wilt thou that we prepare? And he said unto them, Behold, when ye are entered into the city, there shall a man meet you, bearing a pitcher of water; follow him into the house where he entereth in. And ye shall say unto the goodman of the house, The Master saith unto thee, Where is the guestchamber, where I shall eat the passover with my disciples? And he shall shew you a large upper room furnished: there make ready. And they went, and found as he had said unto them: and they made ready the passover."

It has been suggested that this unknown man bearing a pitcher of water may have supplied whatever was necessary for celebrating the feast, and inevitably the question has also been asked why he, like the owner of the colt at Bethphage, should have surrendered his property at the mere request of Jesus. The answer probably lies in the statement of St. John, chapter 12, that many even among the chief rulers of the synagogue believed in Jesus, but because of the Pharisees they did not openly admit their adherence, lest they might be put out of the synagogue.

Jesus knew these friends of his, their loyalty as well as their timidity. One of them was the owner of the colt on which he rode into Jerusalem. The other was the man bearing a pitcher of water, in whose house the paschal supper was celebrated.

To keep the events of the remaining part of the week clear in mind, we have but to think of the supper as occurring late Thursday evening. Still later Jesus was arrested in the garden of Gethsemane and his examination and trial proceeded immediately through the rest of the night and through the early part of the next day. He was crucified on the afternoon of Friday and after a surprisingly small number of hours his body was taken down from the cross and buried in the tomb of Joseph of Arimathæa. Early Sunday morning the tomb was discovered to be empty.

Against the sequence of events here outlined, a number of personal dramas were acted out, which we shall examine in detail, but here the naming of them may help to keep the story in hand. There is of course the tragedy of Judas, and the different tragedy of Peter, the extraordinary dilemma of Pontius Pilate, the revelation of remorseless hate in Caiaphas, the profound answers of Jesus to his examiners, the heroic demeanor during the torture and on Calvary, the episode of the good thief, the presence of friends of Jesus at the cross, the heart-breaking drama of his mother's presence there, brought to the scene and led away by St. John.

2

THE ministry of Jesus began with the selection of his twelve companions. Now in the last week of his life the twelve occupied his thoughts again. He had warned them that he went to Jerusalem to fulfill a tragic destiny, which would have in it elements of power and triumph. Surely they must have known the nature of the tragedy he foretold; they had heard the questions of the scribes and Pharisees, until there was small excuse for not recognizing the kind of enmity he provoked, and they had watched him drive the merchants and money-changers from the temple. But they had also witnessed the entry into the city and the enthusiasm of the mob. After such a beginning, might not the whole week unfold in a crescendo of victory? In spite of all he had taught them they began in their affectionate loyalty to imagine for him an earthly success, and for themselves honors and rewards in various degrees, as each had deserved. It was very human but pathetic, and not a little disappointing. Perhaps Judas Iscariot, listening to the hosannas in the streets, for one moment began to think he had followed the right leader after all. Even the truest of the companions, dazzled by the apparent prosperity of their cause, began to dispute which should have the highest place in the new kingdom. They had argued this question before, and Jesus had rebuked them, but now they began again, Andrew no doubt remembering that he had been the first called, Peter that he had been named the Rock, St. John that he was the beloved disciple. They were not yet ready for their ordeal; though it was almost upon them, they would not recognize it when it appeared. In several great parables Jesus tried to warn them at the last minute to be watchful and to be ready.

"Then shall the kingdom of heaven," he said (St. Matthew, chapter 25), "be likened unto ten virgins, which took their lamps, and went forth to meet the bridegroom. And five of them were wise, and five were foolish. They that were foolish took their lamps, and took no oil with them: but the wise took oil in their vessels with their lamps. While the bridegroom tarried, they all slumbered and slept. And at midnight there was a cry made, Behold, the bridegroom cometh; go ye out to meet him. Then all those virgins arose, and trimmed their lamps. And the foolish said unto the wise, Give us of your oil; for our lamps are gone out. But the wise answered, saying, Not so; lest there be not enough for us and you: but go ye rather to them that sell, and buy for yourselves. And while they went to buy, the bridegroom came; and they that were ready went in with him to the marriage: and the door was shut. Afterward came also the other virgins, saying, Lord, Lord, open to us. But he answered and said, Verily I say unto you, I know you not. Watch therefore, for ye know neither the day nor the hour wherein the Son of man cometh."

This parable, one of the last which Jesus told, did not convey his rebuke clearly enough; the apostles continued to underrate the coming trials, and to exaggerate their courage and endurance, until Jesus warned them that they would suffer severely for their association with him. Peter answered and said unto him (St. Matthew, chapter 26), "Though all men shall be offended because of thee, yet will I never be offended. Jesus said unto him. Verily I say unto thee, That this night, before the cock crow, thou shalt deny me thrice. Peter said unto him, Though I should die with thee, yet will I not deny thee. Likewise also said all the disciples."

None of them realized what he was promising, because they did not yet imagine correctly the sort of attack the enemies of Jesus were about to direct on him and them. The traditional piety and earnestness which pervaded the atmosphere of the paschal ceremonies veiled from them the stark realities he had pointed out, almost under their eyes. They could still think of him as the possible heir to some kind of throne, and of themselves as viceroys in desirable subdivisions of his realm. They clung even now to the boyish ideals they once had of the Messiah. They did not yet believe the statement of Jesus that his kingdom was not of this world.

When they all asserted, echoing Simon Peter, that they would never deny Jesus, was Judas still among them? When the moment of the betrayal arrived, and the soldiers appeared in the garden of Gethsemane, the disciples fled in all directions, but from this panic they recovered by degrees, and some of them were present during certain parts of the trial, and some of them were present at the Crucifixion. Why were they not arrested with Jesus? Since he was charged with inciting revolt, they, as his supporters, might have been considered fellow conspirators. In view of the relentless hostility of the high priests toward Jesus, it is a little extraordinary that his disciples were left untouched. The sudden terror which made Peter the Rock change his nature and for a moment to be weak, seems to have been based on no real danger. For some reason the friends of Jesus were not to be roughly handled nor even threatened. Their tribulations would begin later, after the Crucifixion, when they began to carry on his ministry with a new energy and a new effectiveness.

It may be that this unexplained immunity of the disciples is in some way related to the confused and wretched spirit of Judas Iscariot. For him, as well as for Jesus, the paschal week was his moment of power. His ignominy is that he used his opportunity for a fiendish purpose, yet, as the outcome of his story indicates, he was not completely given over to wickedness, and there must have been in him some admirable qualities, since Jesus originally invited him to be one of the Twelve. His record during the celebration of the Passover was apparently an alternation between his treacherous design to sell Jesus to the high priests, and a hope or at least a wish that the betrayal would result only in profit to himself without serious harm to his friend. Among these mixed intentions was also perhaps the desire of an unhappy conscience to protect as far as possible the disciples who had been his companions, and whose good opinion he was throwing away forever.

3

I F we study carefully the words of the disciples as reported in the Gospel accounts during the week of the Passover, we get the impression that their thoughts were occupied at first by the expectation of a brilliant triumph for their leader, and at the end by the disappointment and the horror of his death. There is no sign that they understood the larger significance of the events and the ceremonies in which they were involved, not even when Jesus, in a form of interpretation which by this time they must have known was characteristic of him, pointed out the symbolic meaning which would attach to this celebration of the Passover.

Even when they began their preaching after the Crucifixion, it was the doctrine of the resurrection which they stressed rather than the profound and primitive truths expressed in the paschal ceremony, the truths of sacrifice and hospitality, which in parable after parable he had tried hard to teach them.

Practically all the great religions of the world have evolved a ritual which expresses the mystery of life, the mystery of food, the sacrament of bread and wine, product of the wheat and the grape out of the soil and the weather and the sunlight. At the ancient ceremony of the Passover, bread was to be eaten and wine was to be drunk by all the participants in the feast. At Eleusis, in the rituals which celebrated Demeter, a barley brew took the place of wine, since Demeter was the goddess of all grains and not of wheat alone, but the symbolism conveyed the same truths as the bread and wine of the Passover.

The great Jewish feast, commemorating the national liberation, incorporated an old Jewish symbol of sacrifice. By sacrifice man could purchase freedom from his baser self, from his weaknesses, from sin. The sacrifice of the lamb had points of resemblance with other purification ceremonies practiced by mankind from the dawn of history. Jesus, celebrating the Passover now with his disciples in Jerusalem, would remember, as they would, the bearing of the ceremony upon the national history, but he seems to have seen in the feast other significances which they missed. We need not fancy that he was familiar with parallel rituals at Eleusis or elsewhere, but with our knowledge of his parables, and with the words attributed to him during the paschal supper, we are certain he was interpreting in his own way at that moment the sacrament of life, the sacrament of hospitality, and the sacrament of sacrifice.

In his earlier meditations and teachings he had already given to the paschal lamb a new significance, active rather than passive. His disciples did not altogether grasp this point, and long after his death they spoke of the lamb of God who takes away the sins of the world. The idea of vicarious repentance had not figured in his teaching. The kingdom of heaven is to be bought at a price, but each one of us must pay the price himself. Jesus had said that the man who finds a pearl of great value will give for it all that he has. During the Passover he was thinking of sacrifice as a purchase which to be complete must be voluntary. He was separating himself from the symbolism of a sheep led to the slaughter.

The sacrament of hospitality, of food-sharing, was so close to the spirit of Jesus that a sequence of incidents might be traced through his life all related to the feasts and dinners, the wedding suppers indoors and the feeding of the hungry out of doors, the celebration over the return of a son, or the entertainment of a great man passing by. Jesus loved hospitality, as a generous virtue in the practice of which human nature always rises above itself. He enjoyed dinner parties for the graces of mind and heart which they call forth. He described the kingdom of heaven as a great banquet which cannot be a success unless the guests consent to come, and if they delay too long their places must be filled from the highways and hedges. In the sacrament of hospitality the guests make the feast.

He thought of life itself as a table spread, where we sit as invited guests with no other obligation but this, to bring with us courtesy and cheerfulness, appreciation and gratitude, wit and noble talk, for the greater delight and happiness of those who are bidden with us. He who accepts the invitation to the wedding must come wearing a wedding garment. The bread and wine will be miraculously multiplied by sharing, but only if they are shared in the right way. The sharing must be done with love.

The ancient world felt that if hospitality is life-giving, an unwillingness to share food is almost a disposition to murder. The stranger on his travels had the right to ask for that which was necessary to keep him alive. "I was an hungred, and ye gave me no meat; I was thirsty, and ye gave me no drink; I was a stranger, and ye took me not in." The guest at the table who did not bring with him the wedding garment of good cheer and courtesy and gratitude was withholding a portion of life from the others, and to that extent he represented an element of murder, or at least he was a death's head at the feast. When Jesus sat down with his disciples at the paschal supper, Judas was among them.

xvii

The Last Supper

T HE HAPPENINGS at the Last Supper which impressed the disciples most deeply were the treachery of Judas and the ceremony of the feet-washing. Without these exceptional incidents the supper would have been memorable only as a celebration of the Passover, and as an illustration of the sacrament of hospitality. The paschal lamb was prepared, there was the ceremonial bread and the cups of ceremonial wine, and all twelve disciples were present, representing, as Jesus had said, his personal family. But the meal took place in an atmosphere of extraordinary serious-ness, since Jesus had recently been speaking, and now continued to speak, of his separation from them, and of the breaking up of their company. He had used terms which to them were vague, yet they may have realized that this was the last occasion on which they should all eat together for a long time. Perhaps he would retire in search of solitude, as when he had traveled north toward Sidon and the other cities of Phœnicia. The talk at the table was at first what dinner conversation should be, friendly, courteous, and graceful, and much of the courtesy persisted in the words of Peter and the others even after the evening had turned serious and the words of Jesus became ominous.

The Evangelists do not tell us to what extent, if at all, the other disciples on that evening suspected Judas. Perhaps he had gradually lost their confidence, but they could hardly have known that when he sat down with them he had already made his bargain with Caiaphas for thirty pieces of silver to deliver Jesus into the hands of the high priests at some moment when there would be no crowd around to protect him. Looking back on the evening afterwards, the disciples did not entirely agree on what Jesus had said to Judas at the supper, or on what Judas had replied.

St. Matthew tells us that Jesus sat down with the Twelve, and that during the meal, whether at the beginning or toward the end, he told them that one of them would betray him, and they were exceeding sorrowful and each began to ask, Lord, is it I? Jesus answered, "He that dippeth his hand with me in the dish, the same shall betray me. The Son of man goeth as it is written of him: but woe unto that man by whom the Son of man is betrayed! it had been good for that man if he had not been born. Then Judas, which betrayed him, answered and said, Master, is it I? He said unto him, Thou hast said."

This account is a bit too condensed to be convincing. If Jesus said that the disciple who dipped his hand with him into the dish would betray him, there would be no reason for Judas to ask later whether he was to be the traitor. And it would be hard to understand why Jesus should announce then to the company the secret of the traitor's plan. Some commentators understand St. Matthew as intending to say that Jesus spoke privately to two or three of his favored disciples, perhaps to Peter and St. John, who were sitting near him at the table. To them he confided that there was murder at the feast. When they asked who the traitor was, Judas had only the moment before dipped his hand in the same dish with Jesus. The expression, he that dippeth his hand, refers therefore to a past action. Judas, not hearing the words, would not know that he was identified. His question, Lord, is it I?, may have revealed a guilty conscience, or it may have indicated an even more terrible confusion as to what he had promised Caiaphas to do.

Though St. Luke tells this part of the story much as St. Matthew does, he adds the strikingly dramatic information that immediately after the disciples were asking which one of them was to be the traitor, they began their now familiar argument over which should be greatest in the kingdom of heaven, Peter protesting his devotion, and drawing down upon himself the prophecy that on that very night, before dawn, he would three times swear that he did not even know Jesus.

St. John tells with peculiar magnificence the series of events in which the treachery of Judas was announced at the supper, making the disclosure follow immediately upon the washing of the disciples' feet. He says that Jesus rose from the supper, chapter 13, "and laid aside his garments; and took a towel, and girded himself. After that he poureth water into a bason, and began to wash the disciples' feet, and to wipe them with the towel wherewith he was girded. Then cometh he to Simon Peter: and Peter saith unto him, Lord, dost thou wash my feet? Jesus answered and said unto him, What I do thou knowest not now; but thou shalt know hereafter. Peter saith unto him, Thou shalt never wash my feet. Jesus answered him, If I wash thee not, thou hast no part with me. Simon Peter saith unto him, Lord, not my feet only, but also my hands and my head. Jesus saith to him, He that is washed needeth not save to wash his feet, but is clean every whit: and ye are clean, but not all. For he knew who should betray him; therefore said he, Ye are not all clean. So after he had washed their feet, and had taken his garments, and was set down again, he said unto them, Know ye what I have done to you? Ye call me Master and Lord: and ye say well; for so I am. If I then, your Lord and Master, have washed your feet; ye also ought to wash one another's feet. For 1 have given you an example, that ye should do as I have done to you. Verily, verily, I say unto you, The servant is not greater than his lord; neither he that is sent greater than he that sent him. If ye know these things, happy are ye if ye do them."

As Jesus spoke, of course he had Judas in mind. The washing of the feet was a symbolic ceremony expressing the kind of love which Jesus had taught as the rule of life, and which he came to Jerusalem to illustrate in the sacrifice of himself—love to the utmost, without any limitation or holding back. But at the Last Supper with his disciples he found this love severely tested. Peter had been deeply moved at the sight of his master performing for him a service so humble. But what were the emotions of Jesus as he washed the feet of Judas? This moment is the dramatic climax of the Last Supper. It committed Jesus to the great sacrifice to come, and it was sure to have upon Judas the effect either of saving him or of driving him further toward perdition. If he could accept this ministration from Jesus and still persist in his plans to betray him, he was lost beyond all saving.

It was of him that Jesus was thinking as he concluded the ceremony. Having pointed out the meaning, and having given his blessing to the disciples so long as they followed the example of humility, he suddenly reverted to dark thoughts about the coming treachery, exclaiming that his words did not apply to them all. Here again we must suppose that he spoke in a low tone to the nearest disciples, and that Judas was beyond the sound of his voice. "I know whom I have chosen: but that the scripture may be fulfilled, He that eateth bread with me hath lifted up his heel against me." Here Jesus recalls a verse from the forty-first Psalm and sees in it a parallel to the treatment of him by Judas. The words of the Psalm perhaps tell us more than the rough paraphrase here ascribed to Jesus. "Yea, mine own familiar friend, in whom I trusted, which did eat of my bread, hath lifted up his heel against me." We are not accustomed to the idea that Judas ever was the familiar friend of Jesus, yet if we had the complete record of their relations from the beginning, we might find that the phrase in the Psalm described accurately a remarkable sympathy which later deteriorated and became, on one side, a diabolical enmity.

Jesus remained troubled in spirit, and by the expression on his face quite as much as by his words, those disciples nearest to him were profoundly disturbed. St. John was seated so close, in the reclining fashion of the Orient, that he describes himself as leaning on Jesus' bosom. Only a few feet away sat Peter. Judas Iscariot may have taken his place from the first moment of the supper at the end of the table, or he had retired there in his embarrassment after Jesus had washed his feet. Peter now beckoned to St. John that he should ask Jesus to whom he referred when he spoke of a traitor. John whispered, Lord, who is it? Jesus answered, He it is to whom I shall give a morsel. He gave the morsel to Judas Iscariot.

It was by an act of hospitality, therefore, that Jesus indicated the man who had violated all hospitality. Whether or not Judas understood that this sharing of food was a gesture intended to point out his depravity, at least it was hard for him to accept the courtesy, as of course he had to. He could stay no longer at the supper, but rose from his place, and Jesus, seeing him rise, and guessing his intention, said, "That thou doest, do quickly." He was willing at last that Jesus should know the treachery was understood. The other disciples at the supper, even John and Peter, thought the words referred to some errand in connection with supplies which Judas, as treasurer, was expected to procure. But Judas went out immediately into the night.

Perhaps he had not intended to stay so long at the supper. He had estimated accurately the length of time the meal would consume, and afterwards, as he knew, Jesus would spend the night in the garden of Gethsemane. No doubt some of the disciples would be with him, but not all, and no matter how many there were, they could not protect him against arrest. When Judas disappeared from the table, therefore, he went looking for Caiaphas, and prepared to lead him to the garden in an hour or so, when Jesus could, without difficulty, be taken.

2

T H E Last Supper ended not on the note of treachery, but with a sublime emphasis on the sacrament of hospitality. As they were eating, "Jesus took bread, and blessed it, and brake it, and gave it to the disciples, and said, Take, eat; this is my body. And he took the cup, and gave thanks, and gave it to them, saying, Drink ye all of it; for this is my blood of the new testament, which is shed for many for the remission of sins."

All the ideas of the Passover, of sacrifice and of hospitality, are echoed in these famous words upon which the followers of Jesus established the sacrament which perpetuates the paschal feast as the Lord's Supper. Christendom has torn itself asunder debating just what kind of sacrament he intended to institute, whether he wished to institute something quite new or only to carry on in a developed form the ancient ceremony of the Passover. It is best perhaps to engage as little as possible in such controversies, but rather to assemble, as we have tried to do, whatever indications from the record may help us to imagine the human experience through which Jesus was passing, and from which he drew profound and strength-giving truths.

After he had offered his disciples the bread and the wine, they sang a hymn and went to the garden of Gethsemane. The evening's emotions had been nervously exciting and exhausting. Jesus wished to meditate and to pray, and he would have been grateful for a comforting word from the three disciples he had with him, Peter and James and John, but they were heavy with sleep. They wished not to fail him, but their inability to stay awake and watch with him, was the beginning of the lesser sorrows leading to his crucifixion. The treachery of Judas and the inadequacy of the others shocked him. If his faith in himself was not weakened, at least he doubted, as any man in the circumstances might doubt, whether the price to be paid might not prove excessive. He knew his three friends were very tired, but they had sat near him and had watched Judas the traitor get up and leave the supper. All that Jesus asked now was that they would watch with him. He urged them to sit down and rest, but he hoped they would stay awake. When he came a second time and found them nodding, he said to Peter, "Could ye not watch with me one hour? Watch and pray, that ye enter not into temptation: the spirit indeed is willing, but the flesh is weak." Again he went aside to pray, and again he found them slumbering. He made no further attempt to arouse them. "Sleep on now, and take your rest: behold, the hour is at hand, and the Son of man is betrayed into the hands of sinners. Rise, let us be going: behold, he is at hand that doth betray me."

As he spoke, he saw Judas and the guards coming through the darkness. Peter drew his sword and struck one of these soldiers of the high priest, cutting off the man's ear. The rebuke that Jesus immediately gave his disciple is particularly interesting when compared with the prayer he had just been making in the garden. Three times he had prayed his Father that if it were possible he might be spared from drinking this bitter cup. Face to face with the sacrifice which deliberately he had been seeking to make, he recoiled as any human being would recoil, and he wished he might be spared. The prayer expressed that part of his nature which according to the doctrine of the Incarnation he had in common with all mankind. Yet having felt the dread and having for a moment recoiled, he continued heroically in the path he had chosen. The heroism of Jesus, his self-devotion to an ideal, we have stressed in these pages before, precisely because it is a side of his character too often overlooked. The importance of the prayers in the garden is that they indicate his spiritual weariness, parallel to the physical weariness of his disciples, and they throw into sharp relief the resolution with which he gathered himself together and went on. That fresh strength is indicated by his words to Peter. "Put up again thy sword," he said. "Thinkest thou that I cannot now pray to my Father, and he shall presently give me more than twelve legions of angels?" The question expressed in this imagery might be translated thus: If what I wished were to escape from evil rather than overcome it, are there not many ways of avoiding the main issue? Before he could put that question he must have had a firm new grasp on his purpose to challenge his enemies to the death, and to wrest from the sufferings they might inflict upon him a greater and wider influence for his teaching throughout the world forever.

The arrest in the garden led quickly to the preliminaries of the trial. After Peter had used his sword and had been discouraged by Jesus from any further attempt at violent defense, all the disciples forsook their master and fled, out of temporary fear or mere prudence. The guard who had accompanied Judas, at once took Jesus to Caiaphas the high priest, to some hall where by pre-arrangement with Judas he had assembled the scribes and the elders. It would have been unlawful for the great Council, or Sanhedrin, to hold a session at night for the trial of any capital offense. This group which Caiaphas had got together was a packed jury. Such important members of the Council as Nicodemus, known to be friendly to Jesus, and Joseph of Arimathæa, had undoubtedly been omitted for the occasion. Caiaphas had provided a number of false witnesses to testify for a fee. Caiaphas himself tried to make Jesus say that he was the Messiah, the son of God, which might be taken as ground for prosecution, for blasphemy according to the old Jewish law, but which would be absolutely no evidence that Jesus had stirred up civil disturbances such as would incur the anger of the Roman authorities. Caiaphas had planned this arrest far in advance, but he had not prepared his case well. Now in the middle of the night his head refused to serve him. He was a man of energy but far less subtle than his father-in-law, Annas. There was nothing to do with Jesus before morning, when a more authoritative court might be assembled and the prosecution renewed on some more carefully thought-out plan. For the time being Caiaphas declared that Jesus, who refused to answer his questions, was thereby convicted of blasphemy and deserved death. Caiaphas himself had no authority to pronounce sentence, but he encouraged his guards and the hangers-on of his soldiery to annoy Jesus by spitting in his face and pushing him around, and jeering at him with the challenge to say what person hit him last.

When Jesus had first been brought to the packed jury, Peter slipped in the door at the end of the procession, and watched the proceedings. Now as he saw his friend and leader insulted and abused, his anger no doubt showed in his face, and a girl came up to him, probably a camp follower of the guard, and said, "Thou also wast with Jesus of Galilee. But he denied before them all, saying, I know not what thou sayest. And when he was gone out into the porch, another maid saw him, and said unto them that were there, This fellow was also with Jesus of Nazareth. And again he denied with an oath, I do not know the man. And after a while came unto him they that stood by, and said to Peter, Surely thou also art one of them; for thy speech bewrayeth thee. Then began he to curse and to swear, saying, I know not the man. And immediately the cock crew. And Peter remembered the word of Jesus, which said unto him, Before the cock crow, thou shalt deny me thrice. And he went out, and wept bitterly."

xviii

The Betrayal, the Trial, the Crucifixion

SINCE Caiaphas wished to arrest Jesus at some moment when there would be no crowd around to create a tumult in his behalf, it seems evident that the popularity which had been his when he entered Jerusalem was still a force to be reckoned with. If that is so, why did the people make no effort to rescue him during the trial, and why did they acquiesce in his execution? We might have the answer if we knew something of the activities of Caiaphas behind the scenes on the night of the arrest and throughout the entire trial. The high priest from the moment of the betrayal had aimed at three objectives: to separate Jesus from his admirers, to convict him of blasphemy in the eyes of the Jews, and to persuade the Romans that he was a political rebel. He wished Jesus killed, but he refused to put on the priestly cast the responsibility of his execution. He must be the victim of the Romans. Jesus from the first understood the mind of Caiaphas, and whenever he foretold his death he named crucifixion, the Roman method. The Jews put to death by stoning. Before the high priest had the mob trained to shout "Crucify him" he had to use a lot of private propaganda. After the midnight arraignment before the packed jury, he consulted Annas, and when the trial got under way next morning, the crafty hand of the experienced old priest could be detected. A council was called to decide the best way to put Jesus to death, and it was voted to make Pilate take charge of the actual killing.

The trial henceforth would be a diplomatic struggle to determine the limits of the ecclesiastical and the imperial powers. The priests would try to make Pilate their tool, and he would try just as hard to avoid responsibility in the case.

"When the morning was come," St. Matthew says, chapter 27, "all the chief priests and elders of the people took counsel against Jesus to put him to death: and when they had bound him, they led him away, and delivered him to Pontius Pilate the governor." Anyone who had followed the debate in the council would know that Caiaphas would not send Jesus to Pilate unless he thought he had prepared the Roman governor to act as the high priests wished. Peter, listening in the hall, must have known that Jesus was lost. St. John says that another disciple was there with Peter, and perhaps he means that he was there himself. He too must have realized that Jesus, if sent to Pilate, must by some pre-arrangement be already doomed. A third disciple, Judas Iscariot, seems to have been present through all the proceedings. St. Matthew says that "Judas, which had betrayed him, when he saw that he was condemned, repented himself, and brought again the thirty pieces of silver to the chief priests and elders, saying, I have sinned in that I have betrayed the innocent blood. And they said, What is that to us? see thou to that. And he cast down the pieces of silver in the temple, and departed, and went and hanged himself. And the chief priests took the silver pieces, and said, It is not lawful for to put them into the treasury, because it is the price of blood. And they took counsel, and bought with them the potter's field, to bury strangers in. Wherefore that field was called, The field of blood, unto this day."

This account of the suicide of Judas is enlarged in The Acts of the Apostles, chapter 1, where Peter is explaining the need to elect a new apostle to take the place of Judas. "He was numbered with us, and had obtained part of this ministry. Now this man purchased a field with the reward of iniquity; and falling headlong, he burst asunder in the midst, and all his bowels gushed out. And it was known unto all the dwellers at Jerusalem; insomuch as that field is called in their proper tongue, Aceldama, that is to say, The field of blood." Here are two accounts, one saying that the field of blood was purchased by the high priests, and the other saying it was purchased by Judas. The first version is probably correct. Whether Judas hanged himself in the field bought with the blood money is less firmly established, though it would be satisfying to poetic justice. The fall of Judas from the gallows tree has been eagerly accepted by the popular imagination everywhere, though outside of these quoted passages there are no reports of his end.

The conscience of Judas drove him to suicide before Jesus was crucified, almost before the trial was completed. The best account of the trial we have from St. John, who was probably present with Peter. When the servants of Caiaphas led Jesus to Pilate it was early in the morning, and they did not care to enter the Roman judgment hall, for fear they might be so defiled by the sight of pagan effigies that they could not eat the Passover. Therefore they remained outside and sent Jesus in guarded by a Roman band. St. John following closely heard the words between Jesus and Pilate. The governor came out to those who had brought the prisoner and asked what the charge was against him. The Jews avoided the question, saying that the man would not have been brought to Pilate if he had not been a malefactor, and that was all Pilate needed to know. "Then said Pilate unto them, Take ye him, and judge him according to your law. The Jews therefore said unto him, It is not lawful for us to put any man to death." On these sentences turns the debate, now centuries old, about the legality of the trial and execution of Jesus. The high priests, as they themselves here said, had no authority to execute Jesus or to condemn him, and Pilate as he repeatedly asserted found Jesus entirely undeserving of death, yet he let him die as though a charge of high treason had been proved. Pontius Pilate remains an enigma. He left the crowd outside the judgment hall, returned inside the building, and had Jesus brought in where he could question him alone. "Art thou the King of the Jews? Jesus answered him, Sayest thou this thing of thyself, or did others tell it thee of me? Pilate answered, Am I a

Jew? Thine own nation and the chief priests have delivered thee unto me: what hast thou done?"

The question of Jesus was very shrewd, so much so that it made Pilate for a moment the defendant rather than the prosecutor, and the Roman governor did not like the position the high priests had put him into. When he asked whether Jesus was king of the Jews he was echoing a charge which he did not understand, and Jesus put him to rout by asking whether he had thought up that question himself, or if he was a mere mouthpiece for others. Pilate abandoned that line of inquiry. He disclaimed any familiarity with theological questions which only a Jew could thoroughly grasp; he took refuge in the purely administrative aspect of the problem. To him as Roman governor the Jewish people and the chief priests had delivered Jesus, a Jew, for punishment, and Pilate thought it reasonable that someone should tell him what crime Jesus had committed.

Jesus knew that he had not been arrested and handed over by his own nation, and perhaps Pilate too saw the whole incident as the work of Caiaphas and his associates. But in some way this man had claimed to be a king, or had given the high priest a phrase to twist against him. "My kingdom," said Jesus, "is not of this world: if my kingdom were of this world, then would my servants fight, that I should not be delivered to the Jews: but now is my kingdom not from hence." He had been arrested not by the Romans but by the high priests, and he reminds Pilate that he had forbidden his followers to resist in any way. No testimony had been offered that he had created a public disturbance.

Pilate, now curious rather than hostile, fastened on the statement of Jesus that his kingdom was not of this world. "Art thou a king then?" As though he had said, "After all, you are some kind of king, aren't you?" Jesus tries again to explain that his kingdom was not of this world, but in the realms of the spirit. "Thou sayest that I am a king. To this end was I born, and for this cause came I into the world, that I should bear witness unto the truth. Every one that is of the truth heareth my voice. Pilate saith unto him, What is truth? And when he had said this, he went out again unto the Jews, and saith unto them, I find in him no fault at all."

At this point the course of the trial changed. Pilate is convinced of the innocence of Jesus, and the high priests see that unless they bring greater pressure the Roman will refuse to act as their executioner. When Pilate said he found no fault in him, "they were the more fierce, [St. Luke, chapter 23] saying, He stirreth up the people, teaching throughout all Jewry, beginning from Galilee to this place. When Pilate heard of Galilee, he asked whether the man were a Galilæan. And as soon as he knew that he belonged unto Herod's jurisdiction, he sent him to Herod, who himself also was at Jerusalem at that time. And when Herod saw Jesus, he was exceeding glad: for he was desirous to see him of a long season, because he had heard many things of him; and he hoped to have seen some miracle done by him. Then he questioned with him in many words; but he answered him nothing." In sending him to Herod Pilate was shifting the responsibility from the Roman back to the local authority. For Herod personally, Pilate had neither friendship nor respect; in fact there was between them at the moment a feud over some matter long since lost to history.

Herod was glad to see the man whose early reputation had made him seem John the Baptist, come back from the dead. What questions did Herod put? Did he ask Jesus if he were king of the Jews? Did he ask if he were the Messiah? Did he mention John the Baptist? In any case he treated Jesus with a surprising degree of consideration, sending him back to Pilate dressed in a gorgeous robe, in mockery of the talk about kingship. And on that day the feud between Herod and Pilate was healed, they having found something in common in the reluctant admiration for Jesus which had been forced out of their cynical hearts.

St. Luke here preserves for us the speech in which Pilate summed up the case so far, declaring Jesus innocent, but indicating his willingness to appease the high priests by some compromise. "Pilate, when he had called together the chief priests and the rulers and the people, said unto them, Ye have brought this man unto me, as one that perverteth the people: and, behold, I, having examined him before you, have found no fault in this man touching those things whereof ye accuse him: no, nor yet Herod: for I sent you to him; and, lo, nothing worthy of death is done unto him. I will therefore chastise him, and release him. (For of necessity he must release one unto them at the feast.)"

The release of a prisoner during a religious ceremony was a Roman rather than a Jewish custom. Pilate is thought to have introduced it some years before the trial of Jesus; the purpose was to permit Pilate to live down a reputation for undue severity with Jewish patriots arrested in revolts. The Barabbas here mentioned had killed a man during some uprising. By offering the choice of Barabbas or Jesus Pilate knew he was sending Jesus to his death. He wished to think he was putting the responsibility on the people, but he understood Caiaphas and his envy or jealousy of this rising leader.

"They cried out all at once, saying, Away with this man, and release unto us Barabbas: (who for a certain sedition made in the city, and for murder, was cast into prison.) Pilate therefore, willing to release Jesus, spake again to them. But they cried, saying, Crucify him, crucify him. And he said unto them the third time, Why, what evil hath he done? I have found no cause of death in him: I will therefore chastise him, and let him go. And they were instant with loud voices, requiring that he might be crucified. And the voices of them and of the chief priests prevailed."

From that moment in the trial St. John's account, chapter 19, is magnificent. "Then Pilate therefore took Jesus, and scourged him. And the soldiers platted a crown of thorns, and put it on his head, and they put on him a purple robe, and said, Hail, King of the Jews! and they smote him with their hands. Pilate therefore went forth again, and saith unto them, Behold, I bring him forth to you, that ye may know that I find no fault in him. Then came Jesus forth, wearing the crown of thorns, and the purple robe. And Pilate saith unto them, Behold the man!"

This great exclamation, "Ecce homo!" was an appeal to the

people, to the crowd as against the high priests; Pilate thought that the spectacle would move human sympathy, and for a moment that may have been the effect, for the chief priests and the officers, when they saw him, cried out, saying, "Crucify him, crucify him. Pilate saith unto them, Take ye him, and crucify him: for I find no fault in him. The Jews answered him, We have a law, and by our law he ought to die, because he made himself the Son of God." The chief priests were changing the accusation again, from treason to Rome to blasphemy against Jehovah. Pilate had quashed the first charge, and now they needed to rouse the people, who were turning sympathetic at the sight of Jesus and the crown of thorns.

"When Pilate therefore heard that saying, he was the more afraid"—not frightened by the people or the chief priests, but puzzled to decide what sort of person Jesus really was. It was about this moment in the trial that he received the message from his wife, of which St. Matthew tells in chapter 27. "When he was set down on the judgment seat, his wife sent unto him, saying, Have thou nothing to do with that just man: for I have suffered many things this day in a dream because of him." We know nothing of Pilate's wife otherwise, whether she had caught a glimpse of Jesus since his entry into the city, and had been drawn as so many others had been by the dynamic and magnetic personality, or whether she was one of those oversophisticated and nervous women of the day, who craved a philosophy which the Roman spirit, practical, materialistic and unemotional, could not give them. But this message from his wife made it hard for Pilate to go on with the strange trial.

He went again into the judgment hall, "and saith unto Jesus, Whence art thou? But Jesus gave him no answer. Then saith Pilate unto him, Speakest thou not unto me? knowest thou not that I have power to crucify thee, and have power to release thee? Jesus answered, Thou couldest have no power at all against me, except it were given thee from above: therefore he that delivered me unto thee hath the greater sin." The words seem to have comforted Pilate, who resented the plot of Caiaphas to force him into a dilemma where he must assume responsibility for the fate of Jesus. "And from thenceforth Pilate sought to release him: but the Jews cried out, saying, If thou let this man go, thou art not Cæsar's friend: whosoever maketh himself a king speaketh against Cæsar." (St. John, chapter 19.) Here the chief priests returned to the charge of treason rather than of blasphemy, and this time they hit on the way to make Pilate do their will; by implication they threatened a kind of blackmail which in those days succeeded entirely too often, as Pilate well knew. The emperor Tiberius was by temperament jealous and fearful, and more than one Roman family had learned from his wrath how dangerous it was to have even a distant relative who was popular or whose ability was notable. If Caiaphas got word to Tiberius that Jesus had tried to organize a new kingdom, with himself at the head of it, and that Pilate had found nothing criminal in the project, even the most amateurish fortuneteller would hesitate to promise Pilate a happy future.

The threat had its effect, and Pilate, afraid to do what he knew was right, lives in infamy. Perhaps he was unnerved by the message which his wife had sent him a few minutes before, but we do not need to draw upon that incident to explain his state of mind. His words to Jesus, and his plain statements to the mob and to the high priests, show what he thought. Now at the last moment, yielding to pressure, he tried to excuse himself by a strange gesture.

"When Pilate saw that he could prevail nothing, but that rather a tumult was made, he took water, and washed his hands before the multitude, saying, I am innocent of the blood of this just person: see ye to it."

The washing of hands is an almost universal symbolism, but here it provokes a deep question. To whom was Pilate making this public apology or self-defense? Certainly not to the mob, nor to the high priests, nor to Jesus. Was it to himself? Since the hand-washing was done in public, it may be that Jesus, captive and bound, was looking on. If so, he alone in that extraordinary audience may have caught the terrible irony. Pilate, representative of the greatest earthly power, Pilate, who thought himself a realist, and who had small respect for the mysticism of the East, was trying in advance to cleanse his soul of the injustice he intended to commit. We should like to know whether from that moment he was able again to look his prisoner in the face.

"He brought Jesus forth, and sat down in the judgment seat in a place that is called the Pavement, but in the Hebrew, Gabbatha. . . . and he saith unto the Jews, Behold your King! But they cried out, Away with him, away with him, crucify him. Pilate saith unto them, Shall I crucify your King? The chief priests answered, We have no king but Cæsar. Then delivered he him therefore unto them to be crucified. And they took Jesus, and led him away."

First they put his own clothes on him, in place of the purple robe, and they compelled a passer-by, Simon a Cyrenian, to carry the cross. St. Mark says, chapter 15, that Simon was coming out of the country when they pressed him into this service, and that he was the father of Alexander and Rufus. Perhaps he was suspected with reason of being a secret disciple. "And they bring him unto the place Golgotha, which is, being interpreted, The place of a skull. And they gave him to drink wine mingled with myrrh: but he received it not." This drink, usually administered to those about to suffer, contained a powerful narcotic, but Jesus refused the drug. And when they had stretched him on the cross and nailed him there, they parted his garments, casting lots upon them, what every man should take. "And it was the third hour, and they crucified him. And the superscription of his accusation was written over, THE KING OF THE JEWS. And with him they crucify two thieves; the one on his right hand, and the other on his left."

2

CRUCIFIXION was a Roman method of execution, one of the most diabolical ways ever discovered by man for torturing his fellow man. The nailing of the body to the cross served to inflict some initial pain, but it was not in itself fatal, and sometimes the desired torture and ultimate death were secured by binding the victim to the cross with ropes at the wrists and the ankles. Death in any case resulted from continuous suspension in a constrained and agonized posture. Death on the cross was for the average victim mercilessly slow.

The flesh of the hands could not sustain the weight of the body dragging down on the nails. It was customary therefore to build into the main shaft of the cross an elbow, a narrow projecting shelf, on which the body could rest astride. The cross was laid on the ground, the victim was stretched on it so that the hands would reach up as far as possible above the head and the feet downward as far as possible below the projecting support. When feet and hands had been nailed in this posture, the cross was raised and set in the hole previously dug for it.

Part of the torture of crucifixion consisted of exposure. The cross was always placed where many people might see it; the victim would hang absolutely naked, and so close to the ground that his feet almost touched the earth. Every spasm of every muscle was revealed to the bystanders, who would not have been there if they had not been morbid and callous, and who even made bets as to what would happen next in the progressive disintegration of nerves and tendons.

Most painters of the last hours on Calvary, and a good many historians, have tried to soften the horror of the picture by assuming that in the single case of Jesus an exception was made, and at least a fragment of covering was reserved for the body on the cross. It is plainly stated, however, that after Jesus was nailed to the cross the soldiers cast lots for his clothes. Golgotha, the place chosen for the execution, was at the side of a main road, where hundreds of travelers would be passing. There could not be too much exposure to suit Caiaphas; he wanted all his people to see what would happen to a man who challenged his leadership in spiritual matters.

There were women present at the Crucifixion, some unnamed

believers or admirers, some of that curious kind who always in history have haunted the gallows or the guillotine, and still others of a far different type who came in friendship and loyalty to mourn. St. Matthew and St. Mark name them, and add that they watched from a distance, no doubt to avoid being immediate spectators of the agony in its shameful detail. They were Mary Magdalene, Mary the mother of James the less and Joses, and Salome the mother of the sons of Zebedee. It is remarkable that in these two accounts the Virgin Mary is not mentioned. On the other hand, St. John tells us in full about the Virgin's presence at the Cross, but seems less sure about the other women, those who had followed him during his ministry in Galilee, had come to Jerusalem with him, and now stood at a distance in respectful grief. St. John seems to remember them all as grouped around the Cross.

The explanation is that he gave his chief attention to the mother of Jesus. Since she insisted on being at her son's side, the favorite apostle brought her from the home in Bethany, near enough to the Cross for Jesus to recognize her, and to entrust her to his best friend. The words to her and to St. John might have been, and evidently were, interpreted as a request that she should be spared any further sight of the agony, and St. John at once led her home. The descriptions of the women given by other Evangelists are thought to record the scene at the moments when St. John was not present.

The last words of Jesus would from any point of view have a peculiar interest, but the few sentences he uttered on the Cross are in themselves dramatic and thought-provoking; they sum up the situation, they sum up his whole life, they put a final authoritative stamp on his teaching. His unwillingness to answer the questions of Pilate suggests that having fully expounded his message, he wished to say no more. On the Cross his wish was to suffer in silence. His last words seem to be wrung from him.

When the Roman soldiers were nailing him to the wood, he said, "Father, forgive them; for they know not what they do." (St. Luke, chapter 23.) This prayer is often quoted as though it were a blanket excusing of any kind of wickedness on the ground of ignorance, but Jesus spoke of the Roman soldiers only, and in his forgiveness he included neither Caiaphas nor Pilate. The soldiers obeyed orders and had no choice; they had not been called on to hear evidence or to judge the case. Caiaphas on the other hand was deliberately hunting down a man whose life had illustrated many of the principles the high priest was supposed to stand for. Caiaphas was putting out of the way a true critic, whose virtues made him a dangerous rival. And Pilate for personal reasons, through a similar kind of moral cowardice, was permitting an innocent man to die. The words of Jesus should be read with an accent on the personal pronoun, indicating the soldiers. "Father, forgive *them.*" There was to be no betraying of the cause for which he died, no forgiving of the selfish and the cowardly who in all time are the enemies of that cause.

The rulers who had persuaded the people to call for his crucifixion were there by the Cross, leading in the taunts and jeers. The soldiers joined in, since it seemed to be the thing to do, and St. Luke says, chapter 23, that after a while even the two thieves who were dying with him, had something to say. "And one of the malefactors which were hanged railed on him, saying, If thou be Christ, save thyself and us. But the other answering rebuked him, saying, Dost not thou fear God, seeing thou art in the same condemnation? And we indeed justly; for we receive the due reward of our deeds: but this man hath done nothing amiss. And he said unto Jesus, Lord, remember me when thou comest into thy kingdom. And Jesus said unto him, Verily I say unto thee, To day shalt thou be with me in paradise." This second word from the Cross is the kind of forgiveness which had formed the basis of much of the healing and comfort in his ministry, an answer to faith, a release from the nerve-ruining sense of guilt. Was the good thief, as the apocryphal story said, the robber whose heart had been softened by the look on the infant face, when Mary and Joseph were carrying the child into Egypt? Something of the character and work of Jesus the dying thief must have known, or he would hardly have asked to be remembered in the Kingdom.

St. John, chapter 19, records the third speech from the Cross, the words which gave the Virgin Mary into his care. The apostle had brought her where she must be, near the child whose life had unfolded far beyond her early dream. The throne of David had turned out to be a cross, and she had become the Mother of Sorrow. Jesus still strong and thoughtful in his suffering, recognized her as she approached, and wished to spare her the sight of him in agony. "When Jesus therefore saw his mother, and the disciple standing by, whom he loved, he saith unto his mother, Woman, behold thy son! Then saith he to the disciple, Behold thy mother! And from that hour that disciple took her unto his own home."

The fourth word from the Cross is given best by St. Mark, chapter 15, who liked to reproduce when he could the precise syllables Jesus used, and who here is said to come closer than St. Matthew to the sound of the Aramaic. "Jesus cried with a loud voice, saying, Eloi, Eloi, lama sabachthani? which is, being interpreted, My God, my God, why hast thou forsaken me?"

Among the other utterances of Jesus in his last hours this exclamation stands out as human rather than heroic. Many people have been grateful for this swift glimpse into the discouragement and the loneliness which waylay even the noblest of mortals. In the crowd that milled around him, stupid and heartless, in the soldiery and the representatives of Caiaphas, satisfied with progress so far but waiting around till they could be sure he was dead, in the jeers and catcalls from the wayfarers who passed on the road to Jerusalem, he could find nothing but evidence that his mission was lost. He had chosen to die, but it was for the sake of the truth which he had preached, love of man carried to the utmost through sacrifice. He could not see that the doctrine of love, for which he died, had struck any roots in the mob around him. He who had just promised to remember the penitent thief, now wondered if God had forgotten him. His words express mental agony rather than lack of faith. If Jesus could have surveyed the scene as it was at that moment without mental agony, he would not have been human.

The fifth, sixth and seventh words from the Cross followed each other quickly, only a few moments before Jesus died. No one Evangelist seems to have been in position to hear them all. St. John, chapter 19, and St. Luke, chapter 23, supplement each other. It may be that St. John was leading away the mother of Jesus when the seventh word was spoken, as recorded by St. Luke. Each of these sentences was spoken when Jesus was fully conscious that his end was near. "After this, Jesus knowing that all things were now accomplished . . . saith, I thirst. Now there was set a vessel full of vinegar: and they filled a sponge with vinegar, and put it upon hyssop, and put it to his mouth. When Jesus therefore had received the vinegar, he said, It is finished: and he bowed his head, and gave up the ghost." It may be that St. John left the scene as Jesus said, "It is finished," thinking that this was his last word. St. Luke remembered one word more: "When Jesus had cried with a loud voice, he said, Father, into thy hands I commend my spirit: and having said thus, he gave up the ghost."

These three sentences should be read together. The exclamation, I thirst, was wrung from the suffering peculiar to this form of execution—a simple human cry of pain. In the next words, however, Jesus had command of himself again, and he knew that he carried his tremendous purpose through to the end. He had given the example of what he had taught, his doctrine had won. Apparently he gave in a loud voice his cry of triumph, "It is finished." Then more quietly, half to himself, as his strength collapsed, he said, "Father, into thy hands I commend my spirit."

This seventh word, and not the preceding or sixth, was the fitting and inevitable farewell for that life, human and divine, as the marvelous soul returned to the Father, the creator, from whom it came. If you are one of those who today feel on more scientific ground if you avoid the use of ancient vocabularies, perhaps you would rather say that the soul of Jesus was absorbed in the universal life force. Or you may help yourself out with a fine phrase from a poet who liked to be careful, lest the name of God should slip into the conversation; instead of saying that the soul of Jesus now returned to the Father, you may quote—

"*That which drew from out the boundless deep*
Turns again home."

But Jesus loved both God and man, and his love for both was to an extraordinary degree personal. His heavenly Father was so near to him, and he said so in so many tender and beautiful ways, that he was killed for it. "He ought to die," said Caiaphas, "because he made himself the son of God."

3

JESUS died more quickly than was usual in crucifixion. He had endured so much during the Passover week that we cannot explain the brevity of his sufferings by physical frailty; he was a strong man, and even as his nerves and his heart broke, he was making on the unfriendly crowd the same magnetic impression he once had made in his early youth. "When the centurion, which stood over against him, saw that he so cried out, and gave up the ghost, he said, Truly this man was the Son of God." (St. Mark, chapter 15.)

We might as well continue this quotation from St. Mark. "And now when the even was come, because it was the preparation, that is, the day before the sabbath, Joseph of Arimathæa, an honourable counsellor, which also waited for the kingdom of God, came, and went in boldly unto Pilate, and craved the body of Jesus. And Pilate marvelled if he were already dead: and calling unto him the centurion, he asked him whether he had been any while dead. And when he knew it of the centurion, he gave the body to Joseph." St. Matthew, chapter 27, says that Joseph of Arimathæa was one of the disciples of Jesus, and that he wrapped the body in a clean linen cloth, and laid it in his own new tomb, which he had hewn out in the rock; and he rolled a great stone to the door of the sepulcher and departed. St. John, chapter 19, adds that Nicodemus, who long ago had come to question Jesus by night, assisted Joseph of Arimathæa in the burial. St. Matthew says, continuing, that the next day after the day of the preparation, "the chief priests and Pharisees came together unto Pilate, saying, Sir, we remember that that deceiver said, while he was yet alive, After three days I will rise again. Command therefore that the sepulchre be made sure until the third day, lest his disciples come by night, and steal him away, and say unto the people, He is risen from the dead: so the last error shall be worse than the first. Pilate said unto them, Ye have a watch: [a better translation would be, Take a watch] go your way, make it as sure as ye can. So they went, and made the sepulchre sure, sealing the stone, and setting a watch."

When Joseph of Arimathæa came before Pilate for permission to bury the body, the Roman governor may have thought that he was through with this difficult case at last. Perhaps he was annoyed, but not greatly, by the request of the Pharisees for a guard at the tomb. The Pharisees were supposed to believe in the resurrection of the dead, but Pilate was a materialistic skeptic, like other well-bred Romans. What puzzling creatures these Hebrews were, with their fantasies of extravagant perfection, and their fear of miracles, which proved their faith in miracles. This Galilean, now, had been tortured till he could not last another minute, then buried in solid rock with a massive stone on top of him—and here were these other fellows of the rival cult worrying lest a legend might be started that he had got up from his grave and was walking around in broad day, spreading more dissension and getting ready to be crucified again.

Pilate did not believe in miracles, yet if he talked with Joseph of Arimathæa and Nicodemus he saw a miracle, a resurrection in process. Joseph had been a coward. St. John says that he believed in Jesus but secretly, for fear of public opinion. Nicodemus had visited Jesus in the dark, surreptitiously, he too having a reputation for respectability to lose. But as soon as Jesus was dead and apparently defeated, these two men rose from their timidity and in the open were true to themselves. The Pharisees and perhaps Pilate himself thought the doctrine of Jesus was buried with the body in Joseph's tomb. The resurrection of that doctrine would be difficult to guard against, but if it rose and gathered power and at last conquered Rome itself, then the words of the Angel to Mary were true, and her son would prove the great deliverer, and all his people would be free.

xix

The Resurrection

T
HE IDEA of the Incarnation, that the divine
wisdom took on the human form and the human
nature and for a season showed men how to live,
carried with it a question which the followers of
Jesus after the Crucifixion found troubling. What myriads of
men and women had been fated to live and die before Jesus was
born in Bethlehem! Was it just that they should have missed forever the knowledge and sight of eternal Love, only because they
had been sent into the world too soon?

In the first centuries after Christ a legend gradually formed
itself which took final shape in the so-called Gospel of Nicodemus, one of the most striking and for a time most influential
of the apocryphal gospels. In this document the time is filled
in between the death on the Cross and the finding of the tomb
empty on the first day of the week. During this interval Jesus
visited hell, the world of the dead, and carried the Gospel to all
mankind, beginning with Adam. As he approached the dead
they were aware of an unaccustomed light in their shadowy
region, and one of them, John the Baptist, explained what the
light meant; in hell as on earth John served as the herald of
Jesus, leading him to Adam, to David, to Isaiah, to all the patriarchs and prophets, kings and saints.

For a while all Christians accepted this legend, but later it
was put aside, as a fanciful development of a wish, rather than

a record of history. Yet to this day the ancient creed of Christianity contains the clause, "He descended into hell. The third day he rose again from the dead."

2

THE four Evangelists tell the story of the Resurrection with considerable difference of detail. St. John says that he hurried to the sepulcher with Peter as soon as he had learned from Mary Magdalene that Jesus was risen, but St. Matthew, St. Mark, and St. Luke make no claim that anything in their report is from their personal knowledge. By the time the Gospels were written down, the events of the Resurrection morning had become legendary, and the legend was transmitted with inevitable variations, additions, and subtractions.

St. Matthew says that just before dawn Mary Magdalene and another Mary came to the sepulcher. There was a great earthquake, which had the effect of removing the heavy stone from the door of the tomb. The Evangelist says it was a great earthquake, but he immediately explains it in other terms by saying that the angel of the Lord descended from heaven and came and rolled back the stone from the door, and sat upon it. This angel, seated upon the stone outside the tomb, talked with the women at some length, told them that Jesus was risen from the dead, bade them take the news to the disciples, with the additional information that the risen Lord was going into Galilee and would be found there.

St. Mark says nothing about the earthquake. In his account the women who came to the sepulcher were Mary Magdalene, Mary the mother of James, and Salome—three instead of two. Arriving at the tomb, they found to their delight that the stone was rolled away. Entering into the sepulcher they saw an angel in the form of a young man seated there—inside the tomb rather than outside. He gave them the same information as in St. Matthew's account.

St. Luke says that the number of women at the sepulcher on the first day of the week was rather large. There were Mary Magdalene, and Joanna, and Mary the mother of James, and perhaps other women of the group which had come with Jesus from Galilee. They found the door of the tomb rolled away, but no angel seated outside, and none inside. The tomb was empty. As they stood there, perplexed, two men stood by them in shining garments, two angels, who reminded them that Jesus was to rise again on the third day. Nothing was said about the intention of Jesus to revisit Galilee. The women reported this whole episode promptly to the apostles, but "their words seemed to them as idle tales, and they believed them not."

St. John says that on the first day of the week, when it was yet dark, Mary Magdalene came alone to the sepulcher and saw the stone taken away. She immediately ran and found Simon Peter and St. John. Those two ran together to the tomb, St. John arriving first. He stooped down and looked in and saw the linen clothes lying, but did not himself at that time enter the tomb. When Simon Peter arrived he went in and saw the linen clothes, and the napkin that was about his head, not lying with the linen clothes, but wrapped together in a place by itself. Then St. John too entered the sepulcher. "Then the disciples went away again unto their own home." There is no mention here of any angel at the sepulcher.

These varying accounts of the Resurrection are followed in each Gospel by certain incidents which convinced those who loved Jesus that he was not dead. They met him in the garden which was about the sepulcher, or on the road walking from one town to another, or he came and spoke with them when they were at their work.

In the accounts of Easter morning and of the events which followed, the Gospels differ from each other, or supplement each other, but the story as told by them all centers around the human experience of life after death, one of the commonest of human experiences but also one of the least understood and the most rarely mentioned. If men leave it untouched, perhaps the reason is that they fear some misunderstanding of their faith or lack of faith in a life after this. Without wishing to obtrude my own convictions upon the reader, I shall try to declare myself plainly, in order that I may comment intelligibly upon the final phase of the human life of Jesus.

I believe that the soul is immortal, and that there is another life beyond this earthly existence. When I say another life beyond this I do not mean that this life must be over before we can have knowledge of that other life. I believe that even here we can enter into the presence of God. I believe—let me say I know by precious experience—that the dead whom we have loved do not leave us, but in some fashion continue here as faithful companions, sustaining and inspiring us. We find them again in familiar places, in the home, in the garden, on the village street; I believe we find them most often in occupations which once we shared with them. This constant resurrection of the dead is for me a simple fact, part of any human acquaintance with the daily mystery and beauty of life. Jesus spoke of it to his disciples before his death, but they did not understand, and because they took his words amiss they had to learn gradually what resurrection is. Afterward St. John, chapter 14, remembered that he had said, "I will not leave you comfortless; I will come to you. Yet a little while, and the world seeth me no more; but ye see me: because I live, ye shall live also."

Mary Magdalene turned around in the garden, and saw him standing there, but did not recognize him until he spoke. He walked with the disciples along the road, and they knew him at the end of the journey, when they sat down to eat. One of the most touching appearances occurred to Peter and some other apostles who had begun as fishermen, and who for a moment in the nostalgia of grief returned to that early occupation. St. John, who was one of the group, tells the incident in chapter 21. "There were together Simon Peter, and Thomas called Didymus, and Nathanael of Cana in Galilee, and the sons of Zebedee, and two other of his disciples. Simon Peter saith unto them, I go a fishing. They say unto him, We also go with thee. They went forth, and entered into a ship immediately; and that night they caught nothing. But when the morning was now come, Jesus stood on the shore: but the disciples knew not that it was Jesus. Then Jesus saith unto them, Children, have ye any meat? They answered him, No. And he said unto them, Cast the net on the right side of the ship."

3

THESE men who had been subject to doubts and fears before the Crucifixion, became firm and daring afterwards through the continued companionship of Jesus. The miracle of the Resurrection was in the transformation of the apostles. The spirit of Jesus went with them all their days, until it seemed that in them he was risen from the dead. It would be well for us to understand that the idea is human rather than mystical. When followers of his followers studied the records of his human life and loved him, and learned that his presence as companion and brother could be realized by good will and practice, mankind dared to hope that the hatreds which crucify may some day indeed be finished, and the kingdom of God may come.

Bibliography

JESUS began to live again in the accounts of his life and his work which constituted the missionary message of his disciples. Some had known him better than others, or they had better memories, or their skill in narrative was greater. As a result there were variations in point of view, and sometimes disagreement as to facts, but all the accounts succeeded to a remarkable degree in conveying the portrait of a single personality. These first preachings about Jesus were the basis for the later authentic Gospels. After much repetition the versions settled down into recognizable patterns, and four versions gradually emerged as the most authoritative or otherwise the most attractive. They are known as the Gospel according to St. Matthew, according to St. Mark, according to St. Luke, and according to St. John, the name in each case standing for the chief source. Though the four Gospels are believed to preserve the story approximately as the four Evangelists told it to their immediate audiences, yet their hearers made notes and circulated copies of those notes among the faithful, and doubtless an occasional error or unintended variation crept in.

These fragmentary copies of notes of what originally was oral discourse were known as the "Good Tidings," or the "Good Word," or in older English, the "Gospel." These earliest records were in Aramaic or Hebrew. Later they were translated, with other Christian scriptures, into Greek, the language of that part of the Gentile world in which the message of Jesus first established itself. Still later they were translated into Latin, the language of the mastering Roman power.

The first, second, and third Gospels are called synoptic because they all give a synopsis of the life of Jesus, using common material and standing, as it were, together. The fourth Gospel has qualities peculiar to itself. The material in the Gospels is supplemented by The Acts of the Apostles, the account of the early missionary work of the disciples, chiefly of the work of

Peter and Paul. This book was probably written by St. Luke. Further light on the life of Jesus is thrown by the Epistles, letters sent by the apostles to their various churches or parishes, or to each other.

The early Christians wrote much about the new faith, much more than is now included in the authorized text of the Bible. There are apocryphal gospels and apocryphal epistles, some of which contain legends not easily forgotten, legends which reinforce doctrines which the followers of Jesus gladly believe. The first members of a new religion are more likely to be enthusiasts than critical scholars, yet the Christians, before their Church was very old, with extraordinary care and restraint selected as the inspired and authentic body of their scriptures only works now included in the New Testament. Drawing on a great passage in Paul's First Epistle to the Corinthians, they called the doctrine of Jesus the New Covenant, in contrast with the Old Covenant, the doctrine of Moses. By a mistranslation the Greek for Covenant became the Latin for Testament.

If you look at your copy of the Bible you see that the New Testament is much shorter than the Old. Even if you haven't been instructed in the matter, you discover for yourself that in substance and form the two parts of the Bible differ. The Old Testament is a collection of books, a library of classics containing the history of a great people, their laws, their religion, their poetry. The New Testament, on the other hand, deals with the life and teachings of a single person. The brevity and the essential unity of the New Testament, and the fact also that its composition is of comparative late date, might seem to relieve it of the need of such commentary as bewilders us in the study of more ancient histories. As a matter of fact, all the problems of the New Testament are summed up eventually in one, and that problem is easily stated.

Some Christians feel they are on sure ground if they base their faith exclusively on the written and printed word. From the Gospels, they say, the personal character of Jesus emerges with a vitality and a persuasion which is beyond literary art. Here Jesus is to be found by those who seek him. There are other Christians, however, who, though they treasure every recorded word and act of the Master, cannot ignore the fact that the early Church was in existence for many years before those words and acts were written down. The whole body of early Christians kept fresh the descriptions and the reports of

Jesus which they had from those who had seen him face to face. In their vivid memories the same portrait lived on which we prize now in the written page. It was this living tradition of the early Church which passed judgment on the first accounts and decided what should go into the authentic canon and what should stay out. The world to which Jesus spoke was not a literary world; most of his first hearers knew the ancient law by heart, and they were accustomed to acquire and pass on their history, their poetry, and their philosophy by word of mouth.

Do the authentic accounts of Jesus, then, rest upon documents or upon oral tradition? It's the question of the authority of the Book as over against the authority of the Church. Protestantism once leaned somewhat exclusively on the Book, but in our time Protestant scholarship sees as clearly as Catholic that the Book itself grew together slowly in the first Christian century, and that it was the judgment of the early Christians which gave the New Testament its form, editing it as far as it is edited.

But the members of the early Church, let us remind ourselves again, had none of our standards of precision in written accounts. Since they were accustomed to oral tradition they were accustomed also to discrepancies in the testimony of a number of witnesses. They knew that discrepancies must exist if the witnesses were sincere. So long as the stories agreed in the main, well and good; unanimity in detail would have suggested some dishonest collusion. To read the Gospels correctly and with profit we must regain something of primitive common sense and an elementary knowledge of human nature.

We speak familiarly of St. Mark's Gospel, St. Matthew's Gospel, St. Luke's Gospel, and St. John's, but in our copy of the New Testament the titles are precise, "The Gospel according to St. Matthew," "According to St. Mark," "According to St. Luke," "According to St. John." The claim is not made that any one of these Gospels was written in the form in which we have it by the apostle whose name it bears. Each Gospel, however, is supposed to represent with considerable accuracy the doctrine as each apostle handed it on. The chance for error in transmission was great indeed. Much has been made by the sniping kind of agnostic of the fact, for example, that only two Evangelists described the birth of Christ, and those two give different accounts—or, at the other end of his life, that all four Evangelists describe the Resurrection morning, but no two tell quite the same story—or that one Evangelist puts the episode of the cleansing of the temple at the beginning of the ministry, and another puts it at the end. But it is inevitable that witnesses should disagree in detail, especially in recalling an episode that happened many years before, and inevitable also that further changes in the testimony should be made by those who repeated or copied it through the years, not having themselves been present at the original event. An experienced judge, familiar with the tricks that an honest memory can play, might be amazed that the Gospel accounts agree as closely as they do. Only yesterday in one of our courts a case was dismissed because the accusing witness repeated testimony which he had given more than a year before, and repeated it word for word.

In the New Testament the Gospels appear in what until modern times was considered their chronological order. The Gospel according to St. Matthew was supposed to be the earliest record. It may indeed be so, but many scholars now assert with considerable positiveness that the Gospel according to St. Mark is still earlier, and its influence can be traced in the St. Matthew version. Again it may be so, or it may not. I can't see that it makes the slightest difference, and I'm a bit wary of the arguments on both sides. Textual criticism has busied itself inventing and solving problems as to which of his own plays Shakespeare wrote, the test in many cases being whether the disputed passages are, in the critics' opinion, the sort of thing Shakespeare ought to have written. It is not surprising that criticism of the same kind has tried to explain by purely fanciful hypotheses whatever in the Gospels is perplexing to a logical and perhaps matter-of-fact intelligence. I prefer the testimony of those who were close to the events they reported, rather than the learned guesses of those who are two thousand years away. The followers of Jesus who first heard the Gospel versions, seem to have thought St. Matthew's was the earliest.

In this book I have tried to tell the story of Jesus as it can be learned from the four Gospels taken together. There are also, as we noticed, certain apocryphal gospels, especially the so-called Gospel of Thomas, which probably dates from the second century, and the so-called Gospel of Nicodemus, which dates from the fourth. Along with much error and fantastic folk-lore they contain traditional information about Mary and Joseph and the child Jesus, incidents which have persisted in popular legend, in poetry, and in religious paintings, and which may have a measure of truth, even though they are preserved in doubtful sources.

Our chief source of information about the first centuries of Christianity is Eusebius, Bishop of Cæsarea in Palestine from 314 to 340. He was born about 266, or approximately two hundred years after the time when the apostles were spreading the Gospel by word of mouth. Of his several books the important one is his *Ecclesiastical History*, from the beginning of the Christian Era to 324. It is Eusebius who preserves for us the remarks of Bishop Papias and other chroniclers who were close indeed to the incidents they wrote about.

If I find it very easy to accept the partial accounts of the various Gospels and their frequent contradictions, it is because for most of my life I have been a teacher, and I know that even my most serious students, listening carefully, heard only what each was qualified to hear. Human nature being everywhere at all times the same, I presume to draw on this modest experience of mine for light in the large problem we here consider. To those without teaching experience it is astounding that only one Evangelist should report an incident or a speech which may have been known to all, yet I can understand that some of the parables of Jesus meant nothing to the fisherman of Galilee, and at the same time meant a great deal to Luke, the physician. I can understand how Matthew, the publican, might have been fascinated by the story of the Wise Men, not knowing much about wise men, whereas St. Luke, the ship's doctor, was fascinated by the story of the shepherds, not knowing much about shepherds. The marvel is that the story of Jesus, pieced together from so many sources, all of them to some extent fragmentary, is still a coherent story, and that the character of Jesus, unique yet of universal appeal, emerges as one character from them all.

A convenient account of the present condition of New Testament scholarship from the Protestant point of view is contained in *Literature of the New Testament* by Ernest Findlay Scott, Columbia University Press. This work includes an excellent bibliography, particularly helpful as a guide to the textual criticism of the Gospels and to points of view toward the life of Jesus which are not primarily Christian. The limitation of this book is that it studies chiefly, or exclusively, the documentary sources, with only the slightest attention to the tradition of the Church.

An excellent picture of the political situation in Jerusalem which formed the background for the enmity of Caiaphas and the Pharisees is given in the title essay of a volume of historical studies called *Toward the Understanding of Jesus*, by Vladimir G. Simkhovitch, The Macmillan Company.

The Ecclesiastical History of Eusebius, source of much information about early Christianity, and the works of Josephus, the Jewish historian, are published in an excellent translation in the Loeb Classical Library.

A convenient and scholarly account of the men who wrote the Gospels and the conditions of their writing will be found in *The Four Gospels*, by Dom John Chapman, O.S.B., Sheed and Ward.

The Catholic doctrine as to all the matters touched on in this book may most readily be consulted by the average reader in the *Catholic Encyclopedia*, as well as in special works to which reference is there made.

Various commentaries on the Gospels give the traditional Anglican point of view, which is close to the Catholic, since, like the Catholic, it attaches importance to the traditions about Jesus handed down by the Church from the earliest time. I have used the *Handy Commentary*, by Bishop Charles John Ellicott, a work originally published many years ago, but in its scholarship and its thoughtful interpretations still of great value.

A word should be said about the versions of the Bible, since the Gospels have been transmitted from age to age and from country to country through a series of translations, all of importance to the student, and some of them essential in any study of the life of Jesus. The first preachings of the Evangelists were recorded, as we have described, in manuscripts more or less fragmentary and in the language of the preacher. These records were variously translated into Greek, and the four Gospels were set down in this written form during the period from 60 to 100 A.D. The earliest Greek manuscripts now extant date back to the fourth and fifth centuries.

At the end of the third century St. Jerome translated the whole Bible into Latin, superseding earlier versions in that tongue, which by that time had become the universal or international language. This translation, known as the Vulgate, since it was in the language of the people, remains outstanding among all translations. Modern scholarship compares the Vulgate with the extant Green manuscripts, remembering that St. Jerome had access to Greek manuscripts and other sources which no longer exist.

Since the Renaissance the Bible has been widely translated into the popular tongues. It is often assumed by those who take their history carelessly that the impulse to make the scriptures available even to men and women who could not read Latin was inspired by Protestantism at the time of the Reformation. But the translating impulse showed itself among Catholics also. The Renaissance made available to scholarship in all countries new sources of information about ancient texts, and scholarly Christians everywhere became aware that even the best versions they had might be improved. Even today Catholic and Protestant scholars are still occupied in the careful revision of their translations.

For English-speaking Protestants the great translation is the one called the King James, published in 1611. Its accuracy is far from impeccable, but for literary qualities, for eloquence and poetic spirit, and for masterly command of the English language, it has no rival. The best literary judgment among English-speaking peoples would say, however, that the stylistic beauty of the King James version has not been an unmixed blessing, either to religion or to literature. Verbal sonority is sometimes a poor substitute for accuracy, and the influence of a sounding and colorful style does not always promote good writing.

The so-called Douay Bible, published in 1609-1610, a few months earlier than the King James version, is translated primarily from the Vulgate. It is the version used by the Catholic Church. As originally issued it was inferior to the King James version in English style, but far more scholarly and accurate. Like the King James version, it has gone through various revisions with resulting improvements in style and with increase even of its original accuracy.

From the purely literary point of view the King James version is remarkable as having found for itself a place in English literature almost as high as though it were an original work. The same praise can be given to Martin Luther's German translation, 1522-1532, which is considered by its admirers one of the masterpieces of German literature.

There are many scholarly editions of the apocryphal gospels, but English readers may conveniently consult the *Apocryphal New Testament*, translated by Montague Rhodes James, Oxford University Press.

I should be guilty of a kind of ingratitude if I did not mention a little volume of the Temple Classics, which for many years I have carried around in my pocket for reading and study. It is a collection of the words of Jesus quoted from the Gospels in the Greek, with the King James translation on the opposite page. The full title is *Verba Christi, The Sayings of Jesus Christ*, published by J. M. Dent and Company. The editor was Dr. Charles W. Stubbs, the Dean of Ely. In an Editorial Note Dr. Stubbs gave the titles of works which he had found helpful, and which I have reason to know are illuminating in a study of the life of Jesus.

Those who make even the slightest explanation of this subject will come upon certain works like Ernest Renan's *Life of Jesus*, which once had a startling vogue, which are still reissued, and which for some readers still carry authority. Such books represent a literary and historical skepticism which in literature and history has been outlived. Where the subject is taken from the field of religion, the skeptical historical method makes a striking effect, especially if joined with a personal lack of faith. Ernest Renan, having lost his personal faith, drew on his knowledge of Oriental antiquities to sweep aside anything in the Gospel account which could not be documented by manuscripts or by the findings of archæologists. He described with great felicity the landscape in which Jesus is supposed to have passed his youth, but he stated flatly, with extraordinary dogmatism, that Jesus was not born at Bethlehem, that he had brothers and sisters with whom he did not get on well, that there was some lack of affection between him and his mother. Renan thought he was interested in Jesus as a human being, but since he declined to accept any part of the traditional account of Jesus, and since he had nothing to put in its place, the effect of his book is to obscure the existence of Jesus altogether, even in his human experiences.

I hope I have made it clear that in my opinion the doubts raised by the so-called higher criticism have to do not exclusively with religious biography, but with any biography whatever. To recover from the past the portrait of any man, we avail ourselves of the records of what he did and what he said. We gather the comments of the friends who knew him, and we investigate the attacks on him and the criticisms made by others who knew him. But the praise or dispraise of those who didn't know him, we are inclined to throw into the wastebasket.

In this book I have studied the acts and the sayings of Jesus as recorded by his disciples and by those who had learned from them. I have tried also to tell the story of his enemies, though I have made no pretense at being able to take their point of view.

CPSIA information can be obtained
at www.ICGtesting.com
Printed in the USA
BVHW050807140223
658473BV00009B/227